The Halfway House

On the Road to Independence

By
Sylvia L. Golomb, MSW, ACSW

and
Andrea Kocsis, MS, CSW

BRUNNER/MAZEL *Publishers* • NEW YORK

All examples given in this book are composites; no real cases are described.

Library of Congress Cataloging-in-Publication Data

Golomb, Sylvia L.
  The halfway house.

  Bibliography: p. 231
  Includes index.
    1. Halfway houses—United States. 2. Community
mental health services—United States. 3. Mentally
handicapped—Rehabilitation—United States. 4. Mentally
ill—Rehabilitation—United States. I. Kocsis, Andrea
II. Title.
HV3006.A4G65 1988   362.2   87-26783
ISBN 0-87630-492-7

Published by
BRUNNER/MAZEL, INC.
19 Union Square
New York, New York 10003

MANUFACTURED IN THE UNITED STATES OF AMERICA

10 9 8 7 6 5 4 3 2 1

Contents

Foreword by Allen Frances, M.D. vii

Preface xi

1. The Evolution of Community Care of the
   Psychiatrically Disabled 3

2. The Nature of the Illness 13

3. The Theoretical Model 35

4. Description of a Halfway House 55

5. Intake 66

6. Settling In: The First Three Months 76

7. The Ecosystem: The Day Hospitals and Therapists 101

8. The Full Working Period: Three to 18 Months 121

9. Discharge Planning: The Last Three Months 160

10. Supportive Apartments 171

11. Aftercare 190

12. The Staff 197

13. The Board of Directors 218

14. Conclusion 223

Bibliography 231

Name Index 239

Subject Index 242

Foreword

Despite the many recent clinical and scientific advances in the treatment of severe mental illness, there has perhaps never been a society less equipped than ours to provide for the basic needs of its mentally ill. Our social structure has evolved in a direction that makes it noxious to many of our patients, complicating their course and compromising their chances for symptomatic and social recovery.

Ours is a complex, individualistic, and performance-oriented nation with a relatively low tolerance for personal weakness and behavioral diversity. Extended families no longer provide support for individuals in need and the bureaucratic agencies that have been created to replace the family often are impossibly cumbersome and minimally caring. How many of us could efficiently negotiate a disability hearing or deal with a housing agency? It is no wonder that our patients get lost in the system. Patients also face a competitive work environment that usually requires them to manage complicated interpersonal and/or technical tasks. It is thus no surprise that psychiatric patients are the last hired and the first fired. Housing is scarce and is often dirty, disreputable, and dangerous. It seems clear that although we now have effective medications and psychosocial treatments for the major mental disorders, we do not have a way of providing a decent life for most of our severely ill patients.

The discovery of psychotropic medications 30 years ago encouraged a massive movement away from the inpatient hospitals, but the patients were usually forced to fend for themselves with inadequate support. Life in the community for many patients has been an even worse nightmare than it had been in the large public hospitals. Psychiatric and medical care are often of low quantity and quality, social services are in rare supply, and the minimal amenities of life are nonexistent.

It would be unfair to expect the mental health system to resolve the many societal disadvantages faced by our patients. Mental health professionals are generally politically powerless and they feel forced to treat their patients with whatever grossly inadequate resources are made available. Furthermore, the service delivery system is often fragmented because it is a creation of historical, economic, and political forces rather than the product of a rational and integrated organizational plan. The most serious deficiency in the way our service system has evolved occurs at the transition between inpatient and outpatient care. Many patients are ill equipped to face the rigors of everyday life outside the hospital but do not need, or are unable to find, long-term refuge within the hospital. They are often caught in the middle.

This brings us to *The Halfway House: On the Road To Independence.* Perhaps the most important, and certainly the most missing, link in our chain of service delivery programs is the halfway house. Our inpatient hospitals vary in the quality and dignity of the care they provide, but they do at least have to meet minimum accreditation standards and generally are more or less current in the treatments offered. Our outpatient services are generally underfunded and inadequate but at least they offer maintenance treatment for most people who need it. The crucial hole in the service delivery system is the halfway house—a program that facilitates the difficult transition from the inpatient to the outpatient level of care and that provides a structured living and decent treatment environment for patients who might otherwise be continually readmitted to inpatient status, or might languish in a nonfunctioning outpatient status, or might wind up homeless and on the street. Had our country reinvested the funds that were saved from the wholesale closings of state hospital beds into the halfway house system, we would now have a comprehensive and integrated network of services. Instead many patients who previously received long-term custodial management in hospitals are now lodged in nursing homes, prisons, or single-room occupancies, or are out on the streets.

It was with these thoughts in mind that I began to read *The Halfway House.* This is simply a wonderful book. Golomb and Kocsis are to be thanked and congratulated for it. The book comprehensively covers every conceivable aspect of halfway house treatment. It is written by two authors who have obviously lived through all of the problems, and have created many solutions, in halfway house settings. They not only know the ropes, but also write in a vivid and informative prose. They begin with an overview of the purposes and history of the halfway house movement, explore the varied patient needs that can be served, and then discuss in a systematic way the steps that patients take "on the road to independence." Each aspect of halfway house care is described in such compelling detail that the reader comes away feeling well equipped to begin a halfway house program or to improve greatly one's existing program. The book is enhanced by a wealth of clinical vignettes, each one of which is brief, recognizable, and to the point. These are authors who know patients and know treatment symptoms and know how the two interact.

The Halfway House will be treasured by anyone who works in a halfway house setting, but it should also be required reading for all mental health professionals who treat the seriously ill. It will have special value for administrators responsible for setting up and lobbying for service delivery programs. My great hope is that halfway houses will soon be recognized as the crucial missing link in our current service delivery and that our society will fill the gap it has created for those most in need. This book illustrates beautifully how and why halfway houses work and it should stimulate us all to push for their greater availability. Golomb and Kocsis have described the halfway house with a clarity and depth that define the field and challenge us to expand it.

Allen Frances, M.D.
Professor of Psychiatry
Payne Whitney Psychiatric Clinic
The New York Hospital
New York City

Preface

Community residences offering rehabilitation services for the psychiatrically disabled were slow to appear on the American landscape. When they surfaced, each house, in the individualistic spirit of growth typical of American institutions, evolved its own methodology for helping its residents function more healthfully.

Little has been written about the operation or philosophy of halfway houses. The authors of this book have referred to the major pieces of work extant, beginning with Rothwell and Doniger's work on the Woodley House (1966), the Raushs' seminal work (1968), Glasscote, Gudeman, and Elpers' national survey (1971), Budson's writings in 1978, and the Solomons' contribution (1982).

The thrust of this book is to look at halfway houses as operating within an ecosystem that utilizes a wide array of community resources. The rationale for this approach derives from the fact that mental illness interrupts functioning in so many spheres that rehabilitation demands a wide spectrum of services from all levels of the environment. The community residence is one facet of this effort which reinforces (compliments, supplements) and is reinforced by many other mental health disciplines: nursing, vocational counseling, social work, recreation, psychology, medicine, art, dance and music therapy, and case management. Particular attention is given to exploring the supportive and adjunctive role the community residence can play in the treatment that primary therapists offer to their patients in the community, whether those therapists practice individually or within a clinic or day hospital setting.

Chapter 1 explores the history of community care of the psychiatrically disabled, the crisis of the homeless, and recent changes in inpatient insurance coverage that place strains on the mental health system. Chapter 2 briefly describes the illnesses represented in community residence populations, and the concerns and behaviors most often encountered by residence staffs. Chapter 3 examines the various theoretical and practical approaches adopted by community residences within the milieu of the residence and in relation to the community at large, the ecosystem. Chapter 4 looks at the physical structure of the residence—its layout, furnishings, and equipment—as well as its daily routine, while Chapter 5 considers the process of admission into the facility.

Chapters 6 through 9 describe life within the residence from admission to discharge, what resident and staff experience as they work together toward change. Chapter 7 relates specifically to the complex interactions between community residence staff and two vital components of the resident's ecosystem: his day hospital and his therapist. Chapter 10 examines the various levels of care offered by community residences, focusing on the supportive apartment.

Chapter 11 argues for a comprehensive aftercare program and documents the beneficial effects of such continued contact between ex-resident and agency staff on rehospitalization rates and on community adjustment. Chapter 12 focuses on issues of staffing, and Chapter 13 on the boards of directors of not-for-profit group home agencies. Finally, Chapter 14 recommends key principles which distinguish a superior residential system of care for the psychiatrically disabled, notes funding priorities, and highlights recent innovative community efforts to address issues of homelessness in the United States.

ACKNOWLEDGMENTS

We acknowledge all the halfway houses throughout the United States whose pioneering efforts have contributed to our knowledge and progress in this important, growing field. We especially acknowledge the excellent cooperation received from the entire staff of Futura House (William Burten, M.D., Renate Scheye, Richard Vanderwerker, Deanna De-Gaetano, Patricia Mylan, Dawn Taylor, Faith Shockley, and Barbara Morey). We wish to thank Elizabeth Harris, Edward Tempkin, and Winifred Christ of New York Hospital-Cornell Medical Center (Westchester Division); and the Friends of Futura House who supported the concept of this book with their constant encouragement. We are especially grateful to all those residents who have provided the inspiration for this book. And, last, we thank our families, Irving L. Golomb, Peter E. Tangredi, and Alison and James Kocsis, who lent us endless encouragement as we strove to create a useful tool for helping our residents stop mourning lost abilities and utilize their strengths in adapting to and growing beyond their illnesses.

Sylvia L. Golomb
Andrea Kocsis

The Halfway House
On the Road to Independence

CHAPTER 1

The Evolution of Community Care of the Psychiatrically Disabled

Joan

The seven women sat in a solid semicircle. At the edge of the circle Joan, staring at nobody, was talking incessantly: "My biggest fault is being self-absorbed. Things did not register. I want to come back because I desperately need to change. People do not speak to me and I don't know why . . . I want the help. . . . "

The leader interrupted her: "Joan, you are monopolizing the meeting much as you did before the suspension. You came here tonight to hear what the other women had to say about you."

Blond-haired Colleen swallowed hard and burst out, "You left the light burning in the bedroom when I was asleep. You banged into the bed, walked back and forth again and again. We knew you were too anxious to sleep but you were not using all the available resources."

The dark-haired woman at Joan's left added, "When you talked to me of suicide, you never thought how I felt."

Joan broke in, "I never intended to kill myself when I scratched my wrist. I only wanted people to see how I was hurting."

Helen, who had boycotted Joan since her arrival at the halfway house three weeks ago, burst in with, "People were offering help but you were biting their hands. My way of dealing with you was not to deal with you. That's why I ignored you."

Colleen had not finished her laundry list of unpardonable transgressions. "You took bites out of several cookies and dropped them back into the bag. You talked with a mouthful of food. You sat at the table crying. You left tissues in the sink."

Clara, Joan's roommate, who had been silent throughout this volley of criticism, told her icily, "We should not have to criticize these behaviors."

Joan's face became tight. Her eyes focused on no one but she responded, "I didn't realize what it meant to live in a halfway house. I saw it only as people telling me what to do." Her voice faltered as she said, "I don't want to be like this the rest of my life."

Rose, not quite reassured about Joan's reformation, said, "We are not going to convince you to get better. We have to work on our own problems. You have to convince yourself."

The leader added, "When we act out, we are running away from our hurts."

Joan, overwhelmed by the unanimity of opinion, said in a hesitant voice, "I'm afraid about what to expect."

Rose, sensing her anguish, added the first reassuring words of the session, "This is a safe and OK place to confront pain. There are protective arms out to catch you. But you need the discipline imposed from the outside until you can impose it on yourself."

Helen could not resist a final shot, "Even if you feel like shit, people are not going to put up with your slamming doors."

Colleen raised the critical question in everybody's minds, "Are you going to be able to deal with change? You have to make a lot of changes."

The leader ended the confrontation by complimenting Joan for the way she had listened to all those criticisms, pointing out that a week ago she would have walked out.

Joan agreed and added, "I want to come back because I desperately need to change. I'm working on tuning in."

Sally

"The strangest thoughts are going around in my head like an alcoholic. I walk in circles like Taffy, my Welsh terrier. I'm afraid I'll become an alcoholic."

"What makes you think so?"

"I saw a bottle of cooking wine in the refrigerator."

"Did you drink it?"

"No, but I walk like an alcoholic."

"Sally, no one becomes an alcoholic without drinking alcohol."

Sally lowered her eyes, assumed her rigid posture and said, "I'm afraid I'll become a bag lady. I want to destroy myself by breaking my back."

The social worker asked Sally if she had explored all these thoughts with her psychiatrist at the day hospital.

Sally indicated that she had not because she was afraid to talk to him. "I want to touch him. I want to touch all the men."

This 30-year-old woman began to cry, "I want to go home. I miss my mother. I'm jealous. Taffy sleeps in my mother's bed. My mother cannot get along without Taffy. At the halfway house I want to sleep all the time."

"Why, Sally?"

"Because the bed is too comfortable. At home the bed is too small. I get out more easily. If I sleep a lot, it's like I'm a baby again. It gets worse every day."

Sally, still tearful, begged to leave the house. "I want to be with my mother," she explained. "I feel she is pulling me in. She wants me. I think of her all the time." She admitted that she was also jealous of her parents being together and that she wanted to be her mother's baby. She had trouble finding her way through the trafficked streets. The crowds frightened her.

Joan, who has insight and motivation to change, and Sally, whose dependency is massive and seemingly nonresponsive to interventions, typify two major groupings of mentally ill persons who can utilize halfway house care: those who can respond to treatment to become independent members of the community and those who can grow and stabilize, but who may need a supportive living arrangement for the remainder of their lives.

Thirty years ago, Sally and Joan would have been back-ward inmates growing increasingly dependent upon the institution that sheltered them. That institution would most likely have been a large state hospital, located in a rural area, suffering from chronic shortages of personnel. It would have but limited access to shops, opportunities for employment and schooling, and contact with parents, relatives, or friends. The possibility for discharge back into the community would be remote without treatment to control the acute symptoms, or programs to address the loss of living skills disrupted by the illness or aborted in adolescence.

The psychiatrically disabled were historically considered incurable and unreachable for vocational retraining. Community pressures and funds were utilized to build larger institutions in which to warehouse them. This concept of incurability permeated federal legislation which set aside monies for the rehabilitation of the physically disabled, excluding all mention of the psychiatrically disabled. It was not until 1943 in Public Law 113 that rehabilitation funds were made available to provide services to those who suffered from psychiatric disabilities.

The winds of change came from many directions. The writings of Maxwell Jones (1953) about his work at Belmont Hospital in England had a profound impact on approaches to treatment of the mentally ill. In his book, *Therapeutic Community*, he recommends a rehabilitative setting in which patients retain as much autonomy as possible. Jones's thesis that the entire community shares responsibility for participating in the course of treatment and aftercare plans for the mentally ill was reaffirmed in the 1961 report of the Joint Commission on Mental Health and Illness entitled *Action for Mental Health*. That publication projected a spectrum of treatment and rehabilitation services starting the day a patient is admitted into the hospital and continuing until he or she functions independently. The Commission also underscored that rehabilitation and aftercare constitute essential services to emotionally ill persons. Additionally, outpatient facilities, day hospitals, vocational counseling, and public health services were considered necessary components in the network of post-hospital care.

The availability of psychotropic medications in the mid-1950s heralded a new era in the care of the mentally ill. The use of these drugs paved the way for the accelerated release of patients from mental hospitals who otherwise would have lived out their lives in these sometimes inhuman settings. The 1974 Supreme Court decision, *Dixon v. Weinberger*, mandating that patients be placed in the "least restrictive setting" when requiring care, served as an impetus to even more rapid discharge. In 1955, more than 550,000 inpatients crowded state psychiatric hospitals. By 1981, only 130,000 persons remained, a drop of about 75% (Lyons, 1984).

In 1963, Congress attempted to serve the increasing numbers of recently discharged psychiatric patients by enacting the Community Mental Health Act, which provided for the establishment of "comprehensive community mental health centers" with a multitude of community-based essential services and personnel (Raush & Raush, 1968, p. 198). Although these newly created centers represented significant modifications in approaches to the emotionally ill person, they did not fully help him* navigate the social systems which may have contributed to his initial breakdown and which he, in his troubled state, may have alienated prior to his hospitalization. The Act spoke of "aftercare" home visiting or foster care arrangements, services classified as not "essential but recommended." It made no provision for transitional living arrangements specifically geared to helping the ex-patient with such routine tasks as daily hygiene care, food shopping and preparation, budgeting,

---

*The use of the male pronoun is not meant to disparage either gender, but is used instead of the more awkward "he/she" or "him/her."

and interacting cooperatively with people—skills eroded by the disability and by a period of hospitalization with its protective routines.

The 1963 Community Mental Health Act lacked scope and funding to serve fully the numbers of ex-patients returning to the communities. Neither were the states ready or able to fill the gaps. As an illustration of the skewed proportioning of funds allocated to the care of the mentally ill, from 1978 to 1982 the New York State Office of Mental Health spent $4.5 billion on its state mental hospitals while in the same time period it spent only $540 million on community services for that population living outside those facilities. This spending occurred "despite a 70% decline in state hospital population—a decrease in the census from 85,000 to 25,000" (Lipton, Sabatini, & Katz, 1983, p. 821).

People who had lost their living skills were not retrained or supported as they struggled to survive in a complex, swiftly changing community. Without realistic discharge planning and support for this highly fragile population, the inevitable disasters followed. Many abruptly discontinued prescribed medications, reverting to states of active hallucinations and/or delusions. Some self-medicated with nonprescription drugs or alcohol. Some attempted to work and lived solitary lives in substandard housing or single-room residential hotels. Many became prey to street crimes, loss of jobs, and despair. Some drifted into the criminal justice system or into nursing or adult homes where they received shelter but little or no rehabilitative care. Up to one-third returned to the protection of their families who frequently were overburdened with the struggle of their reabsorption.

The United States never utilized hostels such as those established in England nor had it accepted the Gheel community concept utilized in Belgium since the 13th century, where mentally ill persons were housed with the townfolk until they became capable of maintaining themselves. Except for large rural facilities, such as Gould Farm in Massachusetts or Spring Lake Ranch in Vermont (primarily for men who helped maintain the farm), there were no halfway houses for recuperating mental patients. Rutland Corner House in Vermont, originally established in the 1870s as temporary housing for distressed women, reassessed its function to become in 1954 the first urban halfway house, responding to the profound change in the attitudes toward the care of those who were mentally ill (Glasscote, Gudeman, & Elpers, 1971). Other pioneer facilities were subsequently established: notably Woodley House in Washington, D. C. (1958) and Conard House in San Francisco (1959). Each facility defined itself in terms of the philosophy of the local community or the board that founded it. Each was highly individual, the concept of its function ranging broadly from the basically custodial to an emphasis on a return to normal functioning.

The report written for the U.S. Joint Information Service of the American Psychiatric Association by Glasscote et al. (1971) defines a halfway house for the mentally ill as

> a non-medical residential facility specifically intended to enhance the capabilities of people who are mentally ill, or who are impaired by residuals of or deficits from mental illness, to remain in the community, participating to the fullest extent in community life. (p. 11)

Raush and Raush (1968) broaden the definition to state that

> all facilities defined as halfway houses maintain something of a professional orientation. This might vary from actual staffing of houses with members of one or more of the mental health professions to use of professionally trained personnel solely in an advisory or consultant capacity. (pp. 45–46)

From the handful of halfway houses extant in the 1950s, the number had increased to 40 by 1963, and by the end of the 1960s upward of 125 were in operation. By 1977, in the last national census conducted by NIMH, there were 225 community residences devoted specifically to psychiatric disabilities. In the last 10 years, there has been considerable growth in the number of such residences, but because of reduced federal funding, NIMH has been unable to update these statistics. Many residences intermingled alcoholics, drug abusers, and the mentally retarded with the emotionally ill. Experience thus far indicates no specific advantages or disadvantages to mixing various categories of disability. The trend, however, has been to establish specialized programs for each disability.

If humanitarian interests and scientific gains sparked the growth of the halfway house movement in the 1960s, the political pressure created by the emergence of the homeless persons living in the streets of our large cities has become the catalyst of the 1980s and has increasingly been drawing the attention of the media, of local and national government, and of the mental health establishment. Although it is difficult to gather consistent data on the demographics of the homeless, all sources report that a significant proportion of the homeless suffer from psychiatric illness. In a 1981 study by the New York State Office of Mental Health of men in Manhattan shelters,

> 75 percent were given some psychiatric diagnosis, including 37 percent who were alcoholics and 19 percent who were schizophrenic. A 1983 study of the homeless who came to Bellevue (Hos-

pital) for medical, not psychiatric, emergency help showed that 18 percent were schizophrenic and 20 percent had other major psychiatric illnesses. About 46 percent were alcoholics . . . 50 percent had been in a psychiatric hospital at least once. (Nelson, 1983, p. C2)

Other studies report in the range of 50–84% of the homeless as suffering "significant mental disability" (Lipton, Sabatini, & Katz, 1983, p. 818).

In contrast to the profiles of those released from institutions in the 1950s and 1960s, an interesting change is now occurring in the demographics of the mentally ill, reflecting the use of the psychiatric system by the baby boom generation born between 1946 and 1961. Lamb and Goertzel (1977) report that 36% of patients they studied who were aged 20–30 years have had at least one state hospitalization, while 73% of patients aged 31–62 have had a state hospitalization. This statistic represents the tendency for the younger chronic psychiatric patient to be hospitalized in acute care psychiatric units in local general hospitals or in a local specialty voluntary psychiatric hospital rather than in a state institution. This finding is bolstered by the fact that between 1955 and 1977 the percentage of total patient care episodes (an episode is the treatment period extending from admission to discharge) occurring in state hospitals, as opposed to other settings, fell from 49% to 9% (McCreath, 1984).

Another changing statistic is that "60 to 70 percent of young chronic patients live with family" (McCreath, 1984, p. 436). This compares to an earlier period when only 20–23% of patients leaving institutions returned home, the rest going to other housing arrangements (Talbott, 1981). This latter group may have been more separated from family due to older age at discharge or longer periods of hospitalization and therefore was less likely to return to family for domicile. However, another changing variable in discharge planning for patients and in the burgeoning crisis of the homeless is the shrinking housing stock presently available. For instance, single room occupancy (SROs) beds in New York City are now estimated at 18,000. About 10 years ago they ran as high as 50,000 (Lipton, Sabatini, & Katz, 1983).

A further development affecting length of stay in hospital, and therefore degree of stability at discharge and quality of discharge planning, has been inpatient insurance coverage. Hospital stays have shortened considerably in response to limitations imposed by Medicare, Medicaid, and private insurance plans. With more patients utilizing local general and specialty hospitals as opposed to state hospitals, hospitalizations are briefer, the opportunity to regain stability before discharge is reduced, and treating staff are hampered in discharge planning because they have

not the time to understand each patient's personality (assets and deficits), symptomatology, and course of illness.

This "quick fix" phenomenon promises to complicate the discharge
dilemma even further with the advent of the Diagnostic Related Group
(DRG) and the Peer Review Organization (PRO). The DRG is the basis of
the Medicare prospective payment system introduced in hospitals across
the U.S. on October 1, 1983: "Faced with the projection that Medicare
costs will double between 1982 and 1987, the federal government approved sweeping new policies to curtail further growth of this program"
(Christ & Gitelson, 1983, p. 1) in hopes of "curbing the sky-rocketing
cost of health care that is becoming an unbearable financial burden for so
many" (p. 1). This plan sets reimbursement rates for "classes of patients
with similar resource needs and lengths of stay" (p. 3). The hope is that
physicians and hospitals will have financial incentive to keep patients in
hospitals for only a set period of time, be rewarded for early discharge,
and be discouraged from prescribing expensive procedures that may not
be necessary.

Thus far, DRG standards have been mandated for psychiatric patients
in acute care hospitals (some of which have been granted exemption).
Specialty hospitals (such as psychiatric teaching institutions) until now
have been exempted, but their inclusion within the program is expected
to be mandated by the U.S. Department of Health and Human Services
in October, 1988. It is only a matter of time, then, before DRG limitations
become a force in every psychiatric patient's life.

In those states where DRG programs have been instituted, treatment
staff is beginning to express some reactions. While there is positive feeling about the increase in knowledge and control of data base and spending patterns by hospital administrators, staff has raised questions about
the

> 15 DRG categories that have been designed for psychiatric
> care . . . (feeling) that they don't take the unique aspects of psychi-
> atric patients into account, and they don't address the intensity of
> treatment patients need. . . . For example, the categories don't ac-
> count for the severity of illness that may lead to more intensive
> treatment, the number of admissions the patient has had before, or
> how the patient has responded to medical care in the past. (*Hospi-
> tals*, 1984, p. 52)

There is some feeling among mental health practitioners that under
DRGs, accompanying a deterioration in patient care is pressure to discharge patients before they are ready to leave the hospital. It is the issue

of discharge at a lower level of functioning about which we are particularly concerned and which we shall address here.

A Peer Review Organization is a congressionally mandated body established to supervise the quality of inpatient care given to Medicare patients and to reduce overbedding of Medicare patients. The PRO determines if a patient should, indeed, have been hospitalized, if that patient is receiving active and appropriate care, and if discharge planning is sufficiently vigorous. The PRO can disallow Medicare reimbursement for days of patient care if it determines that certain standards have not been met. Presently, 25–35% of Medicare days for medical problems are being disallowed by PROs in New York City. Figures regarding psychiatric illnesses are not yet available.

PROs do apply to psychiatric hospitalizations at this time, but for Medicare patients only. Hospitals can now lose days of reimbursement on individual cases when the PRO determines, for instance, that a particular patient should or could have been discharged days earlier than his team or physician deemed advisable or was able to accomplish. Thus, the effect on hospital staffs of PROs, like DRGs, is to place more pressure to move patients out of the hospital according to externally established timetables and review standards. Although there is an appeals process that permits some flexibility of care, the thrust will be to discharge patients as early as possible to prevent loss of reimbursement under a time pressure that affects the level of stability at which such patients reenter the community.

If all the efforts of mental health professionals and society at large have only in the past 30 years begun to address the community needs of the thousands discharged from state institutions and, also, the particular challenge presented by the new young chronic population, what is yet to happen in the next few years under DRGs and PROs? With patients being discharged at even lower levels of functioning, can we expect present outpatient services or families to be any better equipped to meet this challenge in the future?

There is neither sufficient housing stock to shelter these patients nor the requisite degree and number of community resources to serve them. Research clearly demonstrates that utilization of almost any community service geared to treatment, housing, or social needs of the former patient reduces the rate or length of rehospitalization. Going beyond, we propose that combining the treatment, social, educational, and case management thrust with the residential component is a most effective and creative tool for protection and rehabilitation.

As we shall illustrate, the community residence rehabilitation program serves to reinforce the therapist's efforts to help his patient function more effectively and independently. It helps to assure medication compliance, works to keep the patient connected to his day treatment program, and provides crucial support as he moves from greater to lesser levels of care and from lesser to greater degrees of independence and stress tolerance. The community residence provides an immediate social network and fosters the skills of maintaining and perpetuating each resident's social support system. It provides a warm place to come home to at night and a structure around which the resident can organize his days. Residence staff serves a rehabilitative and case management function, helping the resident to engage community resources and to construct a life situation facilitative of his best functioning. Finally, if expanded and finely tuned to current needs, the program can offer permanent housing for those who are unable to live on their own, and episodic care and respite for those others who have moved on to independent living.

CHAPTER 2

The Nature
of the Illness

A halfway house may be compared to the old-fashioned mother who could bear, nurture, and tolerate any number of disparate children. She demanded little, accepted what came her way, hoped for the best, but was always ready with the extra shove in the right direction and the warming nod of approval. This same ability to adapt to varied personalities and problems enables the halfway house to make the new resident feel at home.

For many applicants, the halfway house is the facility of choice because social workers or therapists have advised patients and relatives that the conditions that spawned the illness may recur. Some psychiatric hospitals may have helped families feel that the etiology of the illness had its roots in too much parental control or overprotection. Other families have been worn out by the sick member who was irritable and antisocial, ate and slept at odd hours, demanded and rejected care at the same time, and sequestered himself in his room for days. The hospital alleviated his major psychotic problems, such as hallucinations or delusions, but the residue of the illness left him exquisitely sensitive to others' opinions or presumed rejection and with tremendous vulnerability to stress, whether a changed life situation, separation, or new experiences.

Before directing attention to the effects of a major psychiatric illness on the functioning of an individual, let us first examine the additional and unique impact of a stay in a psychiatric hospital. These institutions, by and large, have come a long way from the conditions described in the *Snake Pit* (Ward, 1946). Inhuman treatment has largely been obliterated, but because the patient is at the height of his disorganization and confusion, he may have lost his hold on reality and his functioning in society may be at a standstill. Admission into the hospital provides instant respite from activities he can no longer handle.

Inpatient care offers a "structured setting for evaluation, the induction into treatment and the alleviation of acute symptoms while the crisis subsides" (Frances, Clarkin, & Perry, 1984, p. 10). For the violent, disruptive, or suicidal person who has exhausted his family to the degree that it cannot or will not offer further support, the hospital provides safety and protects him and society from his destructive behavior. Admission to the hospital offers him

> medication management, seclusion, restraint, drug detoxification, and medical care. . . . Here, a trained staff can provide maximum observation, protection, and support under the most structured and carefully monitored circumstances and, if the law permits and the occasion requires, treatment can be implemented if absolutely necessary against the patient's will. (Frances, Clarkin, & Perry, 1984, pp. 7 & 10)

The patient gains much from the medical model of care. His family and even his outpatient therapist can enjoy a respite with the assurance that he is secure, supported, and safe from his own destructive impulses while he rides out the crisis under 24-hour observation and a treatment plan is evolved for him.

All this, however, imprints the "sick role" on the patient. In subtle ways, the reinstitution of normal adult functioning and responsibility cannot be addressed. The organization of the hospital tends to create a society in which rules and regulations are promulgated to ensure its smooth functioning. In such an environment, the patient who is humble, passive, and undemanding is easier for a sometimes overburdened staff to handle. Inwardly, the illness may have fragmented the patient's sense of himself, his personal identity, his role in society. The milieu, naturally, provides all of life's necessities, but the price for this manna is a deepening and widening of the consciousness of the patient that he is the "sick" person, unable to fulfill adult expectations.

The hospital must of necessity be a secure place, one that implicitly protects the individual from unacceptable, antisocial, or life-threatening impulses. Its responsibility, therefore, dictates that all personal items that may be potentially harmful or of value be temporarily forfeited. The patient, upon admission, yields checkbook, house and car keys, nail file, hair dryer and curlers, eyebrow tweezer, cigarettes, and matches. As he empties his pockets, he doffs his sense of identity along with his freedom.

Confidence and trust in others are traits that a major emotional illness often shatters, requiring slow, patient work to reinstitute. In teaching hospitals, therapists assigned to psychiatric patients are regularly rotated—yearly in some hospitals, quarterly in others. Such shifts do not reflect the needs of the patients but the learning needs of the residents. The current trend toward briefer hospitalization stays may mitigate the negative effect of staff rotation. Changes in nursing shifts every eight hours foster inconsistency in behavioral expectations. New staff persons have to be cultivated who will soon leave. The isolated, withdrawn patient has no great motivation to alter his way of meeting a world that constantly changes. When authorities regularly disappear and reappear, much can be lost in communication, offering fertile opportunities for the manipulative person to disrupt a carefully enunciated treatment plan, upsetting staff and other patients, and retarding his own progress.

While large institutions may be structured, rigid, and organized along lines that reflect staff needs for orderliness and compliance, many small psychiatric hospitals have such lovely facilities that it is difficult to leave them for the less luxurious halfway house. One newly arrived resident at the halfway house, staffed with one counselor for nine persons, complained bitterly that she missed the eight mental health workers who had always been available on her floor. She missed the environment in which most needs were satisfied. The first weeks Sally spent in the halfway house were suffused with tears, expressed fears of becoming independent, and wild impulses to "end it all." On some level, she knew that her neediness, fears, and strong suicidal urges were the sure route back to the Garden of Eden from which she had been rudely expelled. Patients need good healthy motivation to leave well-appointed, richly staffed facilities.

DIAGNOSES

Frances, Clarkin, and Perry (1984) have disparaged hard reliance upon diagnostic labels in planning treatment goals. They say, "The psychiatric syndromes of DSM-III are for the most part no more than collections of isolated symptoms that have been observed, clinically" (p. xxiii). They advocate focusing "attention primarily on target symptoms" which point the treatment direction. These authors caution psychiatrists that "the insistence in arriving at a diagnosis of 'schizophrenic' or 'affective' or 'schizoaffective' disorder for the atypical patient will add little of value to the process of treatment selection and reflects rather than resolves our confusion about such patients" (p. xxiii).

For programmatic planning or staffing in halfway houses, assessment of the severity of symptoms or of social functioning produces more relevant data than does diagnostic labeling. Summers and Hersh (1983) have found that "psychiatric chronicity is equally debilitating across categories" (p. 129). Typical schizophrenic symptoms occur in persons with mood disorders and, conversely, depressive or manic manifestations are found in those diagnosed as schizophrenic.

The current thrust of deinstitutionalization tends to populate community residences with growing numbers of chronic persons who need case management, prolonged financial assistance, and training in the skills of daily living. Chronicity may be the aftermath of many psychiatric disorders but is particularly so in schizophrenia. Since the majority of those persons who utilize halfway house care are schizophrenic, the following discussion will include an examination of the problems of chronicity within the diagnosis of schizophrenia. The material presented here is by no means exhaustive, but has been selected as particularly relevant to those who work with the residual deficits of psychiatric illnesses. Therefore, as we discuss each diagnostic category, we shall focus on symptoms and behavior rather than on diagnosis per se.

Schizophrenia

Schizophrenia, the illness that usually has its onset in adolescence or early adulthood, strikes two to three million Americans or about 1% of the population. Since it often follows a relapsing course and can be chronic, with deterioration in social, educational, or vocational functioning, persons suffering its effects frequently need extensive rehabilitation services over time.

The following is an illustration of the behavior which many families encounter when one member experiences the initial impact of a schizophrenic illness.

The Ks spoke of their daughter, Mimi, as they remembered her before the onset of her illness. She was constantly in motion, with more projects to work on than any kid in her high school. She brought streams of young people into the house. She was president of the graduating class, a top student. A sense of life, vibrant activity, and fun filled the house whenever she entered. In college, where she joined a commune, she cooked regularly for 12 people. After college, Mimi achieved success as a busy junior executive. Her crisis occurred when her fiancé, with whom she had lived for several months, announced his decision to break up their relationship. Her parents then learned that Mimi abandoned her promising career to become a dancer. When her functioning deteriorated further, she returned to the parental home.

There she slept for long periods of time; she tried to attend a cousin's graduation but could not tolerate the crowds; she refused to cooperate with the preparations for the guests and expressed resentment that her parents' business diverted their interest from her. Since taking a shower consumed all her energies, she seemed unable to motivate herself to do so.

Wintersteen (1986) describes the ongoing nature of a lingering illness as follows: "The chronic patient . . . is likely to encounter difficulties over a protracted period of time. These problems may include decreasing physical capacity, loss of accustomed social roles, alternating periods of remission and exacerbation, and the ever-present prospect of severe financial hardship" (p. 332). Any mental illness disrupts the life of a person but a chronic illness such as schizophrenia, according to Strauss (1975), leaves seven identifiable problems:

1. Averting crises or learning how to manage them if prevention fails.
2. Understanding symptoms and learning to control them.
3. Learning how to manage life with prescribed regimens.
4. Reducing social isolation.
5. Learning to accept the aftermath of an illness whether it remits or brings in its wake continued reduced functioning.
6. Normalizing life's activities.
7. Finding financial supports for medical, psychiatric and social needs during extended periods of unemployment (pp. 7–8).

Hospitals ordinarily address the acute phase of schizophrenia with the help of psychotropic medication. This is the easiest aspect to treat. Self-care and recreational or social functioning, essential to attain vocational, educational, or social goals, are more resistant to improvement. Psychiatric patients need structure and continuing support to reduce hard-core problems. Halfway houses constitute one form of community care that can help persons with a chronic illness, such as schizophrenia, to grow. They offer an apprenticeship in reaching maturity. When an applicant steps into a halfway house, he has changed his role from "patient," for whom all needs are met by others, to a person who has responsibility for his decisions, his hygiene, his recreation, his finances, his future work, and his life.

Since most psychiatric institutions now regard schizophrenia as a biological disease, halfway houses are challenged with helping each resident adjust not only to the psychological impact of his illness (the dependency, overcompensation, anxiety, loss of esteem, and fear of the future), but also to the effects of the various biological treatments (psychotropic medications and their side effects, shock treatments, etc.).

Halfway house staff seek to help residents drop or reduce their resistances to taking prescribed medications and to accept the reality that their daily functioning and the proper treatment of their illness may depend on the continued regimen of an antipsychotic medication. These medications, usually phenothiazines, are effective in diminishing or reversing such symptoms of schizophrenia as hallucinations, delusions, disorders in thinking, and extremely passive or aggressive behaviors. Residual symptoms such as apathy, flatness of affect, social withdrawal, and others may not respond to antipsychotic medication. A variety of drugs is currently available to treat a diagnosed schizophrenic illness. For those persons more resistant to taking medications, administration by injection guarantees several weeks of compliance.

Antipsychotic drugs are considered relatively safe even though some persons may develop such side effects as dry mouth, impotence or diminished sexual activity, sensitivity to sunshine, weight gain, and blurred vision that interferes with the ability to read. Occasionally, involuntary movements of the tongue, mouth, legs, arms, or torso may appear. These tremors, called tardive dyskinesia, are not always reversible when medication is discontinued. Because of such possible side effects, current good medical practice dictates use of the lowest effective dose of antipsychotic medication.

With some or any of the above side effects, halfway house residents may refuse to comply with prescribed medications. They make the very difficult choice of experiencing the full force of the illness or suffering the painful or embarrassing side effects. At times, there is confusion for patient and psychiatrist as to whether a symptom is a residue of the illness or sequelae of the prescribed medication.

Positive and Negative Symptoms

Positive symptoms are defined as hallucinations (perceptions that occur without objective stimuli), delusions (firmly held or overvalued beliefs not supported by reality), and florid thought disorders which reflect difficulties in processing thinking. Ideas flow in a disorderly sequence. Confusion is most evident when the patient experiences heightened anxiety: "The tendency to mix in ideas and thoughts about personal conflicts at the wrong time makes the schizophrenic patient look inappropriate, and appears to be a consequence of disordered thinking" (Lanin-Kettering & Harrow, 1985, p. 3).

Thought disorders, reduced by medication, may resurface when a situation feels stressful. Under stress, command hallucinations may also emerge. Halfway house staff must be especially alert at such times, as these hallucinations may compel a person to attempt suicide or other destructive or self-destructive acts.

In the following example, Audrey's difficulties in achieving when she returned to college can be attributed, in part, to the residue of "negative symptoms" with which she had to cope after she had overcome the "positive symptoms" of her illness.

Audrey, diagnosed as schizophrenic, stayed five months in the transitional house, chafing constantly because attendance at a day hospital was prescribed. Before admission to a psychiatric hospital, she had been enrolled in a prestigious college, hoping her studies would lead to an accounting career. In the course of her rehabilitation, she was unable to accept the reality that she found herself struggling with simple bookkeeping problems in a volunteer position. Her parents also expected that she would move quickly through the nerve-wracking (to them) rehabilitation period and return to normal pursuits. For Audrey, being normal also meant that she could again compete with her three high-achieving siblings. Consequently, she left her residence to return to her studies at college. Staff cautioned her to start with a reduced academic program, and emphasized that continuing therapy and medication were essential ingredients for progress. In her rush to return to her former life, she could not accept these precautions. Within three months, she found the stress of the highly competitive academic life too strenuous and was compelled to abandon her studies.

Negative symptoms of chronic schizophrenia include indifference, flatness of affect, social uncertainty, lack of energy and drive, residual thought and memory disturbance, and a lowered threshold for nonspecific stress. Frequently, a psychic passivity to life develops, which the demanding world outside the hospital finds unacceptable and which often hinders efforts to adjust in society. With deficits in intellect and cognitive and psychomotor performance, the struggling person often fails in interpersonal contacts since he cannot cope with everyday social expectations. He tends to be isolated, unable to relate to others.

The Ks' description of Mimi's behavior (p. 16) tallies closely to that reported by another parent (Miles, 1983) who describes his son upon exiting from a hospital as not wanting to return to school or find a job. He "lies around the house all day, does not want to eat or sleep at the usual hours, is careless about personal hygiene or appearance . . . has lost the desire or ability to make friends or plan activities . . . "(p. 1). The parent, struggling with these negative (or residual) symptoms, summed up the rehabilitation problem succinctly when he said, "The chronically mentally ill not only find it difficult to respond to these parental expectations, but they are more than ordinarily stressed by normal and natural expressions or expectations" (p. 1).

Researchers have assessed that premorbid social maladjustment and low-level educational attainment may be predictors for the emergence of negative symptoms in the recovering schizophrenic. With these signs, the prognosis for subsequent efforts to help this group of patients establish a better level of social interaction or employment is less certain. These are important factors to evaluate when expectations for a return to near normal functioning within a specified time frame are enunciated programmatically. Those with strong negative symptoms will need a slower track, more social skills training, and more imaginative motivational efforts.

Dependence and Hostility, Stress and Loss

Another characteristic of persons with schizophrenia (and other chronic psychiatric disorders) is, at times, their extreme dependence on family support, concurrent with layers of hostility toward family members, with the ill person often tracing and retracing the presumed wrongs of the far past.

Igor, a young man of 24, was faced with the prospect of moving from the halfway house, into which he had comfortably settled 18 months ago, to a nearby supportive apartment. He expressed delight that he was chosen for the move and would enjoy greater personal freedom. On a functional level, however, he started to experience daily stomachaches which prevented him from pursuing his assigned program at a local warehouse. These were minor indices of resistance and fear compared to the barrage of hostility he directed at his father when he next met with him and his social worker. He excoriated his father for leaving him when he was 14, forcing him to live, without a buffer, with a well-developed, aggressive brother who often pummeled him and with an invalid mother who was unable to protect him. Igor could not relate in the here and now to the imminent change in his living quarters or to his fear of a new assertive roommate much like his brother; but he easily dredged up the period that had previously stressed him and he blamed his father with the same intensity that he felt 10 years ago for the fear he now experienced.

Some residents are often so plagued by their sense of hopelessness that suicidal thoughts are difficult to contain. With all these self-doubts, they are frequently exploited by others because their feelings of worthlessness prevent them from protesting inequities.

On the other hand, the symptoms in the paranoid schizophrenic, with which community residence staff must deal, include "unfocused anxiety, anger, argumentativeness" (American Psychiatric Association, 1987, p. 197) or, in the extreme, accusatory behavior, which may lead to violence as a self-protective stance. The paranoid person needs distance and is difficult to treat because he often cannot tolerate contradiction. He feels more protected if he relates on a task-oriented basis.

Paradoxically, susceptible as the mentally ill person is to stress, the stress he cannot tolerate is defined more by how he experiences it subjectively than by how disastrous the event actually is.

Juan was a tall, slim, nonaggressive young man, diagnosed schizophrenic. Usually withdrawn, isolated, and passive in his social relations, he was rudely muscled out of the use of the shower by Gordon, a short, belligerent young man who always felt abused by his associates. As the argument about priorities to use the bathroom heated up, threats turned into fisticuffs and in the fracas five-foot-three-inch Gordon threw six-foot-one-inch Juan to the floor. Other residents intervened to separate the antagonists and no one was injured. Within a week, however, Juan started to show signs of isolation and extreme withdrawal. He had not told staff about the degradation he felt he had suffered when the smallest man in the house wrestled him to the ground. None of the residents mentioned the incident. By the second week, Juan assumed a rigid, catatonic posture. One of the few verbalizations he uttered referred to himself as "the Tin Man." He had fallen not only literally but also in his own self-esteem and he could not confront or integrate this defeat as another person might have. Because Juan never faced his anger and his deep humiliation, these reactions stayed underground and emerged as illness instead.

On the other side of the ledger, when an emergency not related to core problems occurs, a resident frequently can be depended upon to assume responsibility and offer full cooperation.

Elvira was blocked in moving assertively in the world. She was frightened of men, of crowds, of selling her talents. However, when her housemate swallowed a bottle of pills, the massive efforts she made to assist the resuscitation team were a study in heroics. She worked exhaustively for three hours, side-by-side with the rescue team, to restore circulation and to induce vomiting. She volunteered her services because the counselor on duty was so overwhelmed by the bodily changes in a formerly handsome man that she became inoperative and helpless. Elvira jumped into the breach to assist. This life-threatening situation momentarily broke through her immobilization in functioning. With the disappearance of the emergency, her inability to move forward resurfaced. She felt unable to cope in a competitive world.

One of the most painful sequelae of schizophrenia with which a resident must struggle is the deterioration from previous levels of intellectual functioning. Family and friends often observe that the person is not the same, as the Ks' remembrance of Mimi underscored. A drop in the quality of social relations or self-care may be gradually accepted by the person who has become ill, but he finds it tortuous and demeaning to accept the fact that he cannot read or concentrate, that his dreams of a career in medicine, law, science, or business have plummeted, and that his future vocational sights, if any, must be set below those of his friends, his siblings, his cousins, or his parents. The young, recovering mentally ill person brings this burden of loss to the halfway house. He is further hampered in setting new goals by his tremendous fear of achieving independence. Study or work which points the way to independent functioning is viewed sometimes with fear or suspicion. Because of poverty of speech, an exaggerated fear of authority, or an inability to present assets, job or school leads often cannot be adequately pursued.

Motivation to take risks in any field is in short supply in many who have battled a major psychotic illness. Ambition to learn, to socialize, to work, or even to care for personal needs has been devastated by illness. A frequent scenario is a young person sitting idly in front of the television, smoking one cigarette after another, interrupted only by sips of strongly brewed coffee.

Course of Schizophrenia

Persons recovering from schizophrenia can be assessed along a continuum from low to high functioning. Those who decompensated slowly or around puberty and who suffer from many negative symptoms most likely belong to the former group. Motivation for growth may be at a low level. With skillful case management, the quality of life such persons enjoy may be improved; they may be helped to accept a medical regimen, to acquire more life skills and more productive work habits, to socialize, and to travel locally. For some, the sheltered workshop may be the optimum work achievement. In contrast, for those for whom an acute crisis precipitated the illness and who had surmounted many of the developmental tasks before the illness struck, therapeutic goals may include a return to almost normal functioning.

In addition to residual deficits, psychosocial factors affect the course of a major psychotic illness such as schizophrenia. Schizophrenics have difficulty sorting out, screening, or synthesizing emotional stimuli. A recovering schizophrenic patient, reentering an environment replete with negative attitudes, is vulnerable to relapse. Such a highly charged climate of expressed emotion (EE) "includes measures of criticism, hostility, and emotional involvement" (Doane et al., 1985, p. 34). Research has established that environments rated as high on any of these reactions are called high EE, and "the likelihood of (patient) relapse over a nine-month follow-up period is three to four times greater . . . than for those from low-EE situations . . . " (Doane et al., 1985, p. 34). Since environmental factors contribute markedly to the course of schizophrenia, a low-keyed atmosphere such as a halfway house, which has structured expectations for functioning rather than insistent, hostile, critical, or overly eager demands, is an excellent treatment strategy for the sensitive, recovering patient and a respite for his beleaguered family.

Until recently, there was widespread acceptance that schizophrenia travels a downward course in functioning (American Psychiatric Association, 1980). DSM-III-R (American Psychiatric Association, 1987) states that "the most common course is probably one of acute exacerbations with residual impairment between episodes" (p. 191). The findings of the Vermont Longitudinal Study of Chronic Mental Patients (Harding, 1984) raise more optimistic assumptions about outcome, as does the Boston State Hospital 12-year follow-up study, the Iowa 500 study, and others.

The Vermont study, begun in 1953, followed 269 long-term, profoundly ill patients as they moved from hospital to halfway house to life in the community. By 1981, "68 percent no longer had either positive or negative symptoms of schizophrenia. Over two-thirds show no indications in their behavior of ever having been hospitalized. . . . All reside in the community and 81 percent care for their own basic needs . . . about 24 percent are employed . . . 27 percent are retired or occupied with responsible daily activities" (Harding, 1984, p. 3). The factors that contributed to their improved functioning in the community were, "having decent housing, food, clothing and people to be with . . . being given responsibility . . . being required to earn privileges" (p. 3). Also included were factors such as being "productive and learning to manage their own symptoms." In her assessment, Harding considers of major importance to their growth, the continuity of the treatment team afforded this group from inpatient days until their integration into the community.

Schizoaffective Disorder

The definition of a schizoaffective illness is clouded in controversy. According to DSM-III-R (American Psychiatric Association, 1987), this disorder presents on a continuum somewhere between schizophrenia and a mood disturbance. Holzman et al. (1986) have found that the thought disorder in a schizoaffective illness is closer to that found in a schizophrenia than in a manic-depressive illness. Schizoaffective patients tend toward confusion and disorientation, whereas the energetic thought found in a mania is frequently accompanied by mirthfulness or flippancy. In a depressive state the schizoaffective patient may become suicidal and is at great risk at such times.

In a schizoaffective illness, an episode begins suddenly accompanied by turmoil and confusion and impaired reality testing. The anxiety that ushered in the episode can lead to ego fragmentation. At such times, an exploration of conflicts is impossible. These patients are frequently painfully aware of their lack of impulse control.

The task of the halfway house is to help residents channel anxieties that are experienced as fragmentation. The counselor or social worker can question what the resident can do to head off the "craziness" and can suggest reduced activity or the elimination of a stressful plan. He can also ask permission of the psychiatrist for increased medication. The structure of the house and the presence of a trusted counselor can serve as controls for impulsive behavior or affect the reduction of anxiety.

The following vignette illustrates the escalation of this illness when change occurred, medications were discontinued, and the structure of the group home was removed.

Ike, who customarily spent many hours alone in his room asleep or playing chess with himself, was offered a trip to California with his family. His mood started to shift dramatically as he prepared to leave. He was elated and friendly but his thoughts raced. In this frame of mind, he surreptitiously abandoned his medication because "it slowed him down." Despite reservations expressed by staff, the family proceeded with the trip. On the airplane to California, his family was unable to restrain him from racing repeatedly up and down the narrow aisles, dangerously swinging a tennis racquet. Later, when he was again medicated and somewhat stabilized, he described his affect as "happy, playful, and extroverted." He expressed surprise that his karate chops, which he thought were attempts to connect with others in a friendly fashion, were considered dangerous. Ike had arrived at the halfway house with a manic-depressive diagnosis. His treating psychiatrist rediagnosed him as schizoaffective when his long periods of isolation and inability to concentrate were observed. His lower level of social functioning became the reality.

Depression

Persons diagnosed as suffering from a major depressive episode are infrequently represented in a community residence population. Because of their complete withdrawal, such persons ordinarily remain hospitalized until the major symptoms have receded. More often the community residence cares for those who experience depression reactive to the incidence of another major psychiatric illness.

Characteristic of depression, as noted in DSM-III-R (American Psychiatric Association, 1987), are lack of interest in food, sex, or personal hygiene, and sleep disturbances—insomnia or hypersomnia. Depressed persons can often be found pacing the room, pulling their hair or skin, or wringing their hands. Long pauses punctuate their speech or they talk in such a monotone that others in the group are thoroughly bored. Physical activities are often greatly slowed. There are frequent complaints of diminished energy and inability to accomplish the simplest assigned chores. Underlying this physical stasis are pervasive feelings of inadequacy, worthlessness, and exaggerated guilt over past failures. The depressed persons' complete lack of pleasure in any event or discussion isolate them further from other residents, as the following vignette illustrates.

Edith entered a halfway house as she recovered from a suicidal gesture made in the depth of her depression. She had been living alone in a large city, attempting to attend school. She was a tall, awkward young woman whose pale skin and mousy hair, coupled with her withdrawn manner, completed the washed-out impression. With her monotonous voice, her attempts to establish contacts with other students failed abysmally. Finally, she spent her weekends sitting in a chair, staring into space. She had a conflicted relationship with her parents, partially because she believed that their high academic achievements diminished her. She dared not communicate her defeats in the social and academic areas and believed that she was no longer welcome at home because she had let down her parents. She never acknowledged her excellent musical talents or her high-level scouting abilities. Any of these areas which she denigrated might have offered her entry into student activities. Life in a halfway house mimicked a dormitory and by its structure provided a modicum of social interchange, even though Edith did not have sufficient social skills to form other than superficial relationships.

Among psychiatric disorders, depressions are most responsive to medical interventions, with adjunctive psychotherapy. Tricyclic antidepressants are effective in reducing anxiety, sadness, and changes in bodily functioning, all of which are components of a major depression. Less widely effective than the tricyclics, monoamine oxidase inhibitors (MAOIs) are prescribed for atypical depressions. These drugs are especially efficacious for those who suffer from high levels of anxiety. Persons using these medications must eliminate specific foods from their diets. For major depressive disorders or bipolar illnesses, lithium may be prescribed in addition to an antidepressant.

Hospitalization may be essential to protect the suicidal person from harming himself and "to insure adherence to a treatment regimen when the patient is unable or unwilling to comply voluntarily" (Bowden, 1985, p. 1192). When suicidal impulses are severe and there are no responses to psychological or pharmacological treatment, then electroconvulsive therapy (ECT) may be considered.

A person suffering from a depression is difficult for any group to tolerate. The feeling of hopelessness, which is often the core of a depression, radiates out into the group. The depressed resident often perceives himself as a victim and it is the task of the group home staff to help him discover that he has options and that life is not simply a series of "no exits." Staff acknowledges the pain, but provides expectations that the resident will get out of bed, groom himself, attend his programs, and attempt to tolerate others.

A small house can absorb one or two depressed residents provided they are balanced by a few others who bring a sense of life and activity into the setting.

Bipolar Illness

A manic-depressive illness can be viewed as a periodic variation in mood either in the direction of elation or, at the other extreme, of depression. These episodes may occur annually or at irregular intervals. They are characterized by irascible or euphoric moods, lasting at least a period of a week. Manic phases are believed to be a reverse manifestation of depression. When the spiral is upward, activity is heightened, speech is never-ending, and the need for sleep seems to vanish. Self-esteem is high, as is energy. This illness can begin as early as age 20 and is subject to frequent relapses during subsequent years. There are alterations not only in mood but also in thought, personality, and all forms of behavior.

In the depressed state, the pendulum of emotions swings to the opposite extreme. At such times, persons with this disorder lack energy, feel their fatigue, have scant appetite, and are deeply saddened or irascible.

They lose weight and feel hopeless or worthless. Delusions or hallucinations, if present, are usually harsh and punishing. There is confusion at times in distinguishing a bipolar illness from a schizoaffective disorder.

Most persons who are subject to mood illnesses probably need to be stabilized on lithium for the remainder of their lives. The discovery of lithium created a breakthrough in preventing recurrences of major affective episodes in about 75% of bipolar patients.

The manic-depressive usually enters a transitional house as he is trying to climb out of his depression, replete with guilt for his past excesses and the havoc he has caused himself and his family during his manic period. Staff can look forward to periods of good functioning in such an individual who, in turn, can be a rich asset to the group provided he stays on his medication and is integrated into a program structured strongly enough to contain his erratic impulses, unlike Jake who is described below.

Effusive Jake was outgoing and easily lovable. He entertained with colorful verbalizations as he tried to bring the word of Jesus to the group. Chores were acknowledged but never performed since they belonged to life's trivia. He had initiative, a good singing voice, and lively opinions about many subjects. He was the outstanding student in his typesetting school until graduation approached. Recognition and independence troubled him so deeply that he abruptly left the printing program. He tried to limit his goals by taking a job as a warehouseman. Without a warning, the need to move sent him out on the road until he ran out of money, gas, and hope and into a deep depression. Jake, like many manic-depressives, periodically enjoyed an inflated self-esteem, marked grandiosity as a defense against his fears, and, at times, an euphoric mood. The house saw Jake as highly energetic, verbal, having all the answers to existence and eternity, but without a sense of personal boundaries.

The consistent, structured environment of the halfway house might interrupt or diminish a manic episode. A program with set routines provides secure support as the individual enters an active phase of his illness.

Borderline Personality Disorder

Persons suffering from borderline personality disorder are increasingly represented in the population of community residences. According to DSM-III-R (American Psychiatric Association, 1987), outstanding characteristics of the borderline personality disorder include marked instability, unpredictability, and intense anger often inappropriately expressed. Also included are mood disturbances, intense and erratic interpersonal relationships, and self-destructive (often self-mutilating) behaviors. These highly manipulative persons suffer from identity disturbance and fear of being alone, perhaps because of their inner emptiness. A depressed outlook often relates to strong feelings of abandonment in the face of change. Such depression linked with the characteristic instability and impulsivity contribute to the risk of accidents or suicidal gestures.

Because of borderlines' easily disrupted self-control and overwhelming impulsivity, assisting them to structure their daily routines is more helpful than encouraging their fantasies or recitals of past traumas. Since their actions are frequently based on overwhelming reaction of the moment, the most effective treatment is that which deflects such impulsivity. For these reasons, the structured, predictable life in a halfway house provides an excellent resource for attempting to stabilize and organize these persons, provided the facility is richly equipped with patient, low-keyed, stable staff who can tolerate such excesses and rebellion against selves, parents, and everyone in the environment; self-destructive acts; suicidal threats; and/or wild acting-out behavior. Borderlines strain both staff and other residents.

> Joan (whom we met in Chapter 1), is typical of the borderline who seeks admission to a halfway house following discharge from the hospital. Despite the fact that she begged to leave the hospital, when the time came to do so, she acted out so violently that her hospital stay had to be extended.
>
> She entered the halfway house like a whirlwind, engaging everyone in her activities and alienating all. She was well equipped with money supplied by her parents for endlessly long, argumentative telephone calls. Her bedroom was constantly chaotic despite good intentions to become organized. She also managed simultaneously to involve herself sexually with several young men so that they were vying with each other for her affections. She demanded enormous amounts of counselor time, yet dashed out impulsively to new, badly conceived endeavors.

A 17th-century English physician defined with incredible acuity the borderline personality, about whom he said, "All is caprice. They love without measure those whom they will soon hate without reason" (Sass, 1982, p. 12).

At any one time there is usually a full spectrum of the remaining personality disorders represented among halfway house residents. Dependent, narcissistic, avoidant, schizotypal, and schizoid personality disorders are the most frequently encountered. The structure and rehabilitation program of the house are geared toward helping these residents gain a greater sense of personal strength and improve their self-esteem and relatedness to others so that they may learn to function with less restriction.

Eating Disorders

Patients suffering from anorexia nervosa or bulimia nervosa are increasingly referred to halfway houses for help in restructuring their lives. These persons, usually women, have experienced gross disturbances in eating behavior during adolescence.

Anorexics have been characterized as those persons who have lost at least 15% of their expected body weight (American Psychiatric Association, 1987) but who, despite looking emaciated, feel "fat" or whose image of themselves is grossly distorted. No matter how many pounds have been lost, they still view themselves as "obese" and plan still more stringent diets. Usually, women have become amenorrheic. Hospitalization is the treatment of choice when the illness becomes life-threatening.

Many anorexics have a history of being perfectionists—in fact, "the model children." They generally are academic achievers. In the midst of an abundant society and living in middle-class families, anorexic teenagers opt for voluntary starvation. External stresses such as changing neighborhoods, leaving home for vacation or entering college, parental disharmonies, or losses of friends, lovers, or relatives can trigger the illness.

Stringent diets may at times become the springboard to bulimia nervosa. As noted in DSM-III-R (American Psychiatric Association, 1987), those who suffer from this illness have recurrent bouts of uncontrollable overeating. Their gorging is done in secret and is differentiated from overeating in obesity by the use of laxatives or by induced vomiting to prevent retention of the prodigious quantities of food consumed. Starvation or vigorous exercise is also used as a means of avoiding weight gain.

It has been estimated by the New York State Office of Mental Health (Walsh, 1983, p. 2) that bulimia affects 20% of college-age women. These women are characterized by abnormal attitudes toward their weight and body and suffer from excessive irritability, a high level of anxiety, and depression. Their depression has been classified by Walsh (1983) and his associates as "atypical depression" (p. 2), differentiated from a typical major depression by the fact that such persons can respond "with enjoyment to some life events despite the depression" (p. 2) or mood disturbance.

Anne exemplifies typical aspects of the bulimic:

Blond, intelligent, talented, Anne had been concerned about her weight from adolescence. Compared to her high-achieving brother, she felt she was inferior, despite the fact that she was a skilled graphic artist. Her self-involvement and need to control led her from one unsatisfying romance and job to another. These losses she absorbed by binge eating and vomiting. So excessive were her bouts that the next morning she would not be able to function at her work. Hospitalization helped her control the gross symptom, but all who treated her recognized her vulnerability to regression as soon as she was released from hospital constraints.

Anne entered the halfway house, a frightened, anxious woman who needed a binding contract to keep her symptoms in check. Without food as the palliative, this highly obsessional person was restless, anxious, and constantly spending money (with which she was generously supplied) on useless articles of clothing which were quickly discarded. She demanded inordinate time from staff and peers and gave little more than her ready intelligence. She criticized herself ruthlessly because she was unable to live up to her own ideals, but could tolerate little reflection of her own behavior from the other women.

At the halfway house, Anne talked incessantly about food. She needed to hear from her social worker and all the other residents that such talk was not helpful to her. She was asked to concentrate on a range of pleasurable tasks. At the height of her anxiety, as she was weaning herself from her intense absorption with food, she cleaned and organized every drawer in the halfway house. Anne could alternate from passivity and docility to anger and lability, but she could not exhibit real assertiveness.

A weight loss associated with an eating disorder may be confused with a weight loss that results from a depression. However, a depressed young person does not typically engage in the ritualistic behaviors associated with eating disorders, such as collecting recipes, counting calories, or spending long periods of time cooking foods that she does not touch. An eating disorder must also be differentiated from a schizophrenia, in which persons often "have delusions about the food they are eating but are seldom concerned over the calorie content of the food and are rarely preoccupied with the fear of becoming obese. They do not demonstrate the hyperactivity present in the anorexic" (Halmi, 1984, p. 269).

Persons suffering from eating disorders frequently create tension around the preparation of food and at the dinner table. Staff must decide how involved it will be in such behavior to minimize control battles. Efforts to engage these residents in activities that are pleasurable and unrelated to food are more productive.

Substance Abuse

Although it is the policy of many psychiatric halfway houses to exclude those whose primary diagnosis is addiction to alcohol or drugs, many applicants have self-medicated their illness with drugs or alcohol but have been diagnosed as suffering primarily from a psychiatric disorder. Naturally, such persons were weaned from their dependence upon the addiction during their hospital stays, permitting their basic psychiatric problems to be addressed. Those with an alcoholic dependence are brought into the Alcoholics Anonymous orbit and before admission to the halfway house, usually via a written contract, agree to forsake alcohol totally and faithfully attend AA meetings. Such a firmly structured probation may sustain the resident until he has formed new habits and lost his dependency. Presumably, inpatient therapy has begun to address the denial, the chief psychological defense mechanism in alcohol-related problems. The effort of the halfway house is to continue to help the resident pierce this denial.

> Nino, a young Mexican, used alcohol to conceal the intense anxiety he felt in separation from country, language, and family when he entered a prestigious and demanding college. Upon discharge from the psychiatric hospital, he had been stabilized and firmly rooted to his AA support group. When Christmas approached, he was invited to visit the home of an aunt whom he refused to inform of his prior alcoholism. Before staff granted him permission to accept the invitation to spend the holidays in an environment where liquor was included as a major aspect of the traditional holiday celebration, they insisted that he fully inform his aunt of his problem and enlist her aid in total avoidance of alcohol during the visit.

The Young Adult Chronic

The young adult chronic is a generic classification by symptomatology and lifestyle rather than by diagnosis. This group includes persons "with severe ongoing mental and emotional disorders . . . " (Pepper & Ryglewicz, 1985b, p. 1), including the severe personality disorders which present major problems in living. Typically, with hospitalizations now so brief, clear diagnostic differentiations are difficult to establish. Therefore, diagnoses often shift in time with treatment and become more like guideposts in formulating treatment plans at intake. Major emphasis during rehabilitation is on behavior or symptomatology rather than on diagnosis. Many of this group suffer from major emotional disturbances, including schizophrenia, major affective illnesses, personality and behavior disorders, or other psychiatric illnesses that seriously prevent acceptable social functioning for extended periods.

The current generation of chronically ill young adults differs in several aspects from older counterparts. Many young chronics self-medicate with drugs or alcohol, creating difficulties in all areas of living in addition to blurring their diagnoses. During a crisis, substance abuse becomes the palliative. This new group has not been warehoused for long periods of time in state or county psychiatric hospitals with scant programs or treatment. Because they have lived in the community, they tend to expect more from the environment. They have also "tended to be sicker, more hostile, and less predictable than previous groups of young adult chronics" (Weinstein & Cohen, 1984, p. 597). With advances in medications and a richer array of community resources, a substantial proportion has never been hospitalized or else has experienced brief inpatient stays in a local hospital. After a first hospital admission, however, these patients tend, when in crisis, to seek the security of the hospital which soon represents a safe retreat.

A profile of these young persons, aged 18 to 35, might describe them as anywhere from 70 percent to 90 percent single (McCreath, 1984). They are fairly well educated (most of them have at least a 12th grade education, many are college educated) but have failed to adjust to work environments. They are unable to handle interpersonal relations, either running from them or rushing thoughtlessly into them. About 90% live at home though not by choice. The thought of living on their own creates unmanageable anxiety since many have never completed their developmental tasks by resolving conflicts through struggle. Because of their massive dependence, they come to rely on families as their major support system.

The young chronics need both family support and a full array of community services, but they misuse people and resources so wantonly that they tend to alienate not only their relatives but even the professionals who reach out to help them. Many psychiatrists feel that their capacity for change or growth is impaired by their hopelessness and disillusion.

When these young persons are shut out from the use of local agencies because of repeated misuse of facilities or when their parents "burn out," the young adults become "poor in resources" (McCreath, 1984, p. 438). The breakdown of a relationship between a person and his social environment creates what Gruenberg (1982) has termed "the social breakdown syndrome . . . (a) form of disability in which work functions, self-care functions or recreation functions fall to a totally inadequate level, or in which intolerable, aggressive, destructive behavior develops" (p. 45). The combination of the social breakdown syndrome and the resultant dearth of resources because of continued misuse isolates this group further.

STAGES OF MENTAL ILLNESS

Researchers have succeeded in evolving a model for decompensation which charts the phases through which the stressed person passes as he begins to disintegrate. Although the following is a medical model, similar stages of decompensation occur within the halfway house. If these states can be recognized early by halfway house staffs and the more vulnerable persons can be properly assessed, perhaps the environment can be so ordered as to prevent or retard decompensation. Docherty (1985)* delineated the following stages of decompensation observed in hospital wards:

1. In a state of *equilibrium*, the patient exhibits good spirits, takes an active leadership role, feels he is in control of his life, and feels good about his future.
2. In the second stage, *overextension*, he verbalizes concern about recurrent problems of identity and his lack of satisfaction about his self-image, while making an effort to keep up with things.
3. The third stage, *restricted consciousness*, finds the patient feeling dependent, self-critical, and neglectful of his personal appearance. His room becomes disorderly. He has decreased impulse control and feels things will not get better unless someone gives him a helping hand. He feels it is an effort to be with people, is easily bored, thinks about the same facts over and over again, is sensitive to noise, lights or people's voices, experiences strange or frightening thoughts, and feels people are making fun of him.
4. In the fourth, *psychotic state*, he may have visual, auditory, or olfactory hallucinations. He may feel that his face has changed or be confused about who people are and exhibit poor reality testing.

In *recompensation*, the patient moves through these sequences in inverse order. Recovery is aided by the presence of a therapeutic environment. Treatment tasks include the removal of whatever stresses contributed to the patient's vulnerability so that he takes this vulnerability into account and attempts to continue functioning in spite of it. From this research, Docherty underscored that antipsychotic drugs can only place

---

*Dr. John Docherty, Grand Rounds, New York Hospital-Westchester Division, January 11, 1985.

a ceiling on the effect of the illness, but a therapeutic alliance with helpful professional staff is critical in combatting the demoralization and in helping the patient understand the illness. The trust generated through this alliance is a powerful force in creating some hope for the future.

A hostile environment is a variable affecting the course of the illness. Some forms of interaction, especially those that are abrasive and critical, are predictors of relapse. Docherty particularly targeted as unsatisfactory for the recovering psychotic those settings that have high expressed emotion, are intrusive, and surround the person with negative criticism. Men appear to tolerate such an environment less well than women.

Docherty further felt that preparation for reentry into the community dictated a comprehensive program of social skills training and family therapy. For such a program the halfway house is the natural adjunct to the hospital as the patient begins his slow, faltering efforts at restabilization. The halfway house provides the consistency and continuity of care which patients require for stabilization, and the flexible structure of the halfway house offers the widely variable time sequence for recovery which many patients demand.

Group homes are asked to cope with multifaceted illnesses, often genetically based, with recurring relapses that may further impair the functioning and motivation of its victims. The task of a rehabilitation facility is to enable its residents to utilize their residual abilities, to help them select living and working environments facilitative of their best functioning, and to assist them to overcome or reduce their despair at their losses. The subsequent chapters shall describe various rehabilitation pathways.

CHAPTER 3

The Theoretical Model

A halfway house is a melting pot of residents diverse in age, education, family background, and financial circumstances. The common bond, however, is that all have experienced emotional problems.

The house serves as a bridge from the psychiatric institution to the general community. Working together with staff, residents develop homemaking and social skills and move toward vocational and educational goals. Living in a halfway house is a shared experience with built-in friendships. With the security of these support systems, the house can be a stable base from which to try new experiences.

HISTORICAL REVIEW

The literature focusing specifically on halfway houses for the mentally ill is sparse, as the movement is yet so young and funding for such community residences has been limited. As noted earlier, halfway houses developed in the United States in the 1950s and 1960s. Glasscote, Gudeman, and Elpers (1971) studied a representative sample of facilities and published a brief description of their programs. Others have written at length about specific halfway houses—Rutland Corner House in Vermont (Landy & Greenblatt, 1965), Woodley House in Washington, D.C. (Rothwell & Doniger, 1966), Gutman House in Oregon (Gutman House Report, 1962–1965), and Berkely House in Boston (Budson, 1978).

Several of these authors present detailed histories of the halfway house movement and summarize the important technical information necessary to establish and operate these facilities, i.e., zoning regulations, public hearing procedures with neighborhood and community planning boards, financial and safety concerns, and so forth. This valuable information will not be repeated here. We shall focus instead on the theoretical orientation of community residences, the therapeutic concepts and effective clinical applications. In doing so, we shall draw heavily on the work of Budson (1978), Raush and Raush (1968), and the life model construct of Gitterman and Germain (1976).

In surveying the literature, it becomes clear that each halfway house develops its own philosophy and range of services which reflect board, staff, community treatment resources, employment and housing facilities, and clientele. Each residence is sensitive to permutations in its locale and in the needs of its residents.

Raush and Raush (1968), in a 1963 study of some 40 halfway houses then operative in the United States, observed a range of facilities, from those that see their function purely as one of human care and shelter to those that seek to provide intense rehabilitation therapy. In the former, therapy, vocational planning, and socialization in a formal sense are left to other resources in the community. Even those residences that least sought to embody a formal program, however, did offer counseling and support in some manner, either by a caring houseparent or in a weekly visit by a professional staff member. The number of staff available to residents, their professional training, and the intensity of involvement varied among houses.

Gutman House, for example, pledges itself to a program "that embraces emotional support, intensive counseling, and non-coercive encouragement of the client to assume an increasingly active social and vocational role, along with greater and greater responsibility for his own conduct and welfare" (Gutman House Report, 1962–1965, p. 11). This theme of self-determination is a strong principal in each halfway house studied, whatever its therapeutic orientation: "Matching individual needs to the appropriate environment has been found to be more beneficial than seeking one form of care for all. . . . (R)esidential facilities differ in many ways that are relevant to placement decisions, particularly in their socioemotional and structural dimensions" (Coulton, Fitch, & Holland, 1985, p. 377).

Most halfway houses see themselves as serving both a holding and an accelerating function. They offer protection for "occasional lapses into dependency without the danger of rehospitalization that might accrue to the patient living alone in the community" (Gutman House Report, 1962–1965, p. 8). Yet they encourage each resident to move at his or her pace toward increased functioning at home and, if possible, at work. Many houses, therefore, have an interest in the vocational development of each resident. Since employment is considered by Gutman House as the best precursor to adjustment in the community, this facility has a particularly strong vocational thrust, employing its own vocational counselor who develops job possibilities and serves as a liaison between the resident and a multitude of business and community agencies offering employment opportunities.

No overview of the halfway house movement in the United States would be complete without mention of George W. Fairweather and his community lodge societies (Fairweather, Sanders, & Maynard, 1969). In these autonomous residences, former chronic mental patients were contracted out as work groups offering cleaning and repair services. While initially receiving extensive supervision from outside sources, these groups eventually assumed total responsibility for their own operation at home and at work, using consultants when necessary. "Compared with traditional aftercare programs, the lodge society significantly increased employment and time in the community" (Fairweather, Sanders, & Maynard, 1969, p. 7). Self-esteem grew, the program cost per resident was half of what it would have been in hospital and the residents eventually became totally self-sufficient, at which point the program phased out. The researchers also found that the community adjustment of lodge members was more complete than in other community treatment programs even for those members who were most chronic.

> From this study, a series of principles for the operation of community treatment programs was derived. It became clear that as the members developed a greater stake in the social system, they became more responsible. The pride that came with personal independence and the ownership of a business, which is one symbol of successful achievement in this society, was obvious to all concerned. Community-treatment programs thus need to provide as much autonomy to their members as possible. Pride cannot develop with autonomy, however, unless meaningful work, as society defines it, is also available to members, so that the responsibilities implied by autonomy are themselves meaningful. (Fairweather, Sanders, & Maynard, 1969, p. 8)

Other programs have since adopted the Fairweather Lodge format, one of the most recent being supervised by the Institute for Living in Hartford, Connecticut.

Whereas the Fairweather Lodge concept presumes a more or less permanent living arrangement, halfway houses are transitional in nature. Whether they have their own vocational services or assist the resident to obtain them in the community, a major concern halfway houses share with the Fairweather researchers is that of promoting residents' efforts toward self-sufficiency and improved quality of life. Eventually, the majority of residents obtain employment and move to transitional supportive apartments or directly into the community, often with peers in relationships which have developed as a result of growth fostered by the halfway house.

Some residents, however, even when working, may require support and supervision for long periods of time or even indefinitely. For these, the permanent supportive apartment is an option offering a consistent, stable, reduced-stress environment which mitigates against frequent hospitalizations or disorganization leading to homelessness. This option will be explored more fully in Chapters 10 and 11.

In their study, Raush and Raush (1968) describe the halfway house as

> somewhat like family life in its informal atmosphere and style of living, in its demand for participation, and in the promise of comfort and support in difficult times. Yet it is unlike a family in being free from associations with past happenings in the resident's life: emotional involvements are less intense. . . . (p. 192)

The authors also see the resemblance of a halfway house to a small boarding school in that both institutions teach and protect their charges for a transitional period of time until a certain degree of independence and wisdom is achieved.

In the houses that the Raushes studied, the populations varied but ranged in size from 6 to 15 residents. The Raushes recommend that the house be small enough that relations among residents and between residents and staff are immediate, direct, and personal, yet large enough so that the actions of any one resident and/or any one occurrence do not totally disorganize the house. In a small, family-oriented living situation, of course, the demographics of the population selected has great impact upon the structure and ambiance of the house. This crucial area will be explored in Chapter 5.

MILIEU INTERVENTIONS

The Raushes contend in their study that systematic change resulting in improved self-esteem and functioning can occur under certain favorable conditions, i.e., where there are opportunities for learning new behaviors, for physical and intellectual development and maturation and where curiosity and exploration are encouraged and supported. Yet none of the above can occur if the individual's system itself seems to have broken down. In cases of severe psychopathology—as in the schizophrenias, which constitute by far the greatest diagnostic bulk of mental hospital patients—we seem to be faced with such a breakdown. Learning is primitivized; developmental change is inhibited; exploration and information seeking and utilization are sharply restricted. (p. 147)

The bonding with others and the sense of hope and trust that enables a person to shift focus from his/her inner world to look once again at life and to take action to risk its possibilities can occur in few places. The Raushes note that those who have been successful in helping the long-term chronic schizophrenic to change not just behavior but the person beneath the behavior, have all moved to meet the subject in his own world. Their understanding of this troubled world serves as a foundation for the development of a relationship built on trust so that learning and development can proceed. Such thorough understanding can rarely be gained in situations other than living with or spending many waking hours with one's patient. Halfway houses (and as we shall explore in Chapter 7, day hospitals) present the opportunity for such intense and prolonged interaction over time on the part of skilled and caring staff.

A basic ingredient in a halfway house is the care manifested by staff for each resident and for the house as a whole. Each staff member brings nurturing concern and commitment into his/her work with every resident. Support for the vulnerable, pleasure in each achievement, firmness in the face of manipulation, understanding of anger, and encouragement for the downhearted are offered along with a consistent structure. Residents live and work with staff and with each other for periods of from one to as many as four years, allowing ample time for staff to come to know residents and for change to occur. Kruzich and Kruzich (1985) have found that "(i)f staff watch TV with patients, eat with them, celebrate their birthdays, and participate in other activities that diminish the status differences, residents will be more involved in the facility" (p. 382).

Budson (1978) in his work on halfway houses and kinship systems sees the halfway house as operating as a social system in the same way as does the nuclear family, by educating and socializing its members. In his view, the "'patient is not just 'sick' but . . . has . . . a defective or arrested development owing to either his environment or his physiology" (Budson, 1978, p. 21). All residents come to community residences, as did Joan and Sally (Chapter 1), with deficits in important maturational areas so that at times their functioning resembles that of young adolescents. In the case of a major psychiatric illness, after any necessary medications have been determined and the patient is stabilized, the patient can return to the task of emotional growth. "The milieu's role is to help the person grow beyond his point of arrest or to correct areas of distortion that occurred in the initial faulty family or physiological experience" (Budson, 1978, p. 21). The resident has another opportunity to complete the tasks of adolescence—to separate and individuate from parents and home, to consolidate his or her sexual identity, to develop and pursue vocational planning and goals, and to establish and maintain relationships with peers.

Budson (1978) contends that "the psychiatric halfway house prepares a person for living in the community through its communication of self-knowledge, the ability to cope, and altruism" (p. 34). Self-knowledge is enhanced by helping people to "understand and gain knowledge about their psychological reality so they can communicate about it, relate to others in relation to it, and thereby increasingly cope effectively themselves. In the most direct sense they learn how to value themselves instead of regarding themselves as stigmatized outcasts" (Budson, 1978, p. 34).

The development of altruism is one of the more interesting processes of growth fostered by the halfway house. As each member experiences the caring and support of staff and peers and learns how to value herself more, she is able to move from self- to other-care involvement. Senior residents who have already grown in this regard stimulate the process in newer members. In the group (Chapter 1) that sat and heard out Joan in her effort to return to the halfway house were women who had been exhausted by Joan's acting out. Indeed, staff had first refused to consider Joan's return but then left the decision to the women who would live with her. Despite their anger, frustration, and pessimism at the likelihood that Joan could control her symptoms, all but the newest—and most self-involved—members of the group finally voted for Joan's return. They felt she would not easily find such an opportunity to grow and learn as with them at the halfway house. In the end, they identified with her and wanted to give her the opportunity they knew she needed.

Both the Raushes and Budson recommend that therapists assume an active, involved role when working with persons having serious mental and emotional disorders. Indeed, this stance is so widely recommended in the literature that it is surprising how often one encounters clinicians in practice who are distant and neutral with such patients. The rehabilitation work of halfway houses, by nature of the setting, has always been direct, vital, and involved. Because residents live in the setting, the whole spectrum of their behavior is available for intervention. The counselor or houseparent can work with a chronically tardy resident, for instance, on:

1. obtaining an alarm clock;
2. making sure it operates correctly;
3. placing it out of arm's reach;
4. negotiating with roommates about the problems a lengthy alarm ring causes them, etc.

The social worker directs and participates in these efforts and connects them to broader issues such as promptness at daily program, incorporating structure and routine, the impact of one's actions on significant others, and the taking charge of one's life. Because so much of the resident's life is available to staff, it becomes easier to locate sources of motivation and attach thereto behaviors in need of change. If Tom wants to move from the triple room to the double, for instance, he can do so once he is able to make his bed daily and keep his laundry off the floor.

It is unrealistic to expect an isolated, withdrawn, relation-starved resident to reach out for or to initiate a treatment situation. One moves to him with planned and spaced interventions, moderating as one goes, bridging the chasm until he is able to move himself. The less verbal, less focused resident may respond to briefer, more frequent, task-oriented contacts by staff and retreat from lengthy, more formal sessions. No less in need of active relatedness is the demanding, emotionally assaultive resident who distances people by onslaught rather than by withdrawal. Staying with this resident in caring firmness can help him to calm himself.

Often, the ego functioning of the chronic, young halfway house resident is so poor that active intervention from personnel at several different venues is necessary before the resident can hear, process, and act on input, and risk changing behavior or cognitive stances. The developmental lags, the dysfunctional survival manipulations, the disordered thinking, and the tremendous needs for support and nurture are simply too massive to be addressed by one treatment person in one location. Change occurs more quickly, effectively and, at times, *only* when the work is shared by the patient and several others, when staff in one setting reinforce and spell staff in another.

This systemic reinforcement, this ecosystem of efforts to help a patient grow to his potential, engages resources throughout the community on behalf of any one person: halfway house, day hospital, outpatient clinic, private therapist, case manager, OVR worker, vocational counselor, family, medical doctor, friends, volunteer job supervisor, landlord, school advisor, public assistance and/or social security worker, boss, lawyer, and so forth.

Any or all of these resources, the threads in the tapestry of the lives of those with whom we work, are sources of stress or strength, but all impact with and upon the resident and with and upon each other. Like any system, the community ecosystem is a living entity subject to change and molding so as to meet more closely the needs of the person at its center.

The Life Model

Social workers have chosen social functioning, the area of interface between the individual and his ecosystem, as their unique domain (Germain, 1973). Social workers are the clinicians who are most often at the hub of the halfway house operation, which is, as the Raushes (1968) note, the interface between the ex-patient and the community to which he returns. Whatever the diagnosis and degree of chronicity, the halfway house resident has been unable to cope with the environment in which he was living, or was functioning poorly enough that his therapist recommended supervised housing as a rehabilitative measure.

The "life model" of social work practice as developed by Gitterman and Germain (1976) "attempts to integrate two historic social work positions: emphasis on knowledge and skill to effect change in persons, and emphasis on knowledge and skill to effect change in environments. . . . Needs and issues are reconceptualized from 'personality states' and 'environmental states' to problems in living" (p. 601). They further conceive that "the human being and the environment reciprocally shape each other. People mold their environments in many ways and, in turn, must then adapt to the changes they create" (p. 602).

The function of the social worker and the halfway house then becomes to help people strengthen their coping patterns and improve their environments so as to attain a better match between people's needs and adaptive skills and the environments in which they live (Gitterman & Germain, 1976). Thus, problems in living are not seen as residing solely within the individual, but rather as consequences of the interaction of the individual with various elements in his particular ecosystem (Peterson, 1979).

Germain (1973) notes that "people ordinarily do not merely talk to reach resolutions, but also act. Successful action results in ego growth and does not necessarily require the development of self-understanding. Often people seek out and find environments that mesh with their character needs or that mitigate their neurotic symptoms . . . " (p. 327). Halfway house staff are acutely aware that a positive change in the environment can often bring about change in the individual's functioning through the spiraling of positive feedback, as the following vignette illustrates:

Pat, a 31-year-old woman who had been floundering for 10 years due to chronic schizoaffective disorder, came to the halfway house determined to "learn more adult behaviors." She was worse than incompetent in the kitchen. Unable to cook, she would work at a snail's pace, forget to turn on the heat, use dirty utensils in the preparation of food, and create conditions dangerous to herself and others. These behaviors totally exasperated the counselors, especially the main counselor who worked weekdays. This counselor was a woman of a firm and orderly nature who was very uncomfortable with chaos and most concerned with cleanliness.

It soon developed that the counselor spent every minute in the kitchen with Pat, giving her orders she at times didn't hear and at times couldn't or wouldn't follow. Eventually, she scolded Pat and prepared the meals herself. Staff worked with the counselor and Pat to ameliorate the situation, but the counselor was unable to withdraw and give Pat more responsibility. Pat was unable to assume more control on her own since she was too enmeshed in this replication of her childhood situation with her parents and her need to remain in a safe "incompetent child" role instead of risking a more mature stance.

Staff decided to schedule Pat to cook only on weekends with relief counselors who were more able to tolerate confusion, Pat's errors, and the threat that dinner for 10 would be late at best. The counselors were instructed to watch from a distance, ready to divert a dangerous situation, but to permit Pat to proceed on her own. At the same time, after collaboration with day hospital, a mental health worker there undertook to help Pat select a simple recipe and visualize its preparation. Within a month (four meals), Pat was cooking a full meal on her own. Within two months, Pat no longer needed supervision at all in the kitchen, and within three months she was feeling comfort, competence, and pride in her mastery.

Staff had sensed that Pat had the potential to perform well in the kitchen. She was bright and coordinated (a good tennis player and driver). Insight-oriented work had not been effective in changing her kitchen behaviors, so her "problem" of cooking was reconceptualized with Pat's help so as to approach it as a problem in living occurring within a specific environment.

In this conceptualization, the helper role is more broadly defined than in the traditional therapies, with the helper not as socially distant from the one helped. Indeed, the helper may be a team or collaborating agents from different venues and can "include more informal, expressive and functionally diffuse roles. The helping process includes anything that will provide the necessary conditions for clients to work on their defined tasks" (Peterson, 1979, p. 596).

In Pat's situation, no one was defined as "sick." Pat was seen as otherwise competent and the counselor was valued for her qualities of structure, strength, and concern for health and order, so important to the operation of the halfway house. It was their particular interaction that was dysfunctional. In the manipulation of Pat's environment by changing counselor (teacher), the focus was upon the imbalance of the transaction rather than on the "pathology" of the individuals (Peterson, 1979).

In subsequent months, Pat's awareness of her vulnerability to an assertive woman's direction increased, as did her ability to assert herself in such situations. She may continue to grow in this area, but she may also remain vulnerable. If so, when she returns to work, she would best choose her work situation and supervisor in consideration of this vulnerability.

THE ECOSYSTEM

As part of the ecosystem, the halfway house environment is organized to offer appropriate and fluctuating amounts of structure and challenge, support and stimulation, to reinforce growth in coping skills and independence. Additionally, staff, in concert with resident, begins a process of interaction with the community ecosystem to mold it more to meet the needs of the resident, to make a life plan best suited to the individual.

The life plan, of course, is formulated with the input of the many resources available to the resident—day hospital staff, therapist, vocational counselors, and so on, as noted above. The staff social worker serves a case manager function, coordinating all these efforts and staying with the resident through changes in the rest of his program. The relative weight of the roles of each facet of the ecosystem fluctuates according to which part of the ecosystem it makes most sense to address for each life problem. As systems interact, there are inevitable problems of communication, of shared or contested domains, of divergent opinions on planning, and so forth. Complexities of the cooperative effort will be further explored in later chapters.

In addition to case manager functions, social work staff may perform specific rehabilitative interventions within the milieu of the halfway house. This work reinforces, augments, and sometimes overlaps the treatment of the outside therapist. The social worker, in frequent communication with the therapist, serves as the arm of the therapist in the patient's living situation and brings valuable feedback to the therapist who, in turn, can conduct more aggressive treatment knowing such support exists (see Chapter 7). The value of mutually reinforcing treatment influences on a population that tends to be extremely needy and draining cannot be overemphasized.

Halfway house rehabilitative efforts tend to be focused on the here and now. Deeper therapies, when indicated, are left to the outside therapist, as are decisions regarding major treatment directions, biological therapies, and (with some exceptions) rehospitalizations.

Each interaction in the halfway house between staff and residents whether in session, at meals, or in the hallway, presents the opportunity for healthy intervention. The emphasis at one moment may be behavioral, at another, cognitive, and at another, developmental. Indeed, many residents are able at times to utilize sophisticated, insight-oriented techniques, so it behooves the staff member to be articulate in a number of therapeutic languages.

According to William Knoedler, director of the Program of Assertive Community Treatment (PACT) in Madison, Wisconsin, dynamically oriented psychotherapy for the quite chronic population served by his program "is at best no better than and at worst less effective than problem-solving, skill-teaching kinds of therapies, combined with drug management."* Psychosocial treatments are supportive, practical and behavioral, specific, and frequently revised.

REHABILITATION

Any reader familiar with the work of William Anthony will have recognized in the above material some significant rehabilitation principles as defined in work coming out of Boston University's Center for Rehabilitation Research and Training in Mental Health. Anthony, Cohen, and Farkas (1982) define rehabilitation as

> a restoration process, designed to remove or reduce those residual handicaps which interfere with psychiatrically disabled persons' abilities to function in their own communities. Rehabilitation programs attempt to increase or maximize the psychiatrically disabled persons' strengths and assets, and focus relatively little of their direct attention on creating therapeutic insight or alleviating the patients' symptoms. (pp. 83–84)

The following 10 principles as developed by Anthony et al. (1982) are the basis of the rehabilitation thrust:

---

*Knoedler, W. (9/21/85). Speech given at the Third Annual Educational Conference sponsored by the Alliance for the Mentally Ill of New York State.

1. *Functional Assessment in Relation to Environmental Demands*—a formal method of determining client strengths in terms of the skills required in any particular environment.
2. *Client Involvement in the Assessment and Intervention Phases of Rehabilitation*.
3. *Systematic Individual Client Rehabilitation Plans*—the behavioral steps, time frames, and reinforcements necessary to reach a goal.
4. *Direct Teaching of Skills to Clients*—including partialization as to skill definition, purpose, steps, applications and evaluation, and the teaching methods needed to impart the above.
5. *Environmental Assessment and Modification*.
6. *Follow-up of Clients in the Real Life Environments*–monitoring progress and getting feedback.
7. *Rehabilitation Team Approach*—each team specialist has a unique function.
8. *Rehabilitation Referrals*—a goal-directed referral specifying desired outcome and timeframe.
9. *Evaluation of Observable Outcomes and Utilization of Evaluation Results*—for practitioner or agency efficacy assessment.
10. *Consumer Involvement in Policy and Planning*.

These 10 principles, as with most therapies, are adapted by different programs according to the needs of the clientele and of the agency. For a highly chronic low-functioning clientele, the number of skills taught, the degree of partialization, and the time frames selected will differ markedly from those for the high-expectation client whose rehabilitation program will also include a fair amount of insight-oriented, perhaps even analytical work. Kruzich and Kruzich (1985) have found that "offering training in many areas (six or more) has a slightly negative effect on patient integration. One interpretation is that there is a point of diminishing returns in the number of types of skills training offered" (p. 382) in any one facility.

The pace and mix of rehabilitation and/or insight work will also fluctuate over time with an individual client if she experiences episodes of acute illness and periods of remission during which she is quite intact. Each practitioner, ideally well grounded in the techniques of many useful theoretical approaches, finally applies his art as does a craftsman with his tapestry—weaving together in his work what is useful from theory and from practice, according to his client's unique capacities.

Despite all the skills of the program and practitioner, despite the cooperation among facets in the ecosystem, and despite all the intent and perseverance of the client/patient, there are times when even the most carefully constructed and developed rehabilitation plan fails. When a client is stressed by anxiety, sudden changes, unexpected events, and so on, there may occur a resurgence of symptoms, of the inability effectively to screen, sort, process, and control stimuli and emotions. Thus, the learning that has occurred will be short-circuited. This is extremely frustrating for client and practitioner and requires retrenchment, support, and reassessment to determine if there is something in the client, the program, or the environment that can change to avoid a repetition of this particular sequence of events.

Pedro was slowly progressing in his efforts to control the anxiety that overwhelmed him when under stress. His panic made him irritable, extremely negative, and, at its worst, caused him to feel hopeless and drove him to drug himself out or to grasp at the idea of death as a release.

Even though separations were extremely difficult for Pedro, he was able to get through a change of therapists without decompensating by working very hard to control his anxieties. He and his halfway house worker set a program of activities which gave him some outlet for his energies. This and pure discipline on Pedro's part kept him stable for weeks after the change.

Just as Pedro and staff were beginning to relax, he had a chance encounter on the street with a former lover whom he had not seen in six years. The lover wanted to see Pedro again and pressed on several occasions for a date. Pedro became so upset by rearoused sexual and intimacy concerns that over the next two weeks he lost his hold on himself and decompensated.

TREATMENT GUIDELINES

The halfway house program sits squarely on a base of broader treatment guidelines which make for more effective service:

Medication Monitoring

According to Talbott (1981), medication is the best preventer of relapses, in both schizophrenia and the affective disorders" (p. 376). Halfway houses approach medications in a variety of ways, but all take a strong interest in medication compliance.

Continuity of Care

Continuity and integration of services are fostered by the case management function of the halfway house worker who coordinates resources and assures that the resident follows through on planning. In addition, the aftercare services of the halfway house—the continued contact with former caretakers who remain interested in the former resident—provide a source of stability and assist the individual to maintain ties to residents and former residents in the community.

Torrey (1985)* advocates a team management approach to continuity of care. He asserts that the single case manager concept is too limited and has not worked. The one person who has responsibility for continuity of care may be on vacation or be changing jobs just when a knowledgeable decision must be made about a patient's treatment—a decision, for example, about medications which may affect decompensation. Torrey recommends a team of practitioners—psychiatrist, nurse, social worker, mental health aide, and so on, and a dedicated family member—responsible for each patient for his lifetime. This approach has proved extremely effective as indicated in the Vermont State Hospital Longitudinal Study (1984). Torrey believes such a team could absorb a turnover rate of one member per year and remain effective.

Group Approaches

Most chronically ill people respond better and remain longer with programs that have a group rather than an individual orientation. Some clients find individual attention too intense and intimate for their comfort and some experience the therapist in individual psychotherapy as a critical parental figure (Pepper, 1984). Halfway houses are group living arrangements offering peer interaction for social purposes as well as for inducements to change. Most residents take quite seriously their role as friend, support, and monitor of each other's dysfunctional behavior.

Building a Social Network

The group orientation of treatment programs provides social and recreational outlets for a frequently isolated population. In the halfway house, residents have rich opportunities to address their social impairments, to make stronger relationships with the goal of developing a kinship support system to take with them after they leave the transitional residence.

One Change at a Time

Stress-sensitive persons can be overwhelmed by sudden or multiple changes in their lives. Careful, step-by-step stretching of the limits of functioning permits each resident to move with reduced levels of anxiety and at his or her own pace. Growth may well occur in some areas, while others may remain impaired for some time or permanently. Progress is often very scattered for this population.

---

*Torrey, E. Fuller (9/22/85). Speech given at the Third Annual Educational Conference sponsored by the Alliance for the Mentally Ill of New York State.

Flexible Programming

Programs that serve the young adult chronic population must of necessity offer unconventional, individualized care. Treatment resisters or dropouts rarely respond to a "you adjust to my program" attitude. Imaginative approaches to work with the unmotivated or inappropriate patient must accompany acceptance of skewed or episodic progress.

Positive Staff Expectations

Investigators of the Vermont Longitudinal Study of Chronic Schizophrenics (1984) are finding that "people with schizophrenia can recover or significantly improve in their functioning" (p. 5). The researchers feel that staff expectations that patients would get better had significant effect on their progress. The underlying yet unpressured expectation at most halfway houses is that people enter wanting to work and grow and that they can achieve reasonable goals.

Focus on Functioning

For many, attention is best focused on functioning rather than on dynamics or symptomatology. People are quite gratified when they learn how to cope with breakthrough hallucinations or paranoia and not permit these symptoms to disrupt their activities so grossly. Mastery of everyday challenges can come fairly quickly in some areas, with accompanying rise in self-esteem.

Team Approach to Care

From the volatile, hysterical acting out of the borderline to the dragging despair of the depressed, this population with its overwhelming needs presents a challenge to program comprehensiveness and staff stamina. As noted earlier, this challenge is too heavy for one staff member or one agency to bear. The team concept is essential in treating this group, not only to provide for outreach, advocacy, individualized care, and a requisite range of services, but also to prevent staff burnout.

Family Involvement

As evidence increasingly points to genetic and biochemical etiology in the various psychiatric disabilities, clinicians are looking upon the experience of parenting a poorly functioning adult child with more empathy and acceptance. Clinicians and parents are trying to shake the old notions that the parents inevitably have played some role in the genesis of the illness. Families—siblings, as well as parents—are looking for help in management of here-and-now problems of caring for and/or living with an emotionally troubled person and for help in accepting and softening some of their own troubled feelings about the ill family member, including those of guilt, anger, and despair (Group for the Advancement of Psychiatry, 1986).

In Chapter 6 we shall offer some guidelines for work with families. Again, this is an area that often is shared by the several programs which are engaged with a particular individual. The halfway house can be quite flexible in filling in the gaps of coverage. Some involvement with parents is absolutely necessary in the case of most residents, varying from lesser contact with a higher-functioning resident who clearly is maturing and will achieve real independence to more intense collaboration with parents whose young adult's progress will be slower, replete with crises, and who will remain dependent for some time. However, it is preferable that formal family treatment take place in a program other than the halfway house, which is experienced by the resident as his home where he is working to live his life more independently.

Substance Abuse

Given the endemic substance usage among young adults, all programs serving this group must consider what stance they will take regarding substance abuse. Most halfway houses take a firm position that use of any nonprescribed substance is dangerous physically and undermines goals to address painful or complex life concerns rather than to avoid them through self-medication. Halfway houses can more easily control substance abuse on premises than in the community and frequently must confront a resident who is abusing alcohol or drugs and determine with the resident if he can use community support groups to help him maintain abstinence or whether his abuse is out of control. In the latter case, the resident usually must leave the halfway house, possibly to return to the hospital for treatment.

Vocational Planning

As "work is the most meaningful tool of involving people in treatment over the long run" (Knoedler, 1985*), it is vital to halfway house programming. The house may employ its own vocational staff, it may refer out to such a service in the community and/or it may reinforce the vocational thrust of the individual therapist and/or day hospital.

---

*Knoedler, W. (9/21/85). Speech given at the Third Annual Educational Conference sponsored by the Alliance for the Mentally Ill of New York State.

Knoedler's (1979) Program of Assertive Community Treatment (PACT) utilizes a multimodal system of work alternatives for the more chronically ill patients. This system embodies the concepts:

1. that most of the chronically mentally ill cannot work competitively full time and that many of them function best in a subcompetitive role (p. 58)
2. that individual patients can vary greatly over time in their capacity for employment, depending on such factors as the stage of their illness and the strength of their support system (p. 59), and
3. that staff must be largely directive and reality oriented in helping patients work rather than depend on nondirective, expressive techniques. (p. 61)

The elements of PACT's system are as follows:

1. A staff-supervised work training site. . . .
2. A network of volunteer jobs for basic work experience. . . .
3. Sheltered workshops, used both traditionally and nontraditionally. . . .
4. On-the-job training positions in competitive business. . . .
5. The structured teaching of job-attainment skills and assistance in finding competitive work. . . . (and)
6. An intensely collaborative relationship with the Division of Vocational Rehabilitation (pp. 59–61).

The concept of "supported employment" as developed by Wehman (1981), Revell, Wehman, and Arnold (1984), of the Rehabilitation Research and Training Center at Virginia Commonwealth University, and Bellamy, O'Connor, and Karan (1979) of the Specialized Training Program, University of Oregon, is an approach that has placed developmentally disabled persons into competitive employment positions in real workplaces, for real wages, alongside nondisabled workers. Staff of rehabilitation facilities and day programs assist severely disabled clients to gain employment, "learn the skills at the job site, adjust to the work environment, and ultimately retain the job" (Revell, Wehman, & Arnold, 1984, p. 33).

Such support continues to the degree required for the client to maintain employment. This innovative approach has recently been expanded in Pennsylvania to include the chronically mentally ill: "It is a powerful and flexible way to ensure normal employment benefits, provide ongoing and appropriate support, create opportunities, and achieve full participation, integration and flexibility" (Rehabilitation Research and Training Center, . . ., 1985, p. 1).

EXPRESSED EMOTION

Recently, studies have focused on the concept of expressed emotion (EE)—overly intense or involved, hostile or critical communications—as a measure of quality of communication in the immediate environment of schizophrenic patients (Brown, Birley, & Wing, 1972; Vaughn & Leff, 1976; see also Chapter 2). Pepper (1984) carries this thinking into the arena of community treatment programs. He suggests "that program components and treatment modalities . . . may be identified as low- or high-EE, and that low-EE environments and interventions may have a positive relationship to treatment engagement and success, not only for schizophrenic patients but for certain functionally defined subgroups of the young adult chronic patient population" (p. 4).

This is an intriguing hypothesis for staff in any program to consider. Certainly, in a halfway house it is far more effective for staff to concentrate on and reinforce positives, to ignore negatives that are not harmful or vital to structure, and to keep communications clear, direct, and relaxed.

MOTIVATION

Most residents come to halfway houses on a voluntary basis—some with real motivation to make changes in lifestyle and circumstances which they feel will benefit them, others to get away from home or because they have not succeeded in living on their own and they see no other housing alternative. Even those whose goals are clear are often too frightened to move on them, fearful of overstressing themselves, of inviting breakdown, of failing once more. Most often, these goals center on the physical living situation, socialization and relationships, and work.

Staff is attentive to each resident's motivation level. Motivation is crucial for movement. If the resident is passive, lethargic, or uninterested in the world, staff can use the house's structure to create or bolster motivation. This is an interesting challenge, much like a treasure hunt—a looking for clues, a thoughtful determination with the resident of where hope remains within him and to what stimulus it will respond. The stimulus might be connecting a negatively charged goal such as work, with a positively charged one, such as having more money to buy more space, privacy, a trip, and so on. If the steps toward goal achievement are made small enough, if support is there, if the possible positive and negative consequences are fully understood and accepted, and if the rewards are real, a resident can be persuaded to make a move, to take a risk toward his goal.

In later chapters we shall illustrate examples of how a halfway house can use a resident's bonding—his need for his new home and companions—to help him make movement in many areas. If he keeps his room clean, he can move from a triple room to a double room; if she gets a job, she can move to the supportive apartment and have a room of her own as well as more freedom and less structure; if he comes out to the public area to socialize, he can sleep an hour later on Saturday. Staff is forthright about this manipulation of structure and residents know they need help with taking risks to reach their goals, or even to set their goals. Once enough small steps are successfully taken to break into the negative legacy of past fears and failures, the resident can carry forward more independently with his own momentum.

A time limitation on residency at the house can be a motivating force. The expectation that within a year a resident is to be employed, for instance, provides a concrete framework within which to operate and enables resident and staff to plan the year in steps leading to employment. The time frame, the goals, and the structure to achieve them will vary according to the orientation of the house. A residence for the high-functioning will differ from that for the more chronic. Time frames in the former will be briefer and expectations higher. The structure will be organized so that as residents grow healthier, they will begin to chafe, feel infantilized by the rules, and want to move on. If the halfway house or supportive apartment is for those who need long-term care, the atmosphere and structure should be comfortable, as much like "home" as possible. With a functionally mixed population, staff can individuate without undermining structure.

Structure is a key element in support of personality change within the halfway house. Growth sometimes occurs seemingly without thought or effort. At other times it is achieved with great struggle:

> Personality change follows change in behavior. Since we are what we do, if we want to change what we are we must begin by changing what we do, must undertake a new mode of action. . . . The new mode will be experienced as difficult, unpleasant, forced, unnatural, anxiety-provoking. It may be undertaken lightly but can be sustained only by a considerable effort of will. Change will occur only if such action is maintained over a long period of time. (Wheelis, 1969, p. 63)

The struggle is at times so painful that there must be real motivation to stay and endure the changing. People become bonded and committed in their living situation. Housemates and staff become their surrogate family who care for them and accept them as they are, even while they want to see them grow and achieve their goals. While people may leave treatment at other settings when facing a crisis or when pain increases, they stay with the halfway house and this, in turn, helps them stay with their goals and their other programs.

CHAPTER 4

Description of a Halfway House

Normalization at a slow, steady pace is the goal of rehabilitation which several levels of community residence care reflect. For the person newly discharged from a psychiatric hospital who has lived in its structured environment where the meals, beds, recreation, and therapy were readily at hand, fending for himself can be overwhelming. Although discharged as "in remission," his hope for a complete return to his previous life is premature and smaller steps are desirable.

The first level of care, the halfway house, offers a safe way station until the new arrival eases himself back into a highly complex society. He enters a friendly, homelike atmosphere peopled with men and women who have been similarly derailed. He need not, at once, struggle with explanations about his illness. The counselor, on duty 24 hours, offers another margin of security. At his own pace and with nonjudgmental guidance, the newcomer is eased back into taking care of his own basic needs at a rate he can tolerate and absorb. Some new arrivals are fully ready to cook a meal for 10 but are woefully inadequate at starting a conversation. A trip to a supermarket may invite a full-blown paranoid reaction. The acceptance of limitations in functioning, with expectations that abilities will improve in time, moves the resident into rediscovering or relearning skills essential for daily living.

Within eight months to a year, many are ready to assume additional responsibility, but total care of themselves and their housing, struggles with landlords and superintendents, being and becoming economically accountable to themselves, all demand an intermediate step. For this reason, the second level of care is established, the supportive apartments located close by the halfway house. Each provides housing for at least three same-sexed persons who have demonstrated their motivation and ability to progress from a program of day hospital rehabilitation to a volunteer position and then either back to school or to paid employment. They have regularized their habits of daily living, proving to themselves and to staff that they can, at some acceptable level, budget, shop, prepare nutritious, balanced meals, create some friendships, and utilize community resources. They still need and want the several weekly visits of the social worker, but life in these apartments is less restrictive than in a halfway house. Supportive apartment residents gain additional time to continue their growth as capable, independent adults who can struggle with a hostile or indifferent society. Supportive or "three-quarter way houses" provide those highly necessary smaller steps back to normalcy.

PHYSICAL LOCATION—APARTMENT AND HOUSE

The inconspicuous setting of the halfway house in a carefully maintained home or apartment building in a residential area bespeaks "normalcy." Its residents are rarely distinguished from their "normal" neighbors. The community should provide resources nearby, such as major psychiatric hospitals, day hospitals, outpatient clinics, and vocational rehabilitation departments. Psychiatrists, psychologists, social workers, and medical and legal resources should abound in the area. Libraries, shops, and department stores can offer instant space for activity with people or for observing the passing scene.

A varied business community is an excellent matrix for developing a variety of employment opportunities for those vocationally adrift or work-ready. The existence of community colleges, readily invite the resumption of an education interrupted by illness. Business schools teach word and data processing, excellent employment potentials for persons struggling with social problems. Available public transportation is also an asset. The resident who is ready to classify himself as "disabled" can utilize the bus system at half price. Accessible public recreational facilities provide a natural antidote to depression and enable low-income persons to enjoy their gyms, pools, and varied classes.

Community housing offers the new resident immediate anonymity and civilian status. He is no longer a "mental patient" but has merged into a mainstream populace that leaves the building in the morning and returns when the day is finished. He is furnished with a set of keys which open the front doors emphasizing once again the restoration of freedom and independence.

Even a small strip of land can be converted into a community garden for those residents who relate to the soil.

To Melanie, a 21-year-old, newly admitted woman who felt thoroughly ejected from her home and abandoned by her burned-out parents, this pocket-sized garden became the transitional object which helped her restructure herself so as to endure the loss of her family and adapt to her new home. Prior to admission, her one hesitation in entering the residence was that she would be forced to abandon her garden, which she considered her single great achievement. With staff encouragement, she transplanted her strawberry plants. Initially, she watched over them tenderly, weeding and watering them daily. As she became acclimated to life in a transitional house, established a few friendships with women, and enjoyed several dates with the young men, she slowly diminished her care of the heretofore treasured plants until they died of neglect. As she integrated with the group, cooking for housemates replaced horticulture.

A halfway house located in an apartment building has the advantage of instant normalcy, but must yield some of its autonomy to community pressures and prejudices. The building superintendent, hired by and responsive to the landlord, can be a staunch ally and friend or a distorter of facts who plays on the underlying fears of mental illness latent in many lay persons. One superintendent, after initial difficulties, became a most valuable resource to one halfway house. He managed to familiarize himself with the residents, their talents, and problems. He rescued one aged ex-piano teacher from his sense of uselessness by suggesting that he offer free piano lessons to a talented young resident. For both of them this association became an exciting symbiotic relationship in which the young woman provided a sense of continuity of life to her teacher, while in return her musical growth helped reduce her delusion that she was incapable of learning.

During his tenure, the superintendent repaired the broken chairs and tables, installed the bookshelves and helped redesign the layout. He was constantly on the alert for discarded items of furniture—an extra easy chair for a bedroom or a 50-year-old leather couch for the office, which he could repair and resell to the house. Since many senior citizens lived in surrounding apartments, he also became an employment resource. He inquired of staff whether any young person, struggling to survive on a limited budget, could or would be available to help an elderly person maintain his household. For several young women such employment provided a first step toward gainful, nonstressful work. The superintendent was regularly invited to house parties, both because he could join in the fun of the evening and because his presence was a protection against complaints that the festivities were too disturbing to the public peace. Through long association with staff members, he became sensitive to the needs of residents for recognition. When he was selected to judge the best costumes created for the annual Halloween Party, he quietly asked the director to help him choose the residents whose growth and self-esteem needed this extra injection of public recognition. He additionally symbolized to residents a person outside the mental health field who could accept them as neighbors, drop in for a cup of coffee or exchange a few good belly laughs.

Unfortunately, not all superintendents become adjuncts to life in the house. An agency with a budget invites a degree of exploitation. Small repairs that are made gratis for other tenants may be ignored until a price is established. The halfway house residents are a ready target for scapegoating to cover inadequacies in performance on the part of superintendents. If markings are discovered on the walls of the halls, suspicion immediately descends on the residents.

The presence of a psychiatric facility in close proximity to persons with various levels of understanding and tolerance for such an operation dredges up misinterpretation and community intolerance. For example, one highly chronic young man loitered in a building lobby, chain smoking until he ran out of cigarettes. He attempted to solve his emergency by stopping the next person who walked through the lobby door. This person, recognizing him as a resident of a halfway house, felt intimidated, partially perhaps because this young man was six feet tall, physically well developed, and sported a wild shock of black curly hair. The ill-placed but simple request frightened the other tenant as if it were an assault and a violation of his safety.

To short-circuit any problems, all residents of the halfway house were asked to use the lobby only for entry or exit. They were incensed by the prejudicial reaction to one of their members who erred only in judgment and by the loss of the free use of the lobby, a right enjoyed by all other tenants. In the extended discussion at a lively community meeting, the residents were forced to confront the fact that "mental illness" carried a stigma. They recognized that the agency could fight the injunction about the use of the lobby and even win this battle, but in so doing might incur the irreversible wrath of the landlord, thus endangering the residence for the entire agency. The group in its discussion (guided by staff) reached a consensus that occupancy of the apartments fulfilled more urgent needs at this time in their history than asserting their civil rights.

Leighton (1982) states that "all the diseases that are seen as life-threatening and incurable make people uneasy and evoke mental mechanisms such as denial, sublimation and displacement" (p. 4). He adds, "On top of that, insanity as such brings an additional dimension which adds to the intensity and irrationality of the response it inspires" (p. 4). In a changing, heterogeneous community, interpretations of the nature of emotional illness need to be constantly made and remade because of the "intense and unpleasant emotion roused in people by mental illnesses" (p. 4). Most efforts to establish community residences meet with vehement community opposition.

Similar prejudicial, exaggerated reactions are aroused by inappropriate but understandable behavior in houses already established.

Tina and Sanford were two young people who, even before their breakdowns, had never been able to enjoy heterosexual dating or any physical intimacies. Their initial discovery of each other created overwhelming urges. Other residents had objected to their hugging and kissing in the living room of the halfway house. Since they had no private areas, they moved their embraces to the storage room located in the hallway. That room also lacked privacy and a neighbor discovered them kissing. She complained to management about the "inappropriate, unsupervised conduct" of residents of the halfway house.

Staff had no alternative but to impose restrictions on the use of the corridors and the public areas of the building even though, from a therapeutic vantage, the ability to develop a relationship with the opposite sex was evaluated as a sign within these two young persons of natural healthy growth which their illnesses had interrupted. Their peers resented staff's edict that the stairwells (where they regularly left evidence of use via a trail of cigarette butts) were out of bounds. One enterprising couple admitted, several months after this incident, that they had created their private space on the top floor stairwell which led to the roof, where they were safe from chance discovery.

Because of such behavior, staff, much as parents do, had the function of educating and harnessing the emerging healthy drives and channeling them into socially approved forms. Unfortunately, the location of a rehabilitation facility in a close community, which demanded greater conformity from halfway house residents than from all other neighbors, created strains and resentments. The families of adolescents who socialized with the opposite sex in the corridor of the building would not have been threatened with eviction. A stern reprimand to the offending youngsters would have resolved the incident.

"Privacy is necessary as a foundation for normal behavior. The lack of it causes people to feel crowded, to withdraw and to set up psychological barriers. An absence of privacy may also cause people to set up other interpersonal structures such as exclusive cliques" (Bakos et al., 1979, p. 25). These authors add, "Without it, private acts are forced into public view and become inappropriate behavior. . . . Giving people privacy relates to trust and dignity" (p. 20).

In halfway houses located in private houses there are nooks or extra spaces in the basement or attic lending themselves to imaginative uses for private conversations or study. Most houses are, however, usually short of space, requiring that every square foot be utilized to provide separate areas for study, reading, artwork, music practice, or typing. A corner may be furnished with a couch that opens into a bed, a resource for a newly admitted, possibly frightened resident who needs proximity to the counselor's room. Or it may serve as a respite bed for a stressed ex-resident who perhaps can use a brief interlude back at the halfway house. Additional support may be an alternative to rehospitalization.

The living room in a community home is usually multifunctional, furnished, and arranged to invite parallel use of space. After meals are completed, the dining tables are converted to writing tables. Groups of four or six can play Scrabble, Trivial Pursuit, or bridge, with refreshments afterwards. An upright piano invites a practice session or a barbershop quartet. These activities can proceed while a group watches sports events on television and the radio plays, audible only to the young man with earphones. Furniture in one end of the living room, perhaps slightly separate from the main groupings, can be arranged to invite a measure of privacy for small group socializing or for one person quietly reading with a bowl of freshly prepared popcorn nearby. Some persons, newly arrived, need to join the larger group slowly.

In any halfway house the stereo and television are permitted to dominate the living room. Staff patiently mediates the endless squabbles about priorities and type of music played. Music is said to be the most provocative and powerful form of human expression. Rose (1984) asserts that the response to the rhythmic beat starts within the womb and recreates security and contentment. The high volume sound demanded by the young is an attempt to alleviate the abandonment which silence denotes. Sound, irrespective of content, is a return to a former supported state, representing object constancy and an attempt to gain a sense of unity in the face of separation anxiety. This is an aspect of the normal process of living and growth and the function of art. In the person who has experienced a psychotic fragmentation of his ego with feelings of disintegration, inconstancy, and floodings, music may recall a former state when the ego was less fragmented; the person may envelop his music with memories of former oneness with his world, leading perhaps to reconstruction of his sense of self or movement out of his regression and ending, temporarily at least, his sense of aloneness. Listening to music has been described as creative, nonlogical thinking, a together-ness of thinker and thought. It represents a mechanism to cope with environmental inconsistencies.

PHYSICAL SETUP OF HOUSE

When halfway houses first appeared as a resource, the furniture origi-nally collected by founding mothers came from the surplus, overstocked cellars of their friends and neighbors. Happily, the lived-in, miscellane-ous, Salvation-Army-Modern look has been replaced with contempo-rary, coordinated couches and chairs which also readily acquire a "lived-in" look. Attractive curtains and colorful cushions purchased by the residents reflect their desire and absolute need for lively, vibrant sur-roundings. Chipped, miscellaneous dinnerware was also jettisoned for a coordinated set reflecting the philosophy of the house that every resident has worth and dignity.

Theoretically, encouraging residents to select and arrange the interior space in the halfway house is one direct route to reasserting control and ownership of their lives. But as the themes of Chapters 2 and 3 imply, motivation is a scarce commodity in a halfway house. If management waited for it, the residents might be living in largely unfurnished quar-ters.

Nevertheless, it is the policy of most halfway houses to encourage as much independent functioning and self-government as possible. Al-though major pieces of furniture are purchased by staff, residents are urged to accompany the counselor to select and buy items used daily, such as dish towels, pot holders, a steam iron, a broom or mop. Such excursions become exercises in acquiring survival skills, learning value, economy, and budgeting.

Staff attempts, in a variety of ways, to involve the residents in rear-ranging the furniture to reflect their current needs and usage, to create a more homelike atmosphere and to offer more privacy even within shared public space. The arrangement of the bulletin board or the decision whether the tables in the dining area be placed together as one long banquet table to achieve a sense of unity or whether they be separated to encourage more intimate interaction at mealtimes is left to the residents. Pictures are provided for the living room walls but great latitude is of-fered the group in their arrangement. If there is a negative reaction to any picture or group of pictures, they may quietly disappear from the wall. If a talented graphic artist chances to live at the house, he is en-couraged, if he can share with others, to display his art for the enjoy-ment of all and receive recognition.

In most houses, bedrooms are shared by two or three residents. The basic reason is an acute shortage of space and an abiding desire to assist as many persons as possible. Sharing, of course, has its positives and negatives. Socialization is fostered but many personality conflicts proliferate which staff must mediate. Staff is constantly sympathetic to all resident complaints about loss of privacy.

The standard response to complaints that a halfway house does not permit a full range of adult conduct is concurrence. Finding ways to motivate those who are content to be cared for as children and to overcome their resistances to independence is the unsolved problem in rehabilitation. Some discontent with the status quo must be stimulated to spur the too passive recipient of the largesse of society. The shared bedroom, along with a weekday curfew, falls nicely into place. Staff is sympathetic to feelings about such inconvenience, with the expressed hope that the complainant will work harder on the stumbling blocks that retard his progress to the supportive apartment where he will have more freedom to regulate his own behavior and hours.

Frequently, bedrooms are only furnished with essentials: a bed, a chest of drawers, an empty bookcase, a desk, a lamp, sheets, and towels. The walls are left bare to encourage residents to decorate them themselves, overcoming the passivity that may have been spawned by the illness and developed in the caring atmosphere of the hospital. A prolonged hospital stay may have embedded the attitude that persons suffering from an emotional illness do not have the same rights or rewards as others. The resident's inner recognition that he needs and wants the halfway house and is not there by sufferance merely because his "team" at the hospital strongly recommended it or because his parents would no longer permit him to live with them can be perceived when he decorates his bedroom with his favorite pictures, fills the bookshelves with loved books, and unpacks the bags he has pushed out of sight under the bed.

DAILY MAINTENANCE AND HOUSE RULES

Basic training in survival skills in any rehabilitation facility naturally revolves around the preparation of meals and maintenance of the facility, including the sanitization of bathrooms. In these areas lies the test of whether the resident can make the changeover from his sick role as "patient" to the more independent status of "resident." The agency will not act as his caretaker in daily tasks. Instead, the expectations are that he will cooperate in every aspect of the daily routines of running and maintaining the unit.

The residents are expected to take turns planning daily menus for each other. From these menus a shopping list is developed. In many halfway houses the residents attend programs until late afternoon so the counselors shop alone for food on a daily basis. On weekends, counselors can be accompanied by a resident who uses this excursion into the crowded, local supermarket to learn comparative shopping and budgeting. The residents often have latitude about the money spent. Do they want to economize by buying generic brand toilet articles, thus saving money for expensive cuts of meat or fish? Have they scoured the papers for coupons which offer rebates, using the money saved over a period of time to buy a prized piece of athletic equipment or to enjoy a relaxed dinner at a local restaurant? Many groups retain autonomy in these decisions.

In one halfway house, the menu planner is the cook of the day, with responsibility rotated daily. The counselor's presence ensures that safety standards are observed. If a resident has not learned or has forgotten the rudiments of cooking, the counselor offers instruction and guidance, much as a parent introduces a young person into the mysteries of cooking and rejoices with him when the meal is worth the effort and the group acknowledges the success of his efforts. The skill of the counselor rests with evaluating the capabilities of the cook for the day and guiding him to surefire, simple menus which produce edible, well-balanced meals for the group. Small victories chip away at the internalized image of incompetence.

Except for major redecoration efforts, the responsibility for daily maintenance of the quarters usually rests with the unit's residents who weekly rotate the chores, ensuring a high standard of hygiene for all. Counselors assign the weekly duties. To guarantee acceptable work performance, they closely supervise new members of the group, describing in detail how to clean a toilet bowl or why the vacuum cleaner stops functioning when the trap is full. As soon as the resident demonstrates competence and an ability to critique his own performance, supervision recedes and is replaced by appreciation. Participation of all in maintenance of the apartment reduces the budget but on a deeper level invites each person to invest in his own comfort, to feel his own competence, which he may have lost during the course of his illness.

Other house rules may be few, limited to those that ensure cooperative effort and prevent members of the group from sabotaging their own or others' rehabilitation goals. A halfway house usually exerts minimal control over movements into the community. Residents move freely to their programs, to visit relatives and friends, or to shop or engage in recreational activities. The few rules relate to the volume of the television or radio. A thoughtful, good neighbor policy is the motto. Other rules define how late in the evening music or television can dominate the living room. Such limits exist not only for residents, who, under heavy medication, retire early, but for those who suffer from insomnia and who would readily slip into nocturnal habits of eating, sleeping, and entertaining themselves. Reversal of night and day happens easily for many.

To ensure daily attendance at the essential day program, a night curfew may be enforced. On weekends, this curfew may be suspended, permitting normal late night pleasures at a singles' group, a bowling alley, or a rock concert. Such latitude naturally pushes morning activities on Saturday and Sunday to a later schedule. Many residents could readily spend the entire weekend in bed, rising only for meals. A firm structure such as not permitting residents to remain in bed beyond 11:00 A.M. may address such dysfunctional behavior.

Simple as these rules are, they are not easily enforced. Noncompliance is the eternal problem facing every rehabilitation facility. Counselors are permitted to impose a modest fine for violation of a rule, but sometimes a more effective reminder is to assign additional chores around the apartment. Defrosting the freezer may imprint on a person his responsibility to be available to cook for the group when his turn comes. But as Raush and Raush (1968) have stated, the written or unwritten rules and regulations provide a background against which a resident can define himself. How smoothly he can adjust to them and stop struggling senselessly against them indicate to a great extent the progress he is making.

To develop a sense of community, many residences ask that members of the group be present for at least four evening meals each week, one of them the community dinner and the meeting that follows. At that meeting, newcomers are welcomed, those who move to another level of care are feted, house problems are addressed, and residents sometimes ask for support in facing new endeavors. Leadership of these meetings may rotate weekly among the residents. A suggestion box can be provided for all anonymous complaints and suggestions. Even staff might enjoy the option of its use.

Although residents may plan their weekends as they choose, halfway houses often request a limitation on overnights away from the house. This rule is aimed at creating a sense of belonging to a group and limiting interaction with families from whom residents are trying to individuate.

In any halfway house, the majority of residents require medication. By and large, they have accepted their need for prescription drugs and are self-medicating. Upon admission, it is recommended that each resident be supplied with a locked metal box in which to secure his medication from misuse by anyone else. He should be briefed to ask the counselor to hold his medications if he feels suicidal. A counselor, observing agitation as a mood changes, can himself make such suggestion or the request may originate in the day hospital.

Smoking is an issue in any group and in a community residence there are those who would become agitated if barred from smoking and others who condemn the pollution of the atmosphere. For safety, smoking must be prohibited in bedrooms but can be permitted in designated areas. Alcohol and nonprescription drugs are usually barred from the premises. For consistency, even wine may not be used in cooking.

CONCLUSION

The confluence of a halfway house's physical setting and its philosophical tenets points toward normalization of its residents. Findings by Hull and Thompson (1981) are consistent with the format discussed in this chapter. In their evaluation of the important ingredients that promote normalization, these researchers explored:

1. The physical social characteristics of each residence.
2. Attitudes of staff.
3. Characteristics of each community. (p. 111)

Of all these variables "the most critical factor here seems to be the size of the residence itself" (p. 111). A smaller institution offers more opportunity to achieve normalization. A second essential characteristic is the focus on only one disability, mental illness. In addition, the residence's location in a middle-class community provides "more potentially integrating services and resources" (p. 112), which this study evaluated as critical. An independent agency offers the optimal possibility for normalization as such facilities "are typically free of social and physical overprotection, and offer more freedom and autonomy" (p. 111).

It is not surprising that the research found that length of institutionalization was negatively correlated to community utilization scores. The findings theorized that the "more competent and less deviant the clients are in a residence, the more likely the staff, sponsors, workers and neighbors are to treat them in a culturally normative, i.e., normalizing manner" (p. 112). According to all the above criteria, a small, independent institution offers essential ingredients to help those leaving a psychiatric hospital return to more normal functioning.

CHAPTER 5
Intake

A transitional facility is a social, homey, friendly setting in which people may learn to trust, interact with peers and staff, and feel secure enough to take risks. As with any new life experience, separation from an inpatient unit creates more anxiety than many mentally ill persons can comfortably integrate into their fragile self-systems. Admission into this community is an extended process requiring care and sensitive timing. The slow, deliberate pace with which the initial meetings proceed is, therefore, designed to ease the applicant into the new setting without jarring him unnecessarily, suffusing him with too many stimuli, or disrupting the delicate balance achieved during his hospital stay. Each aspect of the intake procedure offers him an opportunity to meet significant people for short periods of time, to take his impressions away with him, to reflect about them, to share reactions with mental health workers, therapists, or families, and to return to the halfway house to meet a wider group and to garner more reactions.

Intake interviews attempt to delineate in fine detail the life of the house, how it functions, and who takes responsibility for specified tasks, impressing upon the applicant that he is joining a community in which he will be finding not only friends but also a new kinship system. Naturally, a part of the process includes an evaluation of the applicant's suitability to join an already existing community and his readiness to invest in his own rehabilitation and struggle with his fears and losses. Some applicants still question the severity of their illness, are not medication-compliant, and wish to deny that they cannot simply pick up the threads of life they dropped when they became ill. Others are ready to take the small steps to improve their daily functioning and to establish reachable goals for growth and change.

These first encounters, usually with a social worker, are designed to touch the applicant with a sense of hope that this is an opportunity to reacquire control over fundamental aspects of life, to take charge of daily routines, and to learn to live interdependently with peers. The interview attempts to reassure the applicant that he will have continued support as he slowly rediscovers the external world which he once felt was unbearable. The attitude emanating from the entire staff is that, despite negative symptoms, everyone in the facility can make progress. Every contact with the candidate attempts to convey the message that he is a deserving, meaningful person who is entitled to enjoy the same rights as others. The attitude and expressions of staff members should overtly or covertly convey the themes that staff has the requisite skills, programs, time, interest, and motivation to engage him in the hard work necessary for his rehabilitation.

Often the reputation of the halfway house precedes an application. During inpatient days the applicant may have heard descriptions about miracle cures or seemingly harsh or rigid aspects of life in the house. These too glowing conceptions or frightening misconceptions are explored with the applicant in order to replace them with a balanced, realistic assessment. Presumably, his hospital team has helped him view admission as a step toward improved functioning. The seriousness with which the intake worker examines the applicant's planned use of the house points the way to normalization. Through the warmth, interest, and relatedness of the intake social worker, perhaps the candidate can begin to visualize residence in the halfway house as offering a healthy structure from which to take those initial steps toward making a niche for himself in the outside world. The first staff member the applicant meets may become the metaphor for the facility.

THE APPLICATION QUESTIONNAIRE

In many facilities an interview is not scheduled until staff has read and analyzed extensive referral material prepared by the hospital team. It is aimed at securing the usual factual information such as residence, age, family structure, developmental and educational histories, and a complete picture of the illness and its symptoms, number of hospitalizations, diagnosis, and medication history. Details of physical problems and premorbid functioning are also requested. Staff is particularly interested in the applicant's use of his time in the hospital and the growth in his perception and acceptance of his disabilities. Parental attitudes are also addressed since they relate to his reasons for choosing a halfway house for his convalescence rather than a return to the bosom of his family.

Many halfway houses request that the applicant consider, and have in place, a viable rehabilitation plan for the weekday hours. Usually attendance at a local day hospital is the day plan of choice. Such a program continues, without interruption, rehabilitation efforts already started during hospitalization. Changing domiciles is a radical enough move for the frightened applicant; resuming an educational or vocational career may follow later.

If funding were freely available, the optimal plan for creating a smooth transition from hospital to halfway house would permit the patient to be enrolled in the day hospital a week or two before the transfer to a halfway house, thus carrying out a basic principle of rehabilitation—making only one change at a time. His adjustment secured in his day program, the patient could move smoothly to his new home. But no government or insurance plan offers such largesse that payments can be made simultaneously to two hospital settings. Visits to the day hospital become the substitutes for the actual experience.

The application questionnaire further inquires what the candidate hopes to achieve during his stay at the residence. Occasionally, the hospital treatment team, in its enthusiasm to formulate a viable discharge plan, may influence the candidate to present to the halfway house specific goals, such as returning to work or school, or developing social skills, to maximize his chances of acceptance. Once these goals are enumerated, however, the applicant may begin to internalize them and make them his own.

Most community residences require a complete psychosocial history of each applicant—a longitudinal study of family, social, and education forces that molded the individual during his premorbid state. From such data a plan for the type of family involvement in the intake process is evolved. Are the family members in accord with the admission plan and will they support the applicant in his first anxious days or will they subtly disrupt the placement?

The application asks for the hospital's comments on the strengths or weaknesses of the applicant, his ability to socialize, to respond to the needs of others, and to grow. The questions encourage full sharing of all relevant data but at times applications from the same source bear a striking resemblance to previous referrals. Occasionally, after admission, staff becomes aware of management problems or uncontrolled behavior still persisting, information that might have been grounds for nonacceptance or further inpatient treatment.

For example, excessive loss of control can rarely be handled in a residence and certainly cries out for airing. If acting-out behavior is shared fully and if a cooperative relationship has been established between hospital team and a residence staff, the rejection for admission can be the catalyst for remotivating a patient to strengthen his control over undesirable behavior. The intake process attempts to select candidates who, in the time frame of one to two years, can make substantial progress toward independent functioning. But even an objective intake worker may be overly influenced by positive credentials. A high educational level, combined with a later onset of the illness, is usually (but not always) a predictor of possible progress toward stabilization. An intake worker may ignore serious deficits resulting from the illness because he is too impressed with past achievements. In the following vignette, Gus's earlier accomplishments were not a predictor for progress.

> Gus had secured a graduate degree in physics from an Ivy League university. With this credential he started to teach in a midwestern college, married, and seemingly settled into a happy, stable life. He never suffered an acute crisis but his behavior slowly changed and so did the structure of his life. His marriage crumbled; his job disappeared. He tried teaching at a lower scholastic level but failed there too. By that time his parents realized he was not functioning and arranged for his hospitalization. When he was admitted to the residence after a long inpatient stay, he verbalized as his goals a return to work and socialization. He made sincere efforts to cultivate friendships, but the closest he could approach social intimacy was to list scores of names of persons he had known in the past. His limited concentration made even rote work impossible. He was unable to recapture his past successes, but he utilized the residence to stabilize and to prevent rehospitalization.

THE INITIAL INTERVIEWS

Intake interviews screen the applicant's readiness to join a rehabilitation community. The process involves about five sessions which encompass one to two individual sessions with the applicant, a family interview and tour of the facility, and an evaluation of the applicant's interaction with the group. Although tentative assessments about the candidate's ability to utilize the facility are continuously made and shared with the referring agency, a final decision is based on the applicant's reactions to each step of the process and on the consensus of staff members who interacted with him.

As was stressed above, the first task of the intake interviews is to help the applicant feel at ease, no simple assignment considering the negative symptoms that some bring with them. The majority of patients who apply for admission to a halfway house are schizophrenics who "tend not to use the most fundamental linking behavior of human interaction, i.e., facing, gaze, eye convergence, voice projection, palm displays and touch" (Scheflen, 1981, p. 60). Scheflen adds that clinicians "unversed in this subject (communications) often do not realize the importance of gaze and other microacts in forming and maintaining relationships. To the communicational scientists, an inability to perform these repertoires adequately is a serious matter, for such deviations and inadequacies make it almost impossible to engage in normal social discourse" (p. 60).

For the above reason it may be difficult for an applicant to begin to establish contact with the interviewer. In addition, the applicant may have a profound distrust of others. Arieti (1980) points out that the ill person's low self-esteem and lack of self-acceptance influence him to project his discomfort. He may think that "it is the others who should not be accepted and he will keep away from them. They will hurt him, make him feel undesirable and unacceptable. Any contact with others will bring harm" (p. 465).

Although much of his symptomatology may have been reduced during the applicant's hospital stay, the stress of an evaluatory interview which probes too deeply into past problems can reactivate old behavior. If sessions are low-keyed and informative, staying close to the here and now, his stability may not be threatened. If the applicant is feeling anxiety, he will be free to relax within a short period of time. Despite all these cautions, the movement out of the hospital into the world of the halfway house, protected environment though it is, may stress the applicant so deeply that he may need several weeks of preparation before he can tolerate actual change. Consequently, information gathering or discussion of symptoms are not items high on the initial agenda. Establishing relatedness and creating an atmosphere of trust come ahead of all needed useful information. As Arieti (1980) states, "Relatedness conveys . . . the feeling that he (the patient) is no longer alone in facing his anxiety" (p. 467). The social worker is "with him to share the burden" (p. 467).

The focus, therefore, moves to the applicant's questions about the operations of the house. Routines are explained and an opportunity is afforded the applicant to evaluate whether he can cooperate in the chores involved in maintaining the apartment. Can he cook a meal for himself and others or is he willing and able to learn to do so? Will he, an adult, feel too demeaned by an 11:30 P.M. curfew or can he make his peace with house rules which structure him to secure sufficient rest for his next day's activities? Is he willing to limit his visits to family so that he can more easily integrate into this new community?

A tour of the residence permits the candidate the opportunity to view the limited closet space and the arrangement of the rooms and perhaps visualize himself performing the expected chores, such as running the vacuum cleaner or working in the compact kitchen to prepare the evening meal and eventually cooperating in producing the weekly community dinner for 20 persons. It is important that the applicant view a bedroom, equipped with two or three beds, so that he can squarely see himself living in that room.

A critical part of the intake process is the applicant's introduction to the counselor who would support and guide him to cope with chores and negotiate with peers. The quality of the counselor's welcome can invest the small institution with homelike qualities. Does she invite the applicant into her room to become acquainted over a cup of tea? Does she engage the wary, timid arrival in a discussion about the pleasant activities of the house, the cooperation that can be expected from other residents? Does she make inquiries about the amount of personal belongings he plans to bring? Does she tune into special dietary needs? Does she describe the other residents so that when they are finally introduced the applicant can feel at ease more quickly?

As mentioned previously, each applicant is encouraged to share reactions to these intake sessions with his hospital team. If a cooperative relationship has been established with the referring social worker, an open discussion of reactions can be helpful. In the following vignette, the halfway house social worker communicated her concerns about Luke's plans to the hospital social worker, enabling important additional exploration.

Luke's life had been fragmented for several years by the divorce of his parents. He had regularly shuttled between their two homes in two different states, feeling lonely, adrift, and rootless in both places and manipulating both parents. He came to the intake sessions with a full-blown plan to attend a day hospital located 50 miles distant from the residence, instead of utilizing the local facility situated within walking distance. This continuation of the pattern of splitting his life clearly indicated his lack of readiness to develop a strong identification with one area, one peer group. The intake worker's perception of Luke's resistance to investing fully in the life of the halfway house was communicated to his hospital team. Luke's therapy sessions at the hospital refocused on his drive to fragment his life.

State regulations require that every applicant to a communal living facility be capable of recognizing signs of fire and have a rudimentary understanding of appropriate reactions in the event he sees or causes a fire. A set of simple questions is administered as part of the first or second interview to test the applicant's awareness of danger signs. His ability to exit quickly from the apartment and run down a flight of stairs to the street within the prescribed time is also tested. Rarely does anyone fail this examination.

If no insurmountable obstacles have arisen, the next evaluatory step is the dinner invitation to the house. Here the applicant can meet the group, share the food and whatever congeniality exists, asking any unanswered questions. This visit offers current residents an opportunity to evaluate whether or not they can tolerate, accept, and assimilate this newcomer into their already established community.

The counselor, too, reports his impressions on a form drawn up to tease out the interaction of the new arrival and the group. A portion of the next community meeting is set aside for reactions and impressions of the candidate. A question can be raised as to how much control the group should exert over intake policy. Answers are not hard and fast. If residents report that an applicant has a "wealth of poor habits" (words of a former resident) and would be grossly disruptive to the harmony of group life, then wisdom might dictate rejecting him. If, however, he has alienated some persons by asking too many questions or aggressively changing a television station without being aware that others were viewing a program, such behavior can be addressed and perhaps modified by the inpatient hospital team. After a period of reeducation, the applicant can be invited to dinner again for a reevaluation. More frequently, residents struggling with their own problems or limitations are sympathetic and willing to give the applicant a chance to work toward change with their cooperation.

Whenever serious doubts have been raised about a candidate's symptomatology or ability to utilize the facility, he is invited to a staff evaluation. The entire staff—consulting psychiatrist, social workers, and resident counselors—attend this session. Usually, the consulting psychiatrist conducts the dialogue with the applicant, attempting to tune sharply into problem areas. No doubt this is a stressful interview, but most applicants are capable of navigating it successfully, partially perhaps because they have experienced many such exploratory sessions during their hospitalization.

Stan's hospital record revealed three involuntary hospitalizations precipitated by his rejection of medications and his consequent irritable behavior which provoked anger against him. When Dr. Hume, the consulting psychiatrist, asked Stan to explain these involuntary hospitalizations, Stan recalled that he regularly went off his medications.

Dr. Hume: Why did you stop?

Stan: I guess I did not know I was a manic-depressive. I spent a lot of money. I made demands of people.

Dr. Hume: Didn't your doctors talk to you about your diagnosis?

Stan: Yes. But I didn't believe them. My relatives and girlfriend told me.

Dr. Hume: Why was it so hard for you to trust all these people?

Stan: I was delusional for several years. I couldn't connect medications and behavior. I didn't take hospitalization seriously. I thought the meds were a placebo and that I only had a neurotic problem, that I was antisocial.

Dr. Hume: And how do you feel at this time?

Stan: I lost my girlfriend because of the way I behaved. Now I am generally agreeable. I don't seek to provoke an incident. In fact I am usually good at reconciling conflicts of others.

Dr. Hume: If we accept you, your social worker will draw up a contract in which you will agree to take your meds on a regular basis. Only your therapist will have the authority to reduce or eliminate medication. Will you agree to this?

Stan: I know now that I need my meds.

This evaluatory session served several important functions. It stressed directly with Stan the importance placed upon medications by the entire staff. He knew without any doubt that his acceptance into the community and his continued residence there would depend upon his even functioning. Without medication, his behavior cycled. The contract signed by him and the intake worker further emphasized the seriousness with which the daily ingestion of his medications was viewed.

Staff also evaluated that Stan had suffered severe losses as a result of his inability to accept his illness and felt that perhaps now he could make a maximum effort to adhere to a structured program. With the support of all staff members and in an environment in which illness and medication were a fact of daily life, perhaps he could stabilize his functioning. Also, with the entire staff in attendance at the session, he knew that it would be difficult to manipulate anyone. Expectations were clarified.

There are no universal standards for admission into a halfway house nor does each applicant need a special contract. Each unit formulates its own criteria. Necessarily excluded from a minimally staffed house are those applicants who have a history of violent or antisocial behavior. In addition, a small, intimate group cannot readily tolerate too highly bizarre, obsessional traits such as exhibited by those, for instance, who barricade themselves in a bathroom for rituals lasting hours. Major suicidal risks are screened out for obvious reasons. Nor do many houses accept persons whose primary diagnosis is substance abuse. These residents usually do not mix well in a psychiatric halfway house as their more aggressive personalities and behavior tend to overwhelm a passive, fragile population. They require a different staffing pattern, as well as a more protected setting. However, it is rare at this time that applicants are without some drug or alcohol history. Applicants who suffer from chronic illnesses are accepted but expectations are that progress may be slower than for those recovering from acute episodes.

Family Interview

In a few halfway houses that admit an adult population, a family interview is an integral part of the intake process. As described in previous chapters, many emotionally ill persons are strongly tied to their parents, the most influential authority figures in their lives. An interview with parents offers staff an excellent opportunity for a firsthand experience with them as people, with their strengths and weaknesses. It further provides the vehicle for parents to tour the facility, verbalize their hopes and fears, and correct whatever misinformation they may have received from their son, daughter, or hospital staff. Visiting rules are explained to them as their cooperation is essential, especially during the first few weeks of residence when the newly arrived resident feels alone, lonely, and insecure in his new environment. Many parents are too quickly overly sympathetic, visiting or calling too frequently and generally prolonging their son's or daughter's resistance to putting down roots and establishing a place in a new community.

Families also need to understand that too much financial largesse can further diminish the resident's already reduced motivation to return to the world of work. In addition, this interview can clarify the financial status of the applicant, whether he needs to apply for some form of funding or the family has the financial means to pay the full cost of care.

A knowledgeable, caring staff member can help parents feel that they are not carrying a very serious problem alone, but that they have acquired a support team to which they can turn when they have a difficult weekend with their adult child or when they perceive conduct that troubles them. At this time they are also advised of the regular meetings of the parents' support group, helping them feel that they are not the only parents struggling with a problem that refuses to go away.

At the conclusion of this lengthy interview process, the entire staff evaluates the applicant's reactions, his motivation for rehabilitation, the course and severity of his illness, and his incipient interaction with the already established community. A decision is then reached as to acceptance or rejection. The smoothest transition is achieved if the new admission comes directly from the hospital. Several weeks back at home, awaiting admission, can weaken his resolve and his willingness to make compromises with group demands.

The goal of the entire intake process is to include a wide range of applicants, to be a community resource for as many persons as possible. From a practical administrative viewpoint, the beds must be utilized to meet budgetary demands. Before an admission date is set, a day program must be in place, a funding source settled. The newcomer has met the entire community, staff, and residents and has had several visits to the house. For those who experience extraordinary anxiety, one or two overnight visits are scheduled. All these steps in the lengthy intake process help achieve an ambiance which one applicant described in the following fashion: "A halfway house is a good place for a soft landing."

CHAPTER 6

Settling In:
The First Three Months

BONDING

The first three months of a resident's stay at the halfway house is a most crucial period for establishing the leverage for all future work. It is during this time that the resident bonds with the house and all its elements—other residents, staff, and structure.

Relatively few demands are made of the new resident. Staff is concerned that he grow comfortable in the house, come to know the routine, chores, other residents, staff, neighborhood, and city. Often, the new resident's discomfort and anxiety at the strangeness of his new home and housemates is compounded by the fact that he is simultaneously acclimating to a new day hospital, job or school program, and coping with the separation concerns of leaving the hospital.

In keeping with the concept that each interaction with residents is potentially therapeutic, staff devotes special attention to welcomes. Sivadon (1957) notes that a purposely individual welcoming of a new patient to his hospital unit greatly promoted the rapid integration of the new arrival into the community. A pleasant living space should await the new resident, a freshly made bed, perhaps a small vase of flowers and a card from the new resident's social worker. The counselor sees that the newcomer gets settled, other residents are aware of her arrival, and perhaps one has volunteered to be a buddy for the first week or two to help her adjust, learn about the house and the neighborhood, and to be there for support. Thus, the new person is made to feel special and wanted.

Admissions are scheduled for early in the week so that new arrivals can spend the first four or five days with the main counselor within a highly structured routine. The first few weekends are often experienced with some anxiety, both because of a looser weekend structure and because the resident does not yet know the rotating relief counseling staff.

David entered the house on a Friday because of pressure from the hospital regarding its discharge needs. Most of the men were out Friday night. They came and went on Saturday but David did not know them well enough to ask to be included. Some men sat and watched TV for periods of time but David was hesitant to bother them and they didn't approach him. Most people were pleasant but David didn't know what to do with himself. He finally went out for a walk.

Later, the counselor played cards with him and suggested some other activities, but the day seemed endless and David was unable to focus himself. On Tuesday, he told the community meeting how empty and upsetting the weekend had been for him and he felt a mistake in planning had been made around the timing of his discharge from hospital.

During the first few weeks the social worker maintains close contact with counselors and an outside therapist or day hospital to chart the new resident's adjustment. What is the level of her anxiety? Is she in bed a lot or out of the house frequently to avoid contact with all the people who are new to her? Is she adjusting so well that staff wonders what she is doing in a halfway house at all? The first two reactions are quite common and staff takes measures to involve the resident in the house—assigning tasks that will require her interaction with and help her to feel a part of the group and asking other residents gently to engage her in low EE (expressed emotion) activities.

It is the resident who breezes into the house, slips easily into new relationships, and appears to be functioning very well who gives staff pause. Through painful experience, staff awaits the inevitable crash—when the façade gives way around some precipitating event. This seemingly effortless adjustment most often occurs with women who have a particular borderline personality structure—a vibrant, well-groomed, charming exterior which camouflages underlying chaos.

More typically, residents have a problematic beginning at the halfway house. There is frequently a regression as the person leaves the safety and comfort of the hospital setting, where he may have become one of the more highly functioning patients, to confront the losses he has suffered around breakdown and hospitalization.

Polly, a depressed woman who had decompensated around the breakup of her marriage and had consequently lost a prestigious career position in which she had functioned exceptionally for many years, entered the halfway house and slipped into a much more painful level of depression. In the hospital, Polly had concentrated on getting herself well enough to leave. Once in the halfway house, she began to mourn in earnest the loss of her marriage and the interruption of her career. She had to confront the reality of living once again among people, some of whom were working and involved in relationships, while she was in despair. Only then could her mourning truly begin.

During hospitalization, surrounded by other regressed persons, the patient cannot fully address the losses she has suffered because of her illness. Not until she leaves the hospital is she fully aware that she is unable to return to life at the point at which she left it. She cannot pick up her studies, her concentration is off, and she may be under heavy medication. She may not be able to resume former relationships, as her friends have moved ahead, and she may have lost her lover. Also, she cannot return to her former job and she cannot account on applications for her time in the hospital. She may no longer be welcome in the familial home because of her former conduct.

All this may surface as she tries to pick up the threads of normal living. She must confront, understand, and begin to accept this condition before she can assess her current assets and make realistic plans for the future.

Docherty (1985)* (as mentioned in Chapter 2) notes the importance of the initial period of recuperation from an episode of illness. If the recovering patient is still gathering energy to begin life again, he may need lots of sleep and may, at first, be capable of only limited response to the demands of communal living. Therefore, the counselor differentially assigns chores in the first few weeks of a resident's stay, is sensitive to small changes in the resident's behavior, and emphasizes and reinforces positive movement.

While understanding that the process of reenergizing or the experience of a postpsychotic depression can interfere with a new resident's initial ability to embrace and assume his full responsibilities in the house, staff gently encourages him to become more active and involved as soon as he is able. It usually takes four to six weeks to adjust to the move from the hospital and begin to feel comfortable with the new

---

*Speech given at Grand Rounds on 1/11/85 at New York Hospital—Cornell Medical Center, Westchester Division, White Plains, New York

surroundings and housemates. The more the resident can become involved, the quicker this adjustment occurs and the more comfortable he feels. Activity, especially with housemates, hastens the establishment of new relationships and deters the resident from brooding about his losses or obsessing around his anxiety.

The principal thrust of staff efforts to help the new resident become a fully functioning house member within a reasonable time is the conviction that the healthiest stance staff can take is to expect residents to function as adults, to care for their own needs whenever possible, and to contribute toward the general welfare of the house. At times, residents will not be able to do so because of acute symptoms or despair. At times, they may refuse to do so because of anger, fear of leaving the child position, or other resistances. As staff does not know the resident well during the early weeks, firm stands on negative behaviors are taken with care. Denial and resistance can be accommodated in some degree for a period of time until bonding occurs, in lesser degree thereafter.

Steven entered the halfway house and began attending day hospital. He had been trained as a medical technician and was a pretty good cook, although he sometimes needed supervision getting his meal prepared on time. In the second week, he was assigned the chore of cleaning the bathroom. The counselor was surprised to see him cleaning the tub with a mop. Steven seemed disorganized around chores and didn't do them completely.

Steven was having difficulties at day hospital—he had a hard time staying in the various groups and doing what was expected of him. He was paranoid, impulsive, and quick to lose his temper loudly and often. At the halfway house, though he had occasional temper tantrums, he was mellower in mood and liked to socialize. As the weeks passed, however, he began to oversleep and was frequently late to day hospital. His room was a constant mess—bed barely made, a pile of laundry on the floor, dust and dirt and clutter on bureaus, and so on.

Because Steven was having difficulty at his program and experiencing such pressure there, staff at the halfway house, while reminding him of his responsibilities, kept the demands at a low key. However, after several months, when staff sensed that bonding had occurred, it began to raise its expectations.

The counselor worked with Steven to position the alarm clock out of arm's reach and to remain up once out of bed. Day hospital reinforced this effort by offering sanctions for tardiness. Steven responded slowly but steadily to this effort and over time this problem behavior diminished. However, the messy room did not change and it was only as specific clutters were pointed out to Steven and specific remedies suggested that he began to change his behavior. It became clear that Steven had either never been taught or never learned to clean effectively. His lagging motivation to learn these new behaviors was boosted by the offer of a move to a more desirable bedroom once he could keep his room in order.

Understanding which behaviors are due to resistances and/or character pathology, which are due to learning deficits (because of family teaching failures or the interference with learning of earlier disease processes), and which are due to disease itself (and therefore, perhaps, are less amenable to change) is an ongoing challenge to staff and cannot really be addressed until staff is familiar with the resident's functioning over a period of time. Even then, it remains a mystery why functioning is one area may be unaffected by disease, while in another there are real deficits.

It is within the developing relationships of the resident with his social worker and the counselor that the resident comes to be "known." The counselor interacts with the resident daily; takes soundings on his mood, connection with reality, and plans for the day; sees that the resident keeps to structure; and is the resident's first line of support if he experiences problems in mood or functioning. The counselor acts as the eyes and ears of the social worker, relays information to the latter about the resident's functioning and implements recommendations regarding the resident's care or treatment.

The social worker, whom the resident sees in weekly session, at community dinner and meeting, and whenever they otherwise meet by chance or design, is the resident's main link to other staff and to many resources in the community. The social worker serves as case manager, mother or father confessor, therapist, authority figure, chief support—as many roles as the resident may need and, indeed, may assign him or her in fantasy.

A healthy reparenting experience is available to those residents who choose to see staff as such. Staff is able to take pride and pleasure in a resident's growth and achievements, to be firm in the face of testing behaviors and to help residents through failures and setbacks, as staff spell each other and because staff's own esteem is not so bound up in the process of a resident's life as may be that of his parents.

The communications between the social worker and counselors, day hospitals, therapists and families, and so on occur with the specific consent of the resident as a condition of living at the house. Such communication is necessary given the amount of rehabilitative work done within the house which must be coordinated with the thrust of the therapy, vocational planning, etc., which is occurring outside of the halfway house. Staff advises each resident of the contacts being made on his behalf, describes the material being shared, and offers the resident the opportunity to participate in that communication as much as possible. Every effort is made within this context to preserve confidentiality on information that does not need to be shared.

When a resident tells his social worker in session that he has some important information about another resident that he wants to discuss but does not want to go beyond the session, the worker advises him that if it is information that indicates that someone's life or safety is in danger, it cannot be held confidential. The resident will be protected as the source, but the information will be passed on to the appropriate persons for action. Usually, upon deliberation, the resident goes ahead to divulge his concerns.

STRUCTURE

The new resident bonds to the structure of the house. All residents feel the relative loosening of structure as compared with that of the hospital and must adjust to greater freedom of space and time. The amount of structure will vary with the house, some programs more structured because of the degree of chronicity of the residents. Others provide more structure in order to allay the anxiety of a high expectation program (Carpenter, 1978).

As noted above, weekends can be very anxious times for new residents as the diminished structure may create the feeling that there is "nothing to do."

Peter, a young man in his mid-20s, had been hospitalized for a year before coming to the halfway house. He had actually been scheduled for discharge to the halfway house on several occasions in the past six months but had panicked and was unable to leave. Staff was not convinced that he would make it this time either but he moved in on a Tuesday, began day hospital on Wednesday, and learned on Thursday of the suicide (on Wednesday) of a former lover, a woman with whom he had had no contact for months but who had been a very important part of his life.

Peter, proclaiming his fragility, became very anxious, began shaking, and shared his fear that he would not make it through the coming weekend. Staff was equally concerned about the lack of structure over the next few days, compounded by the fact that Peter was an unknown entity.

On Friday, Peter's social worker mapped out a plan of action with Peter and the relief counselor. Peter felt he would probably need periods of bedrest during Saturday and Sunday. However, as he was afraid of his depression, he and staff agreed that if he were in bed too long, the counselor would periodically check with him about things he might do to activate himself and break into his mood. Certain tasks were selected—cooking, cleaning, shopping with the counselor—for Peter to do at various times. Peter planned a visit with family or friends on each of the days, the social worker was on call in the event of a crisis, and arrangements were made with the counselor and day hospital for rehospitalization if necessary.

The weekend went as planned except that on Saturday Peter cut his visiting time short with his parents in order to stay around the halfway house. On Sunday afternoon, the counselor called the social worker at home with Peter's request that he be allowed to take an overnight out of town to visit a mutual friend of the suicide victim. The social worker reaffirmed with Peter the structure of the house and the plan that had been established for the weekend, neither of which allowed for the overnight. Peter accepted this fairly easily, noting that it was probably better for him to remain with the safety of the house at this crucial time. The weekend passed uneventfully.

Peter's interactions through the weekend provided staff with a beginning knowledge of how to handle future stressful times. His attempt to violate the plans he and staff had made was a request to be structured, a function he could not provide for himself.

Chores

Chores at the halfway house serve a variety of functions, the first of which, of course, is to maintain a clean and orderly house. For residents who have often allowed themselves to live in filth and chaos, chores are the foundation of the halfway house stance that one's surroundings are a reflection of one's self and that each resident deserves to live in a pleasant, cared-for home and to experience the orderly surroundings that will help him organize himself.

Chores are also a method of imparting to the resident the sense of his community with his housemates. He is responsible for caring for them in the doing of his chores as they are likewise responsible to him. Thus are sown the seeds of his interrelationship with others and a sense of altruism, the flowering of which will become apparent much later in his stay.

The routine of weekly rotating chores enables each resident to master new skills of self-care which are really the key to his future independence. Many residents are so frightened of having to prepare food or clean a bathroom because of ignorance or past failures that they are amazed when they master these tasks. The sense of calm and confidence derived from this mastery can fuel their willingness to risk change and challenge in other areas outside of the home.

Those who have had several psychotic episodes and hospitalizations understandably mistrust the encouragement of the helping professionals to press for return to fuller functioning. Many describe their state of uncertainty as "waiting for the other shoe to drop." Which new step or stress will precipitate another acute episode? More than supportive words, even, the residents need concrete evidence that they can grow and achieve anew without dire consequences. Unger and Anthony (unpublished) note:

> There is an accumulating body of research evidence which suggests that teaching independent living, community resource utilization and career preparation skills to seriously disabled young adults can improve their functioning in the community. Reviews of research have shown that seriously psychiatrically disabled people can learn a variety of skills regardless of their symptomatology (Anthony, 1979). When these skills are properly integrated into a rehabilitation program which supports the use of these skills, they can have a significant impact on the client's independent functioning in the community (Anthony, 1979; Anthony & Margules, 1974). (p. 4)

The performance of tasks around the halfway house is also a great means of moderating a mood state. A person struggling with intense anxiety, hypomania, or rage can get some relief by applying a little elbow grease to the premises. Frequently, even those who are depressed and withdrawn respond positively to efforts to break into their moods by baking a cake, washing the walls, repotting a plant, and so on. The house should have certain tasks which are assigned for the specific purpose of helping a resident discharge tension.

Not all residents at a halfway house need all the structure it provides. Some residents are quite neat and orderly and need no reminders regarding their chores, and so forth. Others slip easily into turning day into night. For them, the 11:30 P.M. curfew and the requirement that they be out to their daily program by 9 A.M. weekdays and be up by 11 A.M. on weekends are crucial supports in their rehabilitation. In order that the house run fairly and equitably as well as reliably, all residents must adhere to all structure. Later in their stay, some flexibility is permitted as people prepare for departure into a less structured life situation.

As much of the daily routine as possible is left to the residents to design for themselves, i.e., how the chores are assigned and rotated, visiting hours for friends, the planning of special events such as parties and holidays. Where there are no issues of house health or safety, staff encourages residents to plan and order their own lives.

SOCIALIZATION

The process of determining their share of house routine enables residents to experience the dynamics of interaction and negotiation which are also cornerstones of halfway house experience. Socialization is the area that most applicants wish to develop while in residence in order to improve their functioning. Most have found themselves isolated, afraid of contact, or unequipped with skills to engage people in their worlds— family, friends, employers, coworkers, and so on.

Living in a halfway house, of course, throws people right up against each other. New residents at the house generally move into a triple room. Later, by seniority and by demonstrating their ability to care for their personal space, they move into the more comfortable double room. By virtue of sharing a room, people begin the process of socialization. Residents are expected to work out such decisions as how late a radio can be played in the room, what to do when one resident wants to go to sleep at 10 P.M. and one wants to read until 11 P.M., and so on. If they need help with negotiating a solution or compromise, they may enlist the aid of the counselor. If the conflict continues despite these measures, the residents may request a meeting with their respective social workers for further conferencing. It is rare that some resolution is not reached.

Miles asked for a meeting with Nick and their social workers to address conflicts that were erupting between the two residents. Nick was reluctant to meet but finally agreed when staff assured him he would not be expected to be Miles' friend. Staff appealed to Nick's senior status in the house (he was about to move to a supportive apartment) and to the fact that he, earlier, had struggled with some of the same behaviors that Miles was trying to change.

Miles was upset because Nick had been angrily critical of him in front of the other men for a derogatory comment he had made about a former girlfriend. Nick argued that Miles does not take responsibility for his words and actions, is a gossip, and doesn't learn from his mistakes. He continues to anger people and tries to avoid confronting his behavior, as if he were a child and wasn't to be taken seriously. Nick said that he, himself, used to behave this way and he understands what Miles is doing but he cannot accept it.

There followed a period of some discussion, with the staff persons helping both men to specify the behaviors that annoyed them as well as the factors each had found attractive in the other. Nick noted that he can get quite rigid, moralistic, and narrowly focused, as he tends to react to the younger Miles in a parental way. He accepted that he perhaps must work on this area himself but did not want his problem to shift attention from the fact that Miles has to stop trying to get away with his childlike behavior. Nick knows this because he used to have the same problem: You have to change, grow up. Miles conceded that he is always making people angry. He doesn't know what to do and he doesn't want to lose Nick's feedback because he knows it could be helpful. It is Nick's anger that has made him stop and think. It matters to him.

Miles decided that he must try to stop and think how people will react before he says things and not say everything he thinks. Nick agreed that this had to be done. They discussed how Miles had been trying to control his impulsivity for some time and was getting better at it, but that it takes a long time to change and you have to keep trying.

Before ending the session, Nick's social worker, Vera, assured both men that they were not expected to like each other and be friends if they did not want this. Staff would want them to be able to live together in the house. From the tenor of this meeting, Vera felt they could do this and they agreed. She raised the issue, though, of their mutual friends.

They are both members of a group of young men who enjoy each other and their social activities. Vera commented that though they are free to decide not to socialize with each other individually, she could not believe that they would not be in each other's company while out with this group and perhaps they should think about how they will handle any conflicts which may arise under these circumstances. Both men felt Vera was right and both wanted to be free to enjoy the group. They decided they would try to give each other some distance while together. They worked out a way of signaling each other if they were bothered by what the other was doing and putting a limit or a moratorium on any potential conflict so as not to ruin the night for themselves or others in the group. They would try using a code word, see how this worked, and they then could discuss their differences in private or use staff again if they wish. Both men agreed to try this.

Staff can develop several principles to facilitate the negotiation process.

1. Residents are asked to try to work out their problem before going for further help. This can include individual work done with their social workers to discuss techniques, to role play, and so on.
2. Residents do not have to like each other but they are expected to live together in reasonable harmony.

3. Each resident's right to have his/her feelings about an issue is highly respected, but compromise will always figure in the outcome of
any disagreement in the house. This principle is stressed so often
that residents come to expect it to occur as a matter of course; they
will compromise their stance in some way to reach agreement and
they expect the other resident will do so also. As they come to feel
supported in the legitimacy of their feelings, so, with time, can
they come to grant legitimacy to their adversary.

The development of social skills is bolstered once the resident experiences and begins to incorporate the above process. The resident who has
been too frightened to reach out to others for fear of the aggression (his
own or theirs) that may result from conflict becomes more assertive
when he is supported by staff and when a reliable means of resolving
differences is mastered. At other times, just living with housemates in a
protected environment over a long period enables friendships—or, more
safely for some, companionships—to develop which often last a lifetime.

There are many interventions staff can use to encourage interactions.
The buddy system—pairing an old and a new resident for the first weeks
at the house—engenders a benevolence regarding relationships. By pairing residents who appear compatible on house projects or as roommates, staff begins the process of shaping their environments, their
ecosystems, to suit their needs.

To discourage isolation and to bring people together in the public
areas, residents are not permitted to bring their own television sets and
stereos to the house. In each halfway house, however, there should be a
small space where an individual or two or more people can have some
privacy for study or conversation. Such space, as discussed in Chapter 4,
can support intimacy among residents if they wish to deepen their relationships.

For reasons of need and expense, private bedrooms are rarely possible
in a community residence. However, many adults find living in a dormitory situation both a blow to their esteem and difficult to tolerate if they
are not with a compatible roommate. When possible, house structure
supports movement toward privacy and choice. Often, during a resident's first few months at the house, more senior residents move out,
creating vacancies in the double rooms and/or possibilities for people to
shift rooms so that friends can arrange to room together. Such moves are
supported as long as people fulfill their general house responsibilities.
As noted earlier, where there are areas of dysfunction, a resident's desire
to move to more privacy can spark motivation for change if staff can
connect the two pieces—the move with the recommended behavior
change.

A new resident is welcome to have a variety of feelings about and interactions with her housemates. If this is not occurring, the social worker initiates differentiation exercises.

During Karen's second month in the house, staff realized that she was not able to identify all of her housemates by name. It became clear that Karen saw the world around her as in a haze. To help her to focus in, she and her social worker developed a game. Each week Karen concentrated on a different resident, observed him or her, sought information, and reported in session who that person was—likes, dislikes, hobbies, strengths, weaknesses. Sometimes Karen found this difficult, other times she reported in some detail. This exercise helped her interaction in the house and in the community as well.

ECOSYSTEM

As the resident and social worker begin to develop their working relationship, they assess the resident's resource needs. The halfway house funding arrangement is determined during intake and initial funding referrals are made. Once the resident is in house, the social worker encourages him to complete as much of this application process with public agencies as he can on his own. If necessary, the worker accompanies him through the steps, observing him in action, educating him in the skills of negotiating the systems, and exploring his feelings as he experiences the bureaucracy. This is the beginning of a process that may lead to eventual hearings in the social services or Social Security hierarchies. The worker may refer for legal assistance if such services are available in the community or may him- or herself guide the resident through the quasi-legal process.

As most residents in their early months at the house are attending day hospital, referrals to vocational or educational resources are frequently postponed until later in the stay. If the day program has a vocational arm, referrals are the province of that facility.

The social arena is addressed early on, however. Each worker assists the resident assigned to him to locate social and recreational resources in the ecosystem which are beneficial and responsive to his needs.

Carla entered the halfway house with a history of passivity and depression, one manifestation of which was a chronic inability to rise mornings and leave the house. She had lost many jobs due to lateness and absences and was socially isolated.

Carla began day hospital, and the structure of house and program enabled her to stay with a pattern of early rising. She was quite fearful about weekends, however. She felt she needed help getting up and activating herself on at least one of the mornings as she feared regressing if her weekly pattern were not maintained. Staff helped her to plan and execute application for an exercise class early on Saturday mornings and to obtain a scholarship.

Carla began the course in her second month at the halfway house and felt strongly that it helped her sustain her new routine. She was proud of her ability to stay with the course and, because she was up and out, to make good use of the rest of Saturday. She valued this piece of good feeling which helped her as she worked on some painful problems at day hospital and halfway house.

The bulk of interaction by the halfway house with the resident's eco-system during the first few months of residency occurs with day hospital and/or outside therapist. The resident gives informed consent for contact with these two resources and the workers establish immediate and ongoing communications, the complexities of which will be explored fully in Chapter 7.

Family

The new resident's family—parents and siblings—is a facet of the eco-system which is the focus of staff's early and considered attention. The family's concept of halfway house care can profoundly affect the new resident's adjustment and length of stay. In intake, the family has been prepared to cope with the concrete manifestations of the separation process which may occur as the program encourages the resident toward greater independence and maturity.

Admission to the halfway house can be both an optimistic and frightening experience for the family. While most families hope that their adult child will be able to adjust to and compensate around his illness to a degree which makes possible more independence and self-direction, they are also painfully aware that progress can be dashed by recurrent decompensations. Families are buffeted by the crests of these episodes, pulling back when advised, giving the adult child space for growth, but knowing they are expected by "helping professionals" and their programs to move in again with support if the adult child's needs fall outside program parameters. Parents do not know whether to move in with support when their offspring is suffering a difficult experience or hold back and permit him to go it alone. Indeed, different professionals will advise different courses, leaving the parents confused and frightened that their action or inaction will prove crucial to their offspring's well-being.

Halfway house staff is prepared to help families adjust to the admission to a new program and the resident consents to contact with parents and/or siblings. The extent of the involvement is influenced by the resident's and family's attitudes and abilities to tolerate such contact, the amount of staff time available for this purpose, and the degree of therapeutic involvement of other resources. Some day hospitals or therapists offer active family treatment and it may be appropriate for those auspices to do the bulk of the work with the family so as not to contaminate the resident's new home with too much family presence while he is moving toward separation-individuation. When the house becomes "home" to the resident, it becomes his special place. He has worked hard to make himself a member of a new family group and some residents are intensely possessive of their hard-won territory.

> Paula had been at the house two months and was slowly moving from her stiff, fairly isolated state to some social interaction with her housemates. She was beginning to relax, was smiling more and it was clear that she was starting to enjoy the house. Her social worker, who had not done the intake and thus had not met Paula's parents, asked if she could have them to a session at her office and if Paula would like to be present. Paula readily gave her consent but felt she did not want to be at the meeting.
>
> After the session, Paula was enraged that the meeting had occurred. She felt she could no longer trust her worker now that contact had been made with these parents who had a pattern of family secrets. Staff encouraged Paula to express her strong emotion and helped her to focus on the feelings behind her rage.

During the early weeks, the new resident is expected to spend his time in the house or in outside activities with housemates. Despite whatever anxiety he feels, he is discouraged from seeking escape from the tension of adjustment in flight off by himself or home to family. The more time he spends at the house, the sooner he will feel comfortable there. The family is asked to help the resident turn his focus toward his new home and peers; the ability to do so is crucial for adjustment.

> Basil's family lived in the next town and he easily visited home by bus several times a week. His parents verbally agreed with staff concerns that such frequent visiting was undermining Basil's ability to establish and invest in relationships at the house. The parents encouraged Basil to return to the halfway house, yet they would also entice him by cooking him meals, taking him hunting, and so on. Despite efforts by the worker and by Basil's therapist, the family was unable to alter its patterns and allow him to separate. Thus,

he never fully invested in the house or with peers and never fully utilized the program.

Sal, who had never been hospitalized, was referred by his therapist because he had confined himself to home for months, wasn't socializing, and wasn't able to attend classes and complete his college assignments. During the first months at the halfway house, he returned home many times at odd hours, to the consternation of his father and stepmother. They felt guilty for having worked toward Sal's move and found it very hard to ask him to return to the halfway house. But they embraced Sal's treatment program, accepted the need for separation from home, and negotiated with house staff, day hospital, Sal, and therapist a formal, structured visiting schedule. With support, they were able to direct Sal back to the house when he broke schedule. In time, Sal began to look to his peers as well as to his parents for support, intimacy, and entertainment.

Given that the amount of interaction with families varies from little to intense contact depending on the variables discussed above, staff of community residences are most helpful to parents when they are sensitive "to the reality of parents' needs and quandaries; to the reality of genetically, biochemically based vulnerability to mental illness; to the reality of limited options in the community; and to the reality of many families' unwillingness to engage in therapy that they experience as diminishing rather than supporting their self-esteem" (Pepper & Ryglewicz, 1984b, p. 3).

The following guidelines may help forge a new, more positive, and fruitful relationship between families and community residence staff when a vulnerable family member depends on their combined support.

1. Involve the family in the admission process. Arrange for an on-site visit and an opportunity to question the functional framework of the residence.
2. Share crises with the family and provide support during periods of rehospitalization.
3. Plan for group and individual family sessions to provide information and psychoeducation. Reduce the suggestion of parental blame for illness, and/or language that creates barriers between staff and family.
4. Refer families to advocacy and support groups and/or to family therapy if indicated or requested.

USE OF STAFF MEETING FOR ADJUSTMENT

Occasionally, a resident has such difficulty adjusting to the house that staff must take special measures to intervene. Inability to accept and work within house structure, to control impulsive behavior or outbreaks of temper, to function despite depression, to separate enough from family to focus on program, to refrain from substance abuse, all present specific problems for residents and staff. Some of these behaviors can be tolerated to some degree; others cannot be tolerated at all. When staff has exhausted the usual methods of effecting change or wishes to have a consultation with the staff psychiatrist, a case conference is called.

The resident is interviewed by the psychiatrist in full staff meeting where the presenting problem and various options are explored. Thereafter, a course of action is selected ranging from behavior modification techniques to suspension or expulsion. The longer the resident is in house, the more effective is the conference, both because staff knows the resident better and because he has had time to bond. The most effective leverage available to staff in helping a resident to modify behavior is his own investment in his new home and peer group.

In the following vignette, staff responds to Beth by removing an immediate stress at a vulnerable time, enabling her to feel supported.

Beth came into the staff meeting looking tired and spaced out. She explained that she felt isolated after Tuesday's meeting. She has been unhappy at the halfway house for some time. She feels the women are "vindictive" although they present a "well-meaning facade. . . . They tend to stab others in the back."

Beth said she has experienced a lot of anxiety living at the house, as well as anger and hostility. She admitted to turning the anger inward so that she feels like hurting herself. Dr. Lee (the consulting psychiatrist) inquired about how she would hurt herself. Beth looked disconnected and sat in silence for some time. Finally, she said that she has never told anyone these things.

Beth went on to say that the halfway house is full of negative feelings and personality conflicts. She felt that she and Ursula were particularly in conflict because Ursula has an eating disorder and fills a room with anxiety when she enters it. She compared Ursula to her mother—also an anxious type. She prefers to stay away from anxious people.

Beth also remarked that Amy, Ursula, and Sue are the "veteran residents" and they control the place. She feels like the intruder. Presently, she is feeling too much hostility from Amy. Beth stated, "Amy is learning to express her anger and I'm her victim." Beth again said she is afraid of being self-destructive. Dr. Lee again asked what Beth would do. Beth was silent and then stated that she would cut her wrists. She admitted that upon seeing a knife last night she had thought of this. She felt that knowing how hurt her friend Daisy would be had stopped her.

Dr. Lee asked if Beth would like to leave the halfway house. Beth indicated that she would like to move to the Y because that is where Daisy lives. Dr. Lee asked if Beth would become a burden to Daisy. Beth answered that Daisy has to watch out for herself. She then reasoned that if she put all her problems into Daisy's lap, then she would lose Daisy as a friend. Dr. Lee asked if Beth had any other people in her life that are close to her. Beth responded that she and her dad are close. Dr. Lee asked what her father thought about Beth's destructive thoughts and Beth stated that he doesn't believe that she will act on them.

Dr. Lee told Beth that staff would like her to stay at the house and asked how staff could help her to do so. Beth stated that eliminating the women's meeting called for tonight (which she felt would be hostile to her) would help, or at least she would like to have a staff member present. The director responded by asking the women's counselor to have this meeting postponed to another time.

Prior to leaving the staff meeting, Beth stated that she was feeling a lot of support from staff. Dr. Lee asked her to be more open and direct to staff about her dissatisfactions in the future so that they do not build up over time.

Staff becomes quite invested in the new resident and searches for creative options to avoid expulsion. Or perhaps the resident has no home to which to be suspended, or returning to family is felt by all treatment arms to be a therapeutically negative choice. When available in the community, a supervised respite bed service can be a viable option in these circumstances.

It is helpful to staff and to resident if the outside therapist can be at the staff meeting or play an otherwise significant role in instances where suspension or expulsion are possible consequences. Not only does such participation provide for effective planning but it also prevents potentially harmful splitting of treatment arms.

THE VIOLENT OR AGITATED RESIDENT

A community of vulnerable persons with minimal available staff cannot tolerate those who will do or threaten violence upon themselves or their property. Nor can the delicate relations with surrounding neighbors bear the strain of too much perceived danger or actual nuisance.

The intake procedure is so designed that the violent or explosive applicant can be identified and screened out. On occasion, of course, the
process fails to adequately identify such persons. Also, there may be
unclear predictive factors regarding those who simply cannot tolerate the
intimacy and restrictiveness of living in very close quarters with others
and who become grossly agitated and lose control.

It is usually in the first few weeks after admission that staff is confronted with an explosive or decompensating resident, often before
enough relationship has been established to exert persuasive control on
the resident's behavior. If the resident is overtly violent and force is
necessary to restrain him or her, police may have to be summoned and
other residents moved away immediately. If the resident is agitated,
pacing, and verbally explosive, it is helpful if a staff member, after clear-
ing other residents from the vicinity, sits quietly by the upset person to
absorb his or her anger or anxiety until it is spent.

> Derek was a schizophrenic young man whose most apparent
> symptomatology took the form of time-consuming, ritualistic, com-
> pulsive behaviors, including handwashing and other bathroom ac-
> tivities. He had been living in isolation at home, unemployed for
> two years, and was in frequent verbal conflict with parents over his
> lack of activity and helpfulness around the house. He had attended
> a day treatment center for a year and had made enough gains that
> program staff assessed him as now ready to move to a peer living
> situation, referring him to the halfway house. Derek was accepted
> with some concern about how he would tolerate the anxiety that
> would occur consequent to the change to an intimate living situa-
> tion with peer pressure to spend less time in the bathroom.
> After a week and a half, Derek had what was to be the first of
> several increasingly menacing temper outbursts, mainly at staff,
> but frightening because of his size (over six feet) and his increasing
> paranoia. In the last and most upsetting episode, Derek exploded
> at a resident who was cooking dinner and had asked Derek to move
> his snack out of the kitchen. Derek began shouting and threatening
> the resident, verbally and physically, and another resident ran to
> the other end of the apartment to summon help from the social
> worker. She asked the other residents to clear the area and ap-
> proached Derek who focused his tirade and threats at her. She
> quickly assessed that speaking to Derek exacerbated his hysteria so
> she stood quietly, permitting him to vent his fury.

In most instances, when the irritant precipitating an outburst is removed and the exploder is not threatened in any way, he will gradually
quiet down. A staff member must stand by when a resident has lost
control in this way and his or her calmness may help the resident to

regain control. The resident may interpret as hostile or confining any speech or movements by the staff member, so it is vital that the staff person assess the effect of his interventions as they occur. Once the resident is quiet, he should be given space while other staff is consulted as to what action should next be taken. There are no quiet rooms or husky aides at a halfway house to help control behavior. Staff must rely on a careful intake policy and a delicate handling of emotional outbursts.

In Derek's case, it was determined that he was unable to tolerate the demands of group living. He had had to decrease his compulsive behaviors and was thus unable to bind up his increased anxiety by his usual defenses. He was relieved to move back to his home with the hope that he might make another try at group living in the future after further treatment in his day program.

COMMUNITY MEETINGS

The new resident is introduced to the entire halfway house—staff and residents—at the weekly community meeting. It is the time when all in the house can eat together and enjoy each other's company in a gathering that is part social, part business.

The meeting is chaired by the residents on a rotating basis and the order of business ranges from discussion of house management issues, such as chores, broken toasters, and roaches, to social events in and out of the house, or issues of therapy and life planning. Residents can raise any issue that concerns them. If they are unable to bring it to the group themselves, they may put an anonymous suggestion into the suggestion box and it will be read at the meeting by the group leader.

Humor is welcome at the meetings to add a light touch to sometimes mundane and other times heavy discussions. Residents are quite warm in their response to those who ask for help in working through a therapy issue or taking a risk such as returning to work, going to school, and moving out to the supportive apartment or to the community. Residents may ask for help in determining how to account for hospital time on a resumé, for instance, or how to handle an upcoming family gathering at which relatives will be asking them how they are and what they have been doing.

At times, the men and women decide to meet separately to address issues specifically related to either house. This was the case when the women met with Joan (Chapter 1) to determine if she would be returning to live with them in the halfway house.

On other occasions, guests are invited to attend—political candidates, board members, representatives of local social or recreational organizations, and so forth. Sometimes the meetings are celebrations of a resident's birthday or graduation from the house. On these family-type occasions, special recognition is given to the growth and achievement of this group member. The halfway house family celebrates holidays together—Christmas parties, Thanksgiving feasts, Passover Seders—and parties for Valentine's Day, Election Day, Fourth of July, or whenever the residents want to organize an event.

At one point in his first three months, the new resident will be asked to lead a community meeting. Some resist this assignment because it is so difficult for them to take the leadership position. During the week prior to his first leadership opportunity, the resident's social worker discusses with him his readiness to assume this role and helps him to prepare an agenda, if necessary. Staff and resident can assess his leadership capacities and polish his skills; later, he can transfer them to other experiences such as work and social gatherings.

EVALUATIONS

At the end of the first three months at the house, the resident evaluates his progress in a special session attended by his social worker, his counselor, and the agency director. The purpose of this evaluation is to assess the quality of the resident's adjustment to his new home, highlight his areas of positive functioning, alert staff to special problem areas, and set goals for the next three months. It also gives the director and resident an opportunity to come to know each other more personally. The director, in view of his/her position and, in most cases, older age, is endowed by residents with an authority onus that his/her brief contacts with residents in community meetings does little to dispel. In fact, the authority issues that are heaped upon the director can interfere with a resident's comfort and ability to contribute to the community meeting. Thus, the evaluation enables the resident and the director to begin a personal relationship.

The resident prepares for the evaluation by studying the following questionnaire:

Guideline to Evaluation Session

1. What chores do you do best?
2. What chores do you need the most supervision in?
3. What are your relationships with staff like?
   a. how have they been helpful?
   b. how could they be better?
4. What are your relationships with other residents like?

a. what is good about them?
b. what needs improvement?
5. What goals did you have when you entered the house and what expectations do you have for yourself during the rest of your stay here?
6. How can the halfway house best help you achieve these goals?
7. What would you like to see different about the halfway house program?
8. Overall, how would you rate your progress since admission to the program?

The resident is asked to evaluate his own progress in the several areas and the director actively explores this further when necessary. The counselor and social worker join in with their comments to ensure full reportage on each area of functioning. The social worker takes notes and prepares a report which the resident reviews to assure that it reflects what occurred in the session. He may then have the report sent to anyone he wishes—for example therapist, day hospital—or simply keep a copy himself.

There is a special portion of the evaluation which looks at staff and agency functioning. It enables all present to critique whether the program is appropriately meeting the needs of the resident.

Staff seeks to make evaluations relaxed and informal with as much effort directed toward highlighting positive functioning and growth as is devoted to helping the resident to change negative behaviors and set new goals. The aim is to ensure that resident and staff are working together toward goals set by the resident and reviewed periodically so that the approach is fresh and consistent. The following is a sample summary of the first evaluation conference.

Pat Wilson's First Evaluation

Present: Pat; director; social worker; counselor

I. Chores

Pat feels she has the most difficulty with cooking as she has little experience. She fears that her meal won't come out right or on time. Ways to ease this general insecurity were discussed, including using a few simple recipes repeatedly until Pat feels very comfortable with them, going through a simple recipe book and choosing recipes herself, consulting with people if she wishes, and cooking more than every other week in order to get more practice. As with most other skills, Pat will gradually feel more comfortable and need less supervision with experience.

The counselor confirmed that Pat is not at all comfortable in the kitchen and that she is thus unable to function without total supervision. Pat also stated that she, as well as other residents, puts chores off till the end of the day in order that the clean room not get messy before the day is out. The problem with this is that then the chore hangs over one all day long and the counselor may feel the need to offer reminders. Staff suggested that Pat try doing her chore early in the day, let the counselor know it's done, and relax. It's not Pat's responsibility if someone dirties the room after her work. The counselor can remind people the chore has been done and it's their responsibility to clean up their mess. The point is to have this communication and planning with counselor so she's not on Pat's back.

Pat noted that when first at the community residence she did a more complete job on her chore but saw that others only did enough to get by and her motivation slipped. She would like to be in an atmosphere that induced people to do their best. She was asked to consider taking on the role of standard setter. She could get together with any other women who also care about how the place looks and through the suggestion box and other noncritical means they could support each other in encouraging all the women to put more effort into their work.

The director wondered how Pat can enjoy chores more because eventually she will have her own place and she'll want the satisfaction to be the force that helps keep the place looking nice. Pat wondered where the enjoyment would come from and the director suggested it might come from the feeling that the halfway house is home and Pat is working to make her home a nice place. Pat at first felt the halfway house was a terrible separation from her family and she finds this is changing. While the house doesn't feel like home yet, it now does feel like a safe place. The director suggested that perhaps by decorating her own space in her room, Pat could further transform what has become a safe place into a place she can enjoy.

The director noted that she isn't hearing from Pat that she is having any fun. Pat agreed, saying that she feels everyone else in the house is more advanced and this is a source of difficult and negative feelings in her—that she can't get to their level of accomplishment. Perhaps she will only be stable here but not grow because she's constantly in a state of inferiority vis-à-vis other residents and she doesn't get the confidence she needs in order to learn. She finds she's self-conscious, it's hard to make conversation, she censors herself.

The director suggested breaking down this big bundle and naming one way in which others are superior. Pat gave as an example the social ease with which Bill relates to Ruth. Pat's confidence is so lacking she assumes she wouldn't be able to relate so easily to anyone. The director asked if she could start with just a five-minute conversation with someone. She likes to write—could she arrange a session where she helps someone? Pat thought this was a good idea—something she might enjoy. The director noted that when one feels safe one can take a little risk—one step at a time toward fun. Then she can analyze with staff what was good about the experience and what didn't work.

Pat feels that to do this she will have to put some of her negative feelings on the back burner—they make things look futile. The director agreed that she will get more mileage out of her more constructive feelings. Other suggestions from Pat and staff are to keep reaching out for the fun in other people, to try to develop more conversation with her roommate—asking about her new job, etc.—to look for opportunities to be with people, as when she offered Mike a ride to school, and perhaps, before going into a social situation, to do some pushups to relieve the tension and become more relaxed and emotionally available.

II. Relationships with Staff

Pat feels her self-consciousness also keeps her distant from staff. She has both positive and uncertain feelings about the counselor. She feels the counselor has preferences for people who have mastered skills already as this makes her job easier. The director asked if Pat could see the counselor as a teacher who gets much satisfaction from working with a person who needs to learn more. Pat hasn't felt free to ask for help often and the director suggested taking this risk and then seeing what the attitude of the counselor is. Pat felt she would also just like to talk with the counselor at times and the director agreed that this is a very legitimate desire. She can learn from the counselor and from the other residents whose skills she admires. When she feels competitive, her anger may get in the way of learning the other guy's abilities and using them as building blocks for herself.

III. What Expectations Do You Have of Your Stay Here?

Pat would like some positive experiences that would help break down her negative attitudes about her future. Staff should realize that she carries the weight of these negative feelings with her. Medications help to keep her reactions to these feelings in some check, but she is still a sad woman who hopes for good things but is not surprised when bad things come. The director noted that Pat is an expert on the negative and from now on she can help the counselors focus on the positive. She is attractive, intelligent, has analytical ability and good insight. But staff needs Pat's cooperation—can she park the negatives? The good qualities are there, but she is trampling on them. If she could focus on them the way she's been focusing on the negative, she'll find them there and others will enjoy them, too.

The counselor added that Pat was really able to handle and enjoy the greater intimacy at the house last weekend. She has seen her involve herself with the men, also. The director added that it will be easier for Pat to develop a life at the house by going home less, making her weekends full and stimulating because Pat's peers are here; she should have peer contact at her age. This could be a goal for the next evaluation that she can achieve for herself.

Pat's process of moving out from her family has established a good beginning. Pat added that she is also looking into a new volunteer job which she hopes will be more stimulating. She deserves this also.

IV. What Would Pat Like to See Different at the Halfway House?

Pat would like more heat in the apartment. She and staff discussed measures to achieve this such as insulated drapes, plastic over windows, etc. Measures will be taken to effect this.

Pat also requested that the director try to be impartial in relating to residents in the group situation. She feels that the director tends to favor the people she sees individually. This is difficult for Pat as she feels the director's approval means she will succeed. The director requested that she come to her if she ever feels this occurring (or to the counselor if it is happening there) and check it out to see if there is anything in it of her not trusting her own abilities and thinking that other people are not either.

V. How Does Pat Measure Her Progress at the Halfway House?

Pat now feels that the house is no longer threatening, but she feels that until she brings out some sense of her own assets she won't be able to tap the house for what it really has to offer. The director reinforced that a strong building has to start with a solid foundation. Feeling safe is a very important achievement; until it is there, nothing else can be built atop it. Pat can use her safe feelings as a base from which to set out for other things she wants.

As is seen in this evaluation, Pat is only now feeling safe enough to look around and see where she is. The major goals of the first three months have been achieved—Pat has bonded and staff has come to know her positive and negative functioning. Hopefully, Pat and staff can now turn their energies toward helping her to achieve more specific goals. In her case, these include becoming functional in the kitchen, developing a more positive image of herself and of the world she inhabits, improving the quality of her relationships with peers and authority figures, and selecting a more challenging daily program. During the next three to eighteen months, the full working period at the halfway house, some of these goals will be met, some dropped, and some new goals set. The central focus, however, will be to help Pat to develop her assets, stretch her limits and build as much as possible a world, an ecosystem, which continues to facilitate her functioning.

CHAPTER 7

The Ecosystem:
The Day Hospitals
and Therapists

No community residence can operate with maximum effectiveness without linkage to a network of day hospitals, therapists, vocational rehabilitation agencies, funding sources, and legal services to share problems and goals and to serve as support systems to each other. Coordinated staff effort is the oil that lubricates the operation of the residence. With it the entire ecosystem, interacting cooperatively, expands the possibility of helping a resident move toward higher levels of self-realization. The natural allies of a halfway house, in addition to families, are the day hospitals, which offer "partial hospitalization," and the therapists (psychiatrists, psychologists, and psychiatric social workers).

DAY HOSPITALS

Day hospitals, established within the community as an alternative to costly inpatient care, treat patients with a formal diagnosis of mental illness. Although the effects of the illness may be modified by medication, patients are usually still symptomatic or functionally impaired. Day hospitals, administered by a psychiatrist who carries legal and clinical responsibility for the operation, offer a spectrum of services and provide their clients with an organized, structured daily program of several hours duration. Its groups and carefully planned social events are geared to transition its people gradually to fuller functioning within the community.

Cohen's studies (1984) of day hospitals located in the New York City area found nontrivial differences in program operation and content. Some accept a majority of higher functioning persons who are motivated but afraid to reenter life. Other facilities accept those who have a minimal interest in life's struggles. Consequently, they differ in their philosophies and programs, some emphasizing social interaction, some stressing the nonfunctional aspects of patient behavior with time limits utilized as catalysts.

Day hospitals that accept highly chronic populations concentrate more intensely on problems of daily living. They are oriented toward training clients to engage in simple work efforts, such as preparing a mailing or sorting or delivering mail, and mastering necessary life skills, such as homemaking (which includes budgeting, shopping, cooking), art, exercise, gardening and plant care, tutoring in mathematics and language skills, and exploring the community and vocational activities. In dealing with clients with severe deficits, day hospital staffs tend to be less confrontive, low on affective expression or interpretation, and high on direct guidance, group activities, and role modeling. Leaders make concentrated efforts to help members understand and correctly identify psychiatric symptoms and to be medication-compliant. Some day hospitals have as their goal keeping these patients out of the inpatient ward and living in the community, a major stress for some ill persons.

For higher functioning groups, day hospitals place greater emphasis on insight development. Other differences in program content relate to the stage of the life cycle of its members.

Most day hospitals review their programs periodically and both staff and patients evaluate and change activities to prevent boredom or depression from dragging down morale. No matter what the model of day program, a strong socialization component is characteristic of all. Some programs focus heavily on scholastic and vocational goals. Sharing, taking responsibility, participating in a recreation program, planning an outing, the publication of a newspaper, or the running of a canteen are often integral aspects of a day program, as is vocational rehabilitation.

High-expectancy day hospitals ordinarily try to help their patients stabilize and become functional within the time frame of three to six months. If, after a few extensions, one is still unready to reenter the mainstream for any variety of reasons, such as denial of his problems or anger at his loss or the depth and nature of his illness, he may be transferred for an extended period to a less demanding day hospital.

A high-expectancy halfway house which offers a time-limited program to its residents is nicely balanced by a day hospital which also has an aggressive philosophy, upholding change, progress, and goal setting as its standard. A day hospital so programmed, however, has relatively limited flexibility in retaining those patients who for some reason cannot motivate themselves within this time frame because the day hospital's Utilization Review Board may exert pressure for patients to move on. Naturally, it is not always possible to anticipate progress when resistance or avoidance have been the daily interaction, nor is it always possible to know when a turnaround in motivation is at the threshold. It is also easier to use this administrative structure to hurry toward the exit those who are hostile, oppositional, or simply too bland and dull. The human equation permeates every professional staff whose rewards for sensitive, related interaction derive from the progress of their clients.

Since day hospital programs are voluntary, the individual on his own can decide to drop out when the pressure for utilizing the groups, the activities, and available counseling grows too burdensome or feels demeaning. When, however, the more difficult or resistant clients lose their day hospital program, the halfway house also loses the professional support and knowledge upon which it has come to depend.

About one half of day hospital patients are in the rapidly growing group of "young chronic adults" (see Chapter 2). Ordinarily, young chronic adults initially resist day hospitals. After a rehospitalization or two, however, they are more ready to accept the slower pace of reentry into the environment. According to Wilner (1985), adolescents make better progress in a homogeneous group, whereas those in their 20s or 30s do well in a heterogeneous one. Older populations are best served in geriatric groups. Partial hospitalization can be a treatment resource for most psychiatric patients, except those who are acutely dangerous to themselves and/or others.

The complex demands of the young chronic adult have taxed the resources of many day hospitals, creating the need for graded service modalities to serve those who resist or are unable to utilize time-honored methods. Neffinger and Schiff (1982) have described a tier system of service which includes "the Acute Stabilization component which acts as an alternative to hospitalization" (p. 77) and the Intensive Day treatment service which utilizes a multistep process including "formal problem-area identification and goal-of-the-week format" (p. 78). With the time frame of 14 weeks, the clinic attempts to set up a working structure for both the client and the clinician which sets clear, explicit goals in which the entire group participates, reviews the step-by-step efforts to achieve long- or short-term goals, and provides feedback of results. It begins "to build a pattern of success by gearing each weekly goal to the client's functioning level. With each completed task, a pattern of success is initiated and the client is encouraged to validate his own accomplishment, so that approval becomes internalized as well as external" (Neffinger & Schiff, 1982, p. 82). For those who are exceedingly low in motivation, shorter programs which are not time-limited but are goal-directed, are utilized, as are aggressive medication monitoring clinics.

Other psychiatric hospitals have established late afternoon programs. Their activities begin at 4:00 P.M. and run until 8:00 P.M. This is a resource for those who, having attended the day hospital, have moved on to partial or full employment or returned to school. It provides them with additional needed support and activity. Those who cannot get out of bed early enough to attend the day program are also welcome. This late afternoon session, which is fully staffed with a nurse, activity worker, social worker, mental health technician and psychiatrist, attempts to encourage motivation and new contacts and to ensure service for all who might sink back into apathy.

Staffs of day hospitals are aware how difficult it is for the insecure, frightened person to take on indifferent or bureaucratic environments. Consequently, staff advocate for such concrete services as social security, public welfare, or steer their patients to medical or housing resources. Staff to patient ratio is high, ranging from 1 : 2 to 1 : 6.

Goldstein's studies (1984) have estimated that 77% of day hospital population is single, 16% is divorced or separated, 6% is married, and 1% widowed. The variety of illnesses addressed in these programs corresponds closely to those found in a halfway house. The population is composed of 67% with a diagnosis of schizophrenia, 10% schizoaffective, 10% major depression, 7% bipolar affective disorder, and 6% have other diagnoses (Goldstein & Phil, 1984, p. 6).

Di Bella et al. (1982) underscore the greater effectiveness of group treatment than individual therapy in promoting adaptation. The therapeutic milieu of the day hospital provides an excellent resource for making inroads into such dysfunctional behaviors as shyness, silence, or withdrawal. Peer and staff interaction provide feedback from a wide range of people. In addition, the commonality of problems in the groups provides a safe arena in which to share feelings or try out new roles. Slowly patients may begin to trust. Day hospitals, as do halfway houses, attempt to create kinship groups, members of which, after discharge, may continue to support each other.

Upon admission to the halfway house, each client is routinely required to grant written permission for the exchange of pertinent information with his day program or treating therapist. Consistent, direct communication between the day hospital and the community residence is one key to successful tracking. Many residents are notorious for not sharing plans, goals, programs, changes in medications, or discharge dates. Each activity is a separate chapter in their lives. The only effective bridge is constant communication between staff of the house and the day hospital. Preferably, contacts with supportive services should be made before a crisis arises. Requests by halfway house personnel for invitations to periodic reviews or diagnostic evaluations at the day hospital are willingly granted but often the pressure of large caseloads and heavy administrative demands interferes with communication of specific events.

One halfway house surmounted this hurdle with a day hospital by an agreement whereby a staff member regularly attends rounds on a biweekly basis. The day hospital reviews the progress of its residents on those designated days. Naturally, the day hospital, in exchange, profits by summaries of client utilization of the halfway house, thus creating a unified world and preventing the client from manipulating or splitting staffs. Further invitations to review conferences, diagnostic sessions, or discharge meetings flow easily from such contacts and both agencies are alert to changes in behavior, medications, or new stresses in the client group.

Walter regularly suffered "colds," "stomachaches," and assorted ailments. These effectively kept him in bed on consecutive Monday mornings when his resistance to his day hospital program was strongest. The house rule that a resident must consult a medical doctor on his second day of illness left Walter free to malinger for a day. By evening he usually enjoyed excellent health.

Staff of day hospital and halfway house met to consider Walter's chronic avoidance of the rehabilitation program on Mondays and his late arrival the remainder of the week. The ensuing dialogue revealed that at the day hospital Walter had strongly bonded with one male social worker, Andrew. In fact, a session with Andrew was the highlight of Walter's day. The conference therefore evolved this strategy: Walter would be assigned a daily session with Andrew promptly at 9:00 A.M. If he failed to arrive at the day hospital on time, he would not be granted any substitute session. The halfway house, too, bent its rules. Walter was required to provide a medical excuse any morning he could not leave his bed. With the cooperation of both agencies, Walter's maladies quickly disappeared.

It is especially helpful that persons at the day hospital who prescribe medications be quickly informed of changes in behavior, such as any indication of pressured speech or activities or signs of tardive dyskinesia, so that medications can be promptly adjusted to ward off a worsening of the condition. Conversely, the halfway house must be informed whenever medications are raised or lowered so as to be able to evaluate properly the resultant behavior and promptly transmit such observation back to the prescribing doctor. Whenever a patient reveals an urgency to suicide, it is imperative that the total ecosystem close in around him to determine whether simply holding his medications will help him feel more secure or whether emergency hospitalization is essential to protect him.

In a less dramatic vein, the close cooperation of the day hospital and the halfway house staff creates an excellent piece of structure to modify maladaptive behavior. With consistent, replicated treatment from members of the dyad, pathological behavior can be addressed, each team reinforcing the other. Some behaviors are too heavy for one person or facility to cope with and burnout can ensue. The following account of a halfway house staff meeting, attended by a day hospital staff member, emphasizes this cooperative interaction.

Staff Meeting on Zena with Day Hospital Staff

Present: halfway house staff (including Dr. Mack, consulting psychiatrist), Zena, and Sue B. (day hospital staff)

Dr. Mack interviews Zena, focusing on a number of incidents which have resulted in counseling staff's frustration and, sometimes, anger toward her. Zena is aware that these incidents reflect poor judgment, a sense of entitlement and a passive-aggressive inattention to detail. She calls this behavior a "helpless child act" and feels it is time to give this up as she sees her living situation coming into jeopardy. She very much wants to remain at the house, feels she has made much progress—she now gets satisfaction from doing some chores, is gaining pleasure from her semiprivate bedroom, is much more functional in the kitchen, is more separated from her boyfriend and more focused in day hospital. All of the latter points are documented in the log reports from day hospital and other records.

Dr. Mack recognizes Zena's significant progress but notes that she still has to be given a "kick in the pants" to encourage growth. Staff is tired of being aggressed upon by her inattention and sense of entitlement. How can Zena accept more responsibility for her own growth and how can staff treat her in a different way? Zena suggests that she make out a checklist of all her responsibilities, have it approved by staff, and then follow through each time until she needs less supervision from staff.

After Zena leaves the meeting, Sue B. reports that at first Zena was very disorganized at day hospital. Now she is much more able to follow through on things such as what is being requested in groups and being on time. She is in less trouble at day hospital than at the halfway house, probably because there are fewer occasions for concrete tasks to be performed.

Dr. Mack says that since Zena has taken the stand that she has control over what she does, we can assume, for now, that the problem is not one of disease but of character pathology. We will put some pressure on her and if she cannot respond and begins to get psychotic, we will know she needs more time in program and perhaps referral to a lower expectancy facility.

Dr. Mack's recommendations are:

1. Require Zena to make detailed lists around chores. (Goals group at day hospital can help her focus on and execute this.)
2. Begin a negative point accumulation program with her, e.g., 10 points for not closing front door, 5 points for deviating from list. When she accumulates a certain number of points in a given time, she is suspended from the house for two weeks. Sue B. commits day hospital to work closely with the halfway house to address specific issues and infractions and to monitor developments.

Psychoeducation

Many day hospitals consider interaction with families as central to their program. This is especially vital when patients return home daily. The nature of the family program, the commitment to work closely with the family, and the degree of staff time allotted for family interventions vary markedly among day hospitals. Philosophical approaches also range from medical models to family systems approaches to carefully delineated psychoeducational approaches, as developed in inpatient units by Anderson, Hogarty, and Reiss (1980) and others. This emerging approach, which is spreading to day hospitals, does not conflict with but builds from the family systems concept. The psychoeducation adherents recognize that a chronically ill person needs his family for support more than others and that therapy should not further increase the isolation and alienation of the ill person from his family.

In the psychoeducational model, families are relieved of the burden of blame for having caused the illness. Instead, the emphasis on their emerging role in rehabilitation empowers them to assist their relative. Through workshops, this approach attempts to create a treatment alliance between the patient and his family, to provide information about the illness and its management, to decrease the family's anxiety, and to enable family members to maintain a low key environment. The psychoeducational model promotes a gradual reintegration of the ill member into the family and an even more gradual return to a work life. It urges cooperation with prescribed drug programs and envisions continuity of the care provided from the inpatient to outpatient status.

The psychoeducational approach was developed for a schizophrenic population in one Pittsburgh hospital, but it can be adapted to other psychiatric disorders. This approach takes the position that the "treatment requirements for schizophrenic patients are shaped by a knowledge base which includes a host of very poorly understood biological, psychological, and environmental factors. Beyond the inadequacy of present knowledge what seems to have been lacking in the treatment of schizophrenia is some psychosocial biological position regarding an assumed pathogenesis from which a reasonable treatment formulation could logically follow" (Anderson, Hogarty, & Reiss, 1980, p. 490). These researchers have isolated a "core psychological deficit" which "appears as problems in the selection of relevant stimuli, the inhibition of irrelevant stimuli, the ability to sustain or flexibly shift focused alertness, or as problems in stimulus recognition, identification, integration, storage, recall and use" (p. 491). In brief, schizophrenics suffer from "attention-arousal dysfunction."

Given these deficiencies and an underlying vulnerability to environmental pressures, a high-intensity environment, whether inpatient or outpatient, in the familial setting or in any halfway house may contribute to the development of such positive symptoms of schizophrenia as hallucinations or delusions. On the other hand, when the environment offers scant stimulation and merely custodial care, negative signs such as isolation, apathy, and loss of motivation are exacerbated.

As mentioned above, the psychoeducational model involves the entire family as early as possible after hospitalization in understanding the nature of the illness, the efficacies of medication, the resultant deficits caused by the illness, and the vulnerability of the afflicted person to the "emotional temperature of the family" (Anderson, Hogarty, & Reiss, 1980, p. 492). Interventions aim to maximize familial knowledge of the illness, reduce "overinvolvement, excessive concern, and exaggerated attempts to support, close ranks, and compensate for real but potentially modifiable deficits" (p. 493). The goals are to diminish parental anger, hostility, blame or guilt, while building a tolerance of the nonfunctional aspects of the adult child to assist him to set limits, and to establish structure within the family setting. The simpler the environment, the less chaos prevails; the clearer the expectations of the ill person, the greater is the potential for improved performance.

This system attempts to strengthen the "quantity and quality of extrafamilial connections for patient and family members" (p. 494). Again, the entire ecosystem is mobilized to form linkages with family, friends, advocacy groups, recreational resources, and work or service contacts. All this "includes the provision of information which attempts to equip the family with a rational guide for interacting that is designed to neutralize the precipitators of relapse and the despair of behavioral deficits"

(p. 502). The techniques employed by Dr. Anderson in the various phases are summarized below:

In the initial phase of treatment the therapist bonds with the family through sharing a history of the illness, and feelings about each crisis. Parental guilt and highly emotional or negative reactions may diminish as families connect with the empathic therapist. Anderson offers them practical suggestions to transform their feelings of inadequacy into effective coping mechanisms. In subsequent workshops families are encouraged to lead normal lives by reengaging with lost social networks, reducing the isolation created by the illness. Known hard facts about schizophrenia and techniques to manage the ill members constitute core discussions in survival skills workshops with the aim of reducing family stress. The psychoeducation method can be a prelude for more intensive family therapy which addresses underlying areas of family dysfunction such as marital discord or unresolved conflict.

Halfway houses have not sufficient staff or budget to institute a full program of family intervention. They ordinarily depend heavily on the cooperating day hospital to carry the bulk of such programming. At those times when a resident is in attendance at a day hospital, familial interaction is best assessed cooperatively to evolve constructive weekend visitation plans, or to interpret to a family why their son or daughter resists all contact with them while struggling to overcome dependence and to individuate, or to ease pressures when contacts with families are excessive or destructive. When, however, a resident leaves or is asked to leave a day hospital program, family work in progress there may also be aborted. If insufficient progress had been achieved during the period of attendance at the day hospital, the halfway house may elect either to refer the family to an outpatient clinic or to provide the much needed service itself.

Social Skills Training

Rehabilitation of the mentally ill focuses on the reinstitution of social skills, lost during and after periods of psychotic decomposition or never acquired in the pre-morbid period. These losses are among the "negative symptoms" which were discussed in Chapter 2. They include processing information, sharing attitudes, thoughts, and feelings, or expressing spontaneous reactions. With such deficits the mentally ill person experiences greater difficulty performing routine tasks, achieving ordinary vocational goals, making friends, or maintaining an intimate relationship. The reemergence of psychotic symptoms or relapse frequently occurs when these inadequate problem solving or coping skills do not permit the mentally ill person to resolve or reduce environmental stress.

Training persons to handle person-to-person interactions, helping them to generalize such learning and to maintain the newly acquired skills is the core of this teaching. Unlike social group activities, it employs, in a structured methodology, behavioral learning techniques to develop needed social skills. This training focuses on the person's ability to cope in the real world and on interactions in the present. A valid question raised about social skills training is whether incremental gains in social responsiveness are long-lasting and whether chronic patients develop the ability to generalize from assigned problems to life's problems. Hierholzer and Liberman (1986) have stated that a maintenance program is an essential ingredient of this treatment. Without periodic reviews, improvements in functioning can be expected to diminish in six to 12 months. Generalization of the new learning to unplanned events has not as yet been demonstrated but for many chronic patients training which provides solutions to everyday problems in living improves the quality of life and reduces relapses.

There is disagreement among authorities whether or not specific skills teaching should be conducted within the confines of a day hospital or whether it belongs in an educational facility. The Psychiatric Rehabilitation Approach at Boston University is carefully designed to provide specific classroom training in social skills. Since a halfway house is a living situation, it can only informally address inadequacies in social performance. It is not the forum for a detailed program for such directed learning.

Vocational Planning

Day hospital programs usually include prevocational evaluation and vocational planning. Testing is administered and goals established to delineate the steps needed to reestablish competence and skills. Such programs further support work efforts through volunteer job placements. Often vocational rehabilitation counseling continues on an outpatient basis after the day hospital program is completed.

THERAPISTS

Although the number of halfway houses has been increasing since the 1960s, private therapists have not usually explored or exploited the therapeutic advantages some of their patients could gain through utilization of such facilities. Many members of the psychiatric profession have not realized that halfway houses offer an excellent preventive resource for those persons having grave difficulties individuating or who are on a collision course in rebellion against parental pressures or expectations.

Psychotherapy may have preceded hospitalization or may have been initiated there. Continuing with a qualified therapist is a major aid in helping an incoming resident adjust to his new, oftentimes stressful and bewildering environment. In addition, the halfway house staff may have a fully informed ally in the person of the therapist whose knowledge of the resident, his fears, his strengths, and his ability to handle new situations can serve to facilitate the transition. Occasionally residents have selected psychologists or psychiatric social workers as their outside therapists. Since these professions do not prescribe drugs, a medicating psychiatrist is usually retained for this purpose. Such an arrangement naturally requires the close cooperation of therapist, medicating doctor, and halfway house staff so that behavior may be carefully assessed and reflected in prescribed medications.

Therapists who have treated persons from the onset of their illness may become security blankets. Some clients feel no hardship traveling four hours, at inconvenient times, to be available for a session. Others have changed therapists as often as they changed seasonal clothing. They may have bonded strongly to an inpatient resident psychiatrist who was transferred to another hospital unit. Hospital rules often do not permit a resident therapist to continue as outpatient therapist and the hospital outpatient psychiatrist may be transferred after a year, or may complete his residency with a plan to set up his private practice out of the area. Yet consistent treatment from inpatient to outpatient status is critical if regressions are to be tempered or averted. Few systems of care have addressed such need.

Psychiatrists need consider halfway houses not only for their hospitalized patients but also for their clients who are living either in a noxious environment, in isolation in a rooming house, in a conflicted family or roommate setting, or who are unable to cope with the stresses of a college dormitory.

Many therapists, however, are historically accustomed to working alone, with the professional ethic of maintaining a closed system between themselves and client, sharing no information with families or outside agencies. Consequently, they frequently may not fully realize that community residences will not only not interfere with their relationship with their client, but indeed may be a strong ally in working toward growth and change. As noted in the vignette below, those who have referred their patients have found that the halfway house, a therapeutic community with its solid structure, low level of expressed emotion, and high expectation of cooperation around chores and activities, can become an organizing agent for their heretofore nonfunctional clients.

Brilliant Florence had dropped out of school and was lying around the house, sleeping her days away. She resented her father's remarriage and was antagonistic to her achieving sisters. She dutifully appeared for her therapy sessions and verbalized extensively about her problems, but was frightened to test herself outside her booklined bedroom. Her therapist had learned about the local halfway house and its readiness to accept young people who were nonfunctional but had no history of hospitalization. Florence's parents agreed that a trial residence might alleviate the strains upon the entire family but Florence experienced extreme difficulty arriving at a decision to enter a halfway house. Perhaps the interest of a patient intake worker was the catalyst which motivated her to test the waters.

In the residence she found several young people, equally troubled, who had been derailed in their progress toward lofty vocational goals. Suddenly she was on a safe turf in which she could admit her deep fears of competing with her aggressive, successful father or of taking risks educationally, vocationally or socially. She moved quickly through a day hospital program to a volunteer position at a rehabilitation agency which utilized her dormant but excellent organizational abilities. She agreed to reenter the college she had boycotted for three years while barricaded in her bedroom. All these moves were made despite painful resistance on her part and with patient support and encouragement on the part of her halfway house social worker, her counselor, her peers, and her private therapist. She could tolerate her risks more readily because several other young women were making similar attempts. The energy she had expended in being oppositional to her parents was placed in the service of her reawakened drives.

Jurisdictional Issues

When several groups in the ecosystem are perplexed about the direction in which a client's rehabilitation should travel, the outside therapist who has a long, continuous experience with the person may provide guideposts and reassurance.

At the day hospital and the community residence, Gilbert had been compliant, eager to please, and undemanding. As he pursued paid employment, he gradually became irritable. His immaculate grooming deteriorated, as did his appetite.

All his support systems met for a scheduled, periodic evaluation session at his day program. Day hospital and halfway house personnel questioned whether Gilbert should slow down his efforts to find work. His psychiatrist, however, supported the move as healthy. The doctor pointed out that staff was seeing normal anxiety around a job hunt in a young man whose feelings were usually sealed over in a most unhealthy way. The psychiatrist further pointed out that Gilbert viewed his past psychotic behaviors as egodystonic. Currently, he was not exhibiting psychotic symptoms. The therapist recommended that the day program and halfway house staffs continue to provide the kind of support Gilbert needed to cope with his heightened anxiety and to sustain the job hunt.

Usually jurisdictional issues can be successfully delineated but disputes can flow from different theoretical philosophies.

Helen, a young anorexic, resented the day hospital's insistence that she weigh in regularly with the goal of a weekly weight gain of half a pound. She was closely tied to her private therapist who did not utilize a behavioral approach but worked solely on her inner anxieties. Although these modalities complemented each other, Helen capitalized upon the different approaches to belittle the expectations of the day hospital. She filled her baggy pockets with stones when her weight was low. When her strategy was discovered, she cited her therapist's lack of concern about her weight. He worked solely with inner dynamics. Unfortunately for her progress, she successfully resisted becoming engaged in any aspect of the day hospital program.

Coordinating Rehabilitation Efforts

No single profession is, by itself, adequate to help a mentally ill person. But mutual treatment goals strengthened by available support and well-placed communication between primary therapist and rehabilitation staff can make psychosocial treatment effective. A halfway house as an ally can ease a therapist's burden and sustain his investment in his patient.

When treatment issues become intense and the resident cannot tolerate his anxiety, the halfway house is a safe, neutral place for some acting out, provided the therapist remains available to the house and to the resident for consultation and support.

Adam tried to change his inordinate need to control others. He ordinarily wore down anyone who resisted his ideas. Neither his friends nor family had been able to tolerate his unmitigated intensity. As therapeutic sessions touched sensitive areas, Adam's acting-out behavior erupted in the halfway house. Only the constant telephone availability of his therapist sustained the counselor as she struggled to contain Adam's angry overreaction. When suicidal urges peaked, the counselor controlled Adam's medication and urgently insisted that he stay close to the residence until his self-destructive ideas subsided. Counseling staff quietly mediated any head-on collisions Adam had with members of the group. The solid structure of the halfway house and the support of the counseling staff permitted the therapist, in sessions, to confront issues of separation, dependency, and anger which Adam had buried. The close cooperation and reciprocal support of these two arms of Adam's support system helped him ride out, without hospitalization, the stormy phases of his treatment. Resolution of critical issues enabled him to reenter healthy community activities, to become a more positive leader, and to establish rewarding friendships with both sexes.

The close coordination between therapist and rehabilitation staff maintained at reasonable levels the flamboyant behavior and careless spending of a resident, as shown in the following vignette.

Donna's wild spending sprees had put her far in arrears in her monthly rent. For a period of time she concealed from her halfway house social worker the extent of her unbridled extravagances because spending had become a form of acting out which relieved her high levels of anxiety. She was unable to comply with a budget because it symbolized parental restraint which she compulsively had to defy.

Donna's halfway house social worker and her therapist worked closely to help this young woman develop more constructive ways to discharge her anxiety and to control her acting out in all areas. Such close collaboration promoted gradual, steady change. An agreement was reached that, upon receipt of her weekly salary, Donna would immediately put her rent money aside. The rest of her income she was free to spend.

The case of Kathleen illustrates a variation of the use of "splitting" (assigning only good attributes to one person and only bad ones to another), which confused both her therapist and halfway house staff.

At the house, Kathleen's affect was shallow, superficial, contradictory and negative. She could not maintain any mood. She impressed all who worked with her as scattered, incapable of meeting the demands of the outside world. Her social worker suggested to her psychiatrist that Kathleen attend a day hospital until she stabilized. He, however, refused to refer her because she presented herself in the brief hour of her therapeutic sessions much as she had been in the habit of relating to her father. While her therapist was the "good guy," she showed only good parts of herself. She was the compliant, achieving girl who fulfilled the goals of the "good parent." For him, she was eager to renew such interrupted experiences as returning to college. Consequently, despite the questions raised by halfway house personnel, to whom she exhibited an inability to concentrate or to remain goal-oriented, Kathleen, with the approval of her psychiatrist, enrolled in a college program.

Within a month, the strain of this new venture proved too taxing. Her social worker encouraged her to share fully with her therapist the failure of the school plan. When Kathleen finally revealed her distress, her psychiatrist agreed to refer her to day hospital. At that program she felt the support she needed during the day. The close cooperation of day hospital and halfway house staff helped her reduce her dependence on the use of splitting and denial as defenses.

As Compton and Galaway (1976) state, " . . . the purpose of coming together as a team is not to 'win' one's way or prove one's 'rightness' but to utilize the different capacities brought by the different members of the team in order to expand our knowledge and our range of skills so that we can offer the client the best service in the direction that the client wishes to go" (p. 455). For Kathleen, slow first steps, symbolized by admission to the day hospital, were necessary to launch her back into the more complex environment.

A strong therapeutic relationship has been called "the glue that binds." Atwood (1985) cautions that "the human dimension of chronic mental illness may best be addressed through the potentially powerful medium of the one-to-one therapeutic relationship" (p. 410) and that patients "need sensitive coaching from a supportive therapist to embolden them to accept and stay involved in services like halfway houses and sheltered work shops" (p. 410). From the vantage point of the halfway house, strong one-to-one relationships are also offered which promote continued use of therapists, day hospitals and other programmatic referrals. In short, it is the entire ecosystem operating in unison which benefits the client and hastens him to improved functioning. The total milieu propels him toward constructive goals, each discipline reinforcing the other (as seen in the following case example), gently pushing and supporting the ego with each new step until maladaptive behaviors diminish or disappear.

Kyla's sad history skirted the edge of homelessness. When her beloved cat disappeared from her home, she could not hear or accept her mother's explanation that the cat was incontinent and blind and had been "put to sleep." Instead, Kyla set out to locate the missing animal. She wandered several weeks before she was located, exhausted, psychotic, highly delusional, and preyed upon by various street people. She was sent to a state psychiatric hospital where she was treated with drugs and therapy. Many months had elapsed before her mother was located and informed of her whereabouts. By that time, the old woman, dying of cancer, was too ill for the relationship. No other relative came forth to reestablish family bonds.

Despite these losses, Kyla stabilized and progressed. Her concentration cleared and her skills in daily living improved to the point where she could transfer to a halfway house. Her primary therapist became an important link in assisting her to acclimate to group living and to the frightening world outside the protective walls of the state hospital. Slowly Kyla started to bond with the halfway house staff.

Three months after Kyla's admission, news arrived that her mother had died. Knowing Kyla's intense reaction to loss, her halfway house social worker was understandably concerned that Kyla would not be able to surmount this tragedy without decompensation. The worker contacted the therapist and together they evolved a plan to support this fragile woman through her ordeal. The consensus was that Kyla needed to replace the lost parent with the new kinship system she was building at the halfway house. Since she tended to be highly concrete, her primary therapist and her social worker planned to inform her of her mother's death together and to share all the known final details. The significant persons in Kyla's ecosystem—the therapist, who represented Kyla's lost self weakened by the illness, and Kyla's halfway house social worker, who was helping her forge the bonds to the new kinship group— spelled out through their cooperative interaction, empathy for her grief and solid assurance that she was not alone. Kyla weathered her loss without the anticipated regression.

The supportive life raft offered Antonio (in the following vignette) provides a workable prototype of several systems. These create a chain reaction to alleviate stress. The entire ecosystem (halfway house, therapist, psychiatrist, day hospital, vocational worker, and family) operated in unison to buttress this ill young man and assist him to ride out his crisis by providing security, feedback, and redirection of energies.

Antonio entered the halfway house with a high level of resolve to socialize with its residents and end the isolation which had surrounded him for many months. His cynical, inappropriate remarks, however, quickly alienated the men. He classified their comments about politics, theatre, or sports events as "simplistic." He felt they did not possess his in-depth knowledge base. He was equally offensive when he tried to approach the women who, in turn, rejected him. His anger surfaced as he experienced these unsatisfactory reactions.

Antonio's halfway house counselor and social worker gave him feedback on his behavior and suggested more satisfactory ways to engage others. Antonio insisted that he enjoyed pinpointing the weaknesses of others or insulting these "crazies."

Since he seemed out of control, untrusting, irritable, angry, and flagrantly paranoid, his social worker communicated his behavior to his outside therapist who offered Antonio emergency sessions. The therapist further agreed to arrange for hospitalization if Antonio's control deteriorated further, thus reassuring the halfway house staff that the other residents would have protection if the young man could not contain his anger. The therapist also contacted the medicating psychiatrist who at once raised the young man's prescription. The changed dosage was communicated to the halfway house where the counselor was advised to monitor its administration to assure compliance.

Antonio's day hospital was alerted to his distress in order to place minimal pressure on him in that setting and to ensure that a program of social skills training be instituted in a more neutral environment. Day hospital staff also agreed to keep the halfway house staff and therapist informed of whether or not Antonio attended regularly and of any significant changes in his moods or attitudes.

Antonio was also counseled by a vocational worker who was fully informed about his behavior. She agreed to slow down a pending referral for an assignment as a volunteer in a medical laboratory until he stabilized and exhibited more readiness to interact appropriately with his peers. She, too, utilized her sessions to help him feel less threatened and more accepted. She communicated her interventions to all systems.

Constant contact was maintained by halfway house social worker, therapist, and day hospital staff with his grandparents to gain their cooperation and to avert or reduce any pressure these relatives might place on him.

The ecosystem working together provided a safety net for this frightened, vulnerable young man. No agency or supportive person claimed territorial perogatives. All felt reassured that Antonio's whereabouts and behavior were constantly checked and that all were helping him reach the same goal. With all cooperating, sharing problems and progress, there was no splitting. Each member of the system felt the responsiveness of other parts and everyone was secure that Antonio's acting-out behavior was being carefully monitored and could be contained, via hospitalization, if necessary. Fortunately for him, his disappointment at his inability to break out of his isolation diminished. As that came under control, his level of irritation and anger receded. He started slowly to cultivate the friendship of two men who accompanied him to church. The protective shield of a nurturing ecosystem had sustained him throughout his crisis.

Decompensation

The most troublesome times at a halfway house occur when a resident decompensates. He becomes argumentative, angry, easily irritable, and responsive to stimuli that are often unknown to the counselor and to the other residents. When an individual is decompensating, counselors, of course, are instructed to reduce all pressures and to adopt a low emotional level. The social worker and counselor are at once in direct contact with the primary therapist since such behavior is often a threat to the safety of the ill person as well as to the group. But beyond that, a member of the community who cannot control his thoughts and actions is emotionally upsetting to all. It implies that the facility is unable to act as a safety net. The sense of hope, which staff has so carefully nurtured, is fractured. The optional approach, if the stressors cannot be alleviated, is to rehospitalize the decompensating person.

The primary therapist may not, however, be in accord with this decision. He may expect that the stress will subside or he may be concerned about alienating his patient by suggesting hospitalization. If he makes this suggestion to his patient and is met with a negative response, his next move may be to look toward involuntary hospitalization.

The dilemma for the treating psychiatrist and the halfway house is illustrated by Stefan who slowly decompensated after he was transferred from one day hospital, where he had made no progress, to a day hospital with a lower functioning population. He could not get out of bed in the morning. His shaving routine engulfed the rest of the morning and wearied him so deeply that he felt compelled to return to bed. He shared recurrent suicidal ideation, kicked holes in the door, and often emitted piercing shrieks during the night, terrifying his roommates and all those within earshot in the apartment building. This behavior was communicated to his psychiatrist who asked for continued patience with the problem. A final crisis occurred one evening when Stefan, for no apparent reason, threatened to throw a plateful of food at another resident and then burst out with threats that he was going "to kill someone tonight."

His psychiatrist now agreed that Stefan's behavior was out of control, but to protect his relationship with his patient he asked the crisis team to hospitalize Stefan. That group declined, however, to act for the primary therapist and the counselor on duty felt impelled to call the police who arrived as the young man quieted down. Observing no violence, the police team would not take him to a hospital emergency room. The counselor had the unenviable job of calming the ill young man and reassuring the other residents that they would not be molested by him. For the safety of the entire house, the director decided that if Stefan were not hospitalized the next morning, he would be discharged to his parents. Fortunately, the psychiatrist at the new day hospital managed to secure Stefan's cooperation for a voluntary hospitalization.

The primary therapist had indeed protected his rapport with his patient. But, physically removed from the halfway house, he was unaware of the damage to the other eight residents. He equated a halfway house to a hospital with manpower and facilities to protect the one who is out of control and reassure the others. Perhaps one method of preventing such misconceptions might be to invite, with some frequency, primary therapists to the facility so that they can become more informed about the nature of a halfway house and its inherent limitations in managing a decompensating resident.

A chronic client represents a dilemma to therapists who have been trained in a profession that focuses on "cures" as an index of effective service. A successful therapeutic treatment plan for the chronic patient, however, may concentrate on adaptation to reduced capabilities or recurrent bouts of illness. For many therapists such limited vistas may produce feelings of helplessness and hopelessness which the chronic, but sensitive, patient inevitably absorbs. Patients, however, may attain a solid baseline if therapists treating them can downplay their diagnoses and help them struggle and adapt to the current reality shaped by their illness.

With modified goals for the chronic patient, psychosocial treatment, appropriately applied, may become a valuable tool. Perhaps successful treatment outcome can then be redefined in terms of the severity of a person's illness, his premorbid personality, and his family system.

The ever-present hope of returning patients to their premorbid states, however, drives some (especially inexperienced) therapists to struggle to move their clients too quickly to healthy functioning in the face of severe, unyielding deficits.

THE FUTURE OF SYSTEMIC COOPERATION

The current policy of shortened hospital stays which quickly return patients to community living will require richer resources to serve a system-dependent population if they are to transition smoothly from inpatient care to life in the community. The mental health network must include funding streams and case management for those who are not living in a halfway house, partial hospitalization, short- or long-term day treatment, clinic treatment, psychosocial clubs, on-site rehabilitation, and crisis services as well as employment training, work, and family support programs. This vulnerable population will need a broad spectrum of community-based residences including those providing long-range care. If the ecosystem can provide and coordinate all these projected services, mentally ill persons will have the continuity they need to adapt to the outside community. For those who cannot or should not live at home, residence in a halfway house will enable them to utilize the above-named services while they work toward stability and independence.

CHAPTER 8

The Full Working Period: Three to 18 Months

The value system of the program should be apparent in all aspects of the milieu. The fundamental principles are that each resident has both healthy and troubled parts of his personality and that the healthy parts can increasingly understand and master the areas of difficulty. The acquisition of new skills strengthens healthy functioning and contributes to an inner sense of mastery. The resident increasingly feels himself to be competent and capable—a person of value. The old concept of the self as defective and valueless slowly withers in response to this growth force. (Budson, 1978, p. 177)

It takes a long time to get used to the idea that you have to say "bye bye" to childhood, that you have to grow up and take responsibility for yourself. You want to keep avoiding that moment when you say, "This is it, no more leaning on Mommy and Daddy."
　　　　　　　　　　　　　　　　—Sam (A Former Resident)

The full working period is the time when mastery commences. Those who are able begin to form their identities, leave behind the sick, inept persona, and emerge with a modified, more capable self. The exchange takes a long time, of course, as a little of the new is taken on and a little of the old slowly fades. It is a process fraught with crises and emotional storms, a process that can take three to four years in the halfway house, the supportive apartment, and aftercare.

In a halfway house, which has a mixture in degree of chronicity among residents, it is expected that the patient who has had but one or two hospitalizations and whose functioning appears to be only minimally impaired will be the one who will be able to make a full life for himself and avoid having a psychiatric rehospitalization.

Indeed, many residents do progress along this course, but for others whose illness is of a more chronic nature, the treatment becomes one of habilitation/rehabilitation. The goal of rehabilitation is to help the resident to function reasonably well despite a continuing vulnerability, to modify maladaptive behavior, to recognize stressors, and to structure his environment to be as facilitative of good functioning as possible. For a third group, the disability is so pervasive that rehabilitation focuses on stabilization, on lessening the degree and/or frequency of decompensation.

As there are no variables at intake predictive of success or failure within a community residence program (Glasscote, Gudeman, & Elpers, 1971), a higher expectation program will always have in residence people who fit variously and at shifting times into the above categories. The program should be flexible enough to serve the needs of its total population. Staff must also prepare itself for the unexpected: the bright, related applicant who gradually slips in functioning on a long decline into chronicity, and the poorly functioning applicant who is able to use the facility with its support, structure, and caring to coalesce his disparate assets, accept some of the limitations of his illness, push on the boundaries of others, and achieve a level of functioning which brings him pleasure, around which he can stabilize, and which allows him, with certain supports, to be independent.

A community residence which is truly rehabilitative offers its clients an appropriate length of stay to effect significant behavior and attitude change. After the first three months of initial adjustment, the stay ranges around a year in the halfway house and two years in the supportive apartment. The time frames can become a piece of structure—manipulated to provide additional support or motivation. It is becoming clear that one year or less is not sufficient time in a supervised facility for people to make real changes in their functioning. Also, it is clear that different levels of care facilitate growth. At some point, the resident will outgrow the 24-hour supervised residence and will graduate to less supervised settings.

Residents more easily address and modify behaviors than attitudes. Once a certain level of concrete functioning is reached in the halfway house, residents need further time in the supportive apartments to integrate their new functioning into their identities, to gain confidence, and to soothe fears before moving on into the community and to total independence.

STEPS IN SEPARATION AND INDIVIDUATION

As the resident feels safe in the halfway house, staff begins to encourage small, paced steps in two major directions: trust of self and trust of others. Trust of self evolves from the gradual growth in self-dependence and the lessening of overdependency on others for the gratification of needs and for direction. Separation from family has occurred physically in the first three months and now proceeds emotionally, with staff encouraging residents to make their own decisions with less involvement of family members.

While most intensive family work is carried by outside treatment facilities, the halfway house can offer occasional sessions to help the family deal with concrete separation issues. The house can also sponsor a family group meeting on an occasional or regular basis to keep parents abreast of agency policy, offer psychoeducation (perhaps with the involvement of the consulting psychiatrist on medication issues, etc.), and offer families an opportunity to develop trust in the agency and support each other, especially in the areas of their offspring's separation or dependency.

There were 18 family members at the group meeting, having coffee as they settled themselves around the room. Several couples exchanged friendly greetings, knowing each other from past meetings and asking after each other's children. A few were attending their first meeting, most of these parents of newly admitted residents.

The director began the meeting by asking for introductions around the room, each person identifying also the age and sex of their youngster or sibling at the halfway house or in the supportive apartment. The director warmly welcomed the newer members and she and some of the older members summarized for the new people the group's tradition of focusing on whatever areas concerned the members on a particular night.

On this night one couple, Mr. and Mrs. Burke, were distraught as their son, John, was in a very anxious period and was coming home too frequently. They had been working closely with John's social worker to try to limit the visits, to structure them so John would transfer some of his needs for intimacy and support to his peers at the house and to his day program. But these parents were frightened. Mrs. Burke described in emotional detail a suicide attempt John had once made in their home—her finding him and getting him, bleeding, to the hospital with a neighbor's help. Mrs. Burke was floundering, wanting to accept agency support in separating a little from her son, yet fearful that he might, in his anger and anxiety, not be able to use the support of staff and peers and might again act to destroy or injure himself.

Some other members of the group tried to reassure the Burkes that there was now an agency around John, monitoring his moods and providing him with structure. Yet several members said that they had experienced similar anxieties about the safety of their youngsters who have threatened or attempted suicide. The group eventually concluded that they had no "right answer" to offer Mr. and Mrs. Burke, that there is, indeed, no "answer" at all for this problem, only a hope that with caring people watching over him, John could move a little away from his dependence on home.

Then, Mr. and Mrs. Steiner, who were attending their first meeting, said they were surprised to hear so many people having trouble with a son or daughter being home a lot, leaning on them too much. They were having the opposite problem. Ever since their daughter had entered the halfway house three months ago, they had hardly heard from her. She became angry when they called and she had not come home to visit. They, too, had turned to Kris's social worker for support and had been told that many times when adult children are trying to become more independent, they find it more possible to make a complete break than to move away in stages. After several explanations, Mr. and Mrs. Steiner were able to understand that Kris apparently feared that if she saw them she might lose her resolve completely and cling to them again. But they, too, were frightened. They felt the loss of their daughter very deeply and were hurt and angered by her apparent anger at them. What should they do, they wanted to know, and what was going to happen?

In this instance, the group meeting provided a very concrete answer. Mrs. Max, whose daughter was older than some of the others and had been a supportive apartment resident for some time, told the group that her daughter had acted similarly. She suggested that the Steiners be patient and allow Kris time to do her growing. Mrs. Max had had to reassure herself that her daughter was safe and hopefully was making new friends and developing new interests. Mrs. Max shared that it was a painful time for her, too, but it helped her to begin to focus her attention elsewhere than on this daughter who had absorbed it for so long. Now, three years later, she reported, things have reached a kind of balance. Her daughter and she see each other regularly and have a pretty good relationship. It just took time and some guidance by staff. She hoped that it would work this way for the Steiners also.

As residents are encouraged by their therapists, their day programs, and community residence staff to turn their attention once again to self-development and to relationships with peers, they are, in effect, being persuaded to consider that there are others in the world besides their families to whom to relate, to trust, and with whom to become interdependent. The very broadening of the social network strengthens the resident as he then has more resources to draw upon in time of need. He begins, of course, with his peers in house and in day program. These are his significant social others, and he is encouraged to develop these relationships as well as those of any friends he may have made during his hospital stay.

Buoyed by the sense of belonging and caring, which are a part of life at a halfway house where the focus is on one's new family and on rehabilitation, the resident can begin to move. Her worker has come to meet her where she is and is beckoning her to take a step. Can she begin to trust herself and/or the people around her enough to risk herself in change? Often, these first steps are taken leaning upon the borrowed egos of the helping professionals in her life. Whether she is a very isolated resident who forces herself to sit alongside others in the living room for an hour each evening or the resident who is struggling to cope with work despite recurrent hallucinations, each makes her move in the symbolic company of the worker. Counselors and other social work staff, having consulted formally and informally on the progress of each resident, are there to reinforce movement. So are other residents, who are quite aware when one of their own is making a move and are there to offer encouragement.

As the resident moves through her program over time, the support extended by staff and peers slowly nourishes the growth of trust through relationships. People gradually learn about themselves and others through the process of interaction. Those who were isolated for years find a group and finally belong. As friendships form and develop and networks grow, so strong are the needs and the bonds that some of these relationships last for many years beyond the community residence.

People are, of course, united in having suffered similar painful failures, hospitalizations, and losses in their pasts. They come together, also, around the present pain and pleasure of common house experiences and change. They are able to accept inconsistency and mood swings in others for they ask the same acceptance during their own "hard times." They can relax and trust each other, not having to worry about concealing a past life or a present symptom, a medication tremor or a compulsive act.

Residents, Ralph, Geoff, Frank, and two other men they met at day hospital began to go out together for coffee, movies, and so on, in twos and threes and gradually coalesced into a group which met each Saturday night at the diner and often went on from there to some activity. When Michael entered the halfway house and attended the same day hospital, he quickly became one of the group. The members continued to meet in smaller subgroups but the Saturday night out became the consistent base of their friendship.

As the months passed, some of the members moved from the halfway house to supportive apartments or to nearby towns, some had crises in their relationships, but the group survived and flourished. A man could be silent all evening because he was stressed or needed to withdraw and the group accepted this and formed around him protectively. Another could be agitated and provocative on occasion and yet the group could usually tolerate that. Almost every one of the men had come to the halfway house quite isolated. For most of them this was their first adult male group experience since the onset of the illness, and they valued it.

A halfway house for men and women offers all residents an opportunity to develop friendships with members of the opposite sex. Some continue to avoid such contact because of shyness or fear of intimacy. Staff creates and supports situations that bring men and women together comfortably in house activities and social events. Holidays, especially, are the focus of celebration of the rebirth of energy and interest in life that such special days represent.

Love Relationships

On occasion, love relationships form among residents at the house. They usually occur with people who have reached a degree of comfort in their social relationships which enables them to move into greater physical and emotional intimacy. Some residents have had prior love relationships, but for many this is their first experience of such depth.

Although staff considers the ability to enter into a love relationship a sign of health, when both lovers reside in the halfway house there are certain inevitable complications which present a real challenge to the agency. Lovers cannot get away from each other in a community residence and their every action—affectionate or hostile—becomes public property. The lovers share a living space, friends, and perhaps the same day program and social worker at the house. The situation is ripe for merging and/or competition. Among a population that has severe boundary problems, such lack of physical and emotional space may feed into the pathology.

Early in the relationship, the lovers spend most of their free time together. Soon, one or the other, or both, begins to feel smothered, overwhelmed, or rejected and frequent fights and crises occur as one or the other strives for distance. There is usually a long period of dissension, of moving toward and apart from each other as the lovers work on issues of identity, separation, intimacy, and merging. This can be a time of crucial personal growth.

As staff is involved with both parties in the relationship, it can provide some objectivity to both the lovers and their therapists in viewing the quality of the relationship. Residents welcome this feedback as they try to understand and work with the emotions they are experiencing. Couples have asked for and received joint counseling sessions from agency workers.

When a couple is living in the same facility, the temptation to be together continuously is very difficult to resist and most couples eventually ask for help to structure their contacts. Staff can assist them to set up a routine, i.e., they will see each other Monday, Wednesday, Friday, and Saturday nights and spend the other evenings apart, in individual pursuits or in social activities with other women or men friends. The lovers are usually unable to keep to this structure, despite the fact that they recognize the value of developing and maintaining the other areas of their lives. However, this inability to be separate then becomes an issue in treatment and is explored over time until the couple can provide its own structure.

Following are some guidelines which staff will find helpful in coping with the complex, sometimes explosive, love relationships:

1. The halfway house should provide a private space in each location which lovers can use to have some alone time, but they are expected to keep the physical part of their relationship outside of the halfway house (and out of the building, if applicable). Other residents may have real difficulties with physical intimacy and/or feelings of rejection or loneliness that arise when they see intimacy enjoyed by lovers. Just as others are expected to work on these areas in their own treatment, so are the lovers expected to comport themselves with consideration for the needs and vulnerabilities of their housemates. Lovers are usually able to find locations (motels, the family home, etc.) in which to have their physical contact. If they feel confined by this structure, they are encouraged to focus on their growth so that they can move out of the halfway house and into more private housing. Their relationship becomes an additional source of motivation for growth to independence.

2. Likewise, lovers are expected to keep their arguments, dissension, and so forth as private as possible. This, again, is something couples are frequently unable to do initially because of problems of impulse control and inability to sit on negative feelings until an appropriate time or place to express differences is secured. On one occasion, staff had to ban a young man from coming to or calling the women's apartment for a week as a consequence of his inability to separate from his woman friend

during times of dissension in the relationship. His hanging on to her at the door and incessant phone calls had disturbed the other women for several nights. The limits on his behavior and on his access to the woman in question served as impetus to focus emotionally in session on issues of separation and his lack of inner controls and concern for the needs of others when he is upset.

3. The same problems and needs arise in homosexual as in heterosexual relationships. Homosexual lovers are expected to observe house structure and respect others' sensitivities.

When there are several intrahouse romances occurring at once, the tensions can run high, as there can be jealousies and conflicts over the affections. Although this proves to be highly demanding of staff time and attention, entering into and maintaining love relationships are great steps toward health for most residents who were once isolated. It may indeed be that the safety and control of the halfway house structure enables some to move into relationships of this nature once again or for the first time in their lives, or to move away from a relationship that impedes their growth.

CONFRONTATION

As relationships of various kinds form in the house, residents often commit themselves to taking firm stands in asking a fellow resident to cease a particularly upsetting or destructive piece of behavior. A combination of not being able to tolerate the behavior any longer and wanting to see the friend or peer move from a no-win situation fuels the confrontation.

> Darlene, a 22-year-old bulimic who had successfully been able to control her symptoms for periods of several weeks at a time since entering the halfway house, had been bingeing during the night for the last week. The other residents were aware that food was missing and they could occasionally hear Darlene vomiting in the bathroom. She was agitated and irritable during the day and looked puffy and swollen.
>
> As the week wore on, the women became increasingly upset. They were annoyed by Darlene's irritability and frightened at her lack of control, knowing that she was putting her life in danger. Several women began informing staff members of the binges, asking for help for themselves and for Darlene. While staff worked with Darlene separately to help her regain control, four of the women asked for a meeting to confront her with their concerns.

Two staff members were present to offer Darlene support during the meeting.

The women asked Darlene to stop snapping at them in the kitchen, monopolizing the bathroom and neglecting her chores. They acknowledged that she was in a crisis and said they were upset not only because she was making life difficult for them but also because they cared for her. They knew how hard she had worked to increase the length of her symptom-free periods, they admired her for that, and they wanted her to win her struggle. They were asking her to stop—insisting on it—for her good and theirs.

Darlene became very upset, heard only the negative, and eventually ran from the room. However, over the next few days, even though she withdrew into herself more and had little to do with her peers, it was clear that the binges and vomiting had stopped. Darlene entered into a new, even longer symptom-free period and gradually returned to more normal interaction with the women.

The development of the ability to confront in an assertive, reasonable manner and to support in an altruistic manner is fostered by the structure of the halfway house and bolstered by a similar thrust in day hospital and in therapy. Each individual is simultaneously cared for and supported by staff and yet encouraged to care for and support herself, to assert herself on many levels. Initially, the staff feeding is heavy, but during the process of the years in residence, the balance gradually shifts to the resident's doing the bulk of her own nourishing, staff slowly withdrawing. Thus does the inner "emptiness" felt by so many struggling with emotional illness become filled. And from that sense of fullness comes substance to give to others.

Elise, in her first months at the halfway house, had an extremely difficult time leaving her outside therapist after sessions. An overwhelming emptiness engulfed her and she panicked to the extent that she returned to the house tense, shaking, and talking a stream of consciousness for several hours. With staff attention and with some sleep, she eventually regained control. While she worked in her treatment hours on the dynamic issues of the emptiness, her social worker and counselor at the house worked in tandem to help her develop means of overcoming these periods of emptiness. A series of tactics were selected by Elise and staff for her to use during these terribly disordered times.

Among them were:

1. Elise was to hold an item given her by her therapist and summon up a mental image of the therapist and of the session.
2. She was to activate herself—do a chore, read, take a walk,

bake a cake—anything to interest herself in something and to discharge tension.

3. She was to engage herself with another person—focus on someone else—even if "not as good as" the therapist.

4. She was to remind herself that this awful feeling state would pass. She would feel better in time.

Elise could select any of these and other tactics to help herself. At first she required much staff support during these times. She needed reminders and she needed company. She was very angry at her therapist for not being available to her at all times and she resisted taking charge of her own care. However, as she worked through in therapy the issue that she could not possess and merge with her therapist, nor could that therapist become her perpetual feeder, and as she came to learn her own power for self-care, her floods of feelings lessened in intensity and frequency. She came to experience periods of anxiety rather than of desperate disintegration.

Were Elise not in the care of the halfway house during this period, she surely would have required further hospitalization. She lost track of her medications, had suicidal wishes, and feared she would fall apart. Indeed, there were occasions when neither day hospital nor halfway house staff were sure Elise could make it through the night. However, she gathered strength from surviving these episodes and from the expectation that if she acted to help herself, she would feel stronger.

Staff's calm expectation that residents will "make it through" a crisis, will grow, and will do what they have to do to make that next step is an extremely important variable in the equation of recovery. Hope and expectation are absolutely essential ingredients for rehabilitation. Residents have frequently reported that it was staff's conviction that they could have a better life that gave them hope and enabled them to keep going.

THE REHABILITATION MODEL

A significant component of the growth of confidence, self-esteem, and self-trust that is the thrust of halfway house life is the attention given to skills mastery and environmental manipulation in the interest of better functioning.

The initial step in the process of planned change according to the rehabilitation model of Anthony, Cohen, and Cohen (1983) is the completion of a functional assessment in which the social worker and resident identify the latter's skills, strengths, and deficits and develop together a plan of sequenced steps toward the resident's goals. The degree of partialization and the time spent on specific steps and skill development increase with the degree of functional impairment. As noted in Chapter 3, with the severely chronic resident the work is much more concrete and task-oriented both in day program and at the house than with the person who has more insight and ego strengths.

The process of goal selection presupposes at least a minimal level of motivation. At times, the goals selected by residents may seem inappropriate, unrealistic, and/or grandiose to the worker, family, vocational counselor, or others involved. However, after some reality testing, it may be clear that the resident is firmly wedded to his goal and that this is the only motivation available to him. It is thus the only motivation available to the staff member.

A primary value in rehabilitation therapy is that the client take the lead and define the priorities. Creative staff can break down even a grandiose goal into steps, which touch, in turn, on many areas of potential improvement. Time frames are applied by mutual agreement of worker and client and work begins. At times, the worker may take a directive or persuasive role to help the client keep to task and to schedule.

Marcy wanted to make a major impact on international efforts to secure world peace and avoid nuclear disaster. She was bright, articulate, and a very good writer, although socially isolated, quite rigid, and easily frustrated. She could not accept working in the antinuclear movement at a local level—only the top echelon would do. She was unmotivated to move out of day hospital until she and her worker devised a plan that focused on developing her writing skills to use as a tool to get her to a position of influence.

Marcy's first step was to obtain a volunteer job editing public relations copy for a local public service agency. She did well there and developed references that helped her to secure a part-time paid job as a "stringer," a reporter who covers police news for the weekly town newspaper, while she also took courses in typing and stenography. These latter skills helped her obtain a paid position as secretary for a company which published works devoted to securing world disarmament. During this process, which took several years, Marcy's goals became less grandiose and she was able to accommodate somewhat to working, at least temporarily, at a level below which she had originally set as her goal.

Where there is little or no motivation to improve functioning, remaining in the halfway house can become the source of motivation, i.e., one cannot stay if one is not up and out to program by 9 A.M. This stance presupposes that the resident wants to stay and thus staff will avoid inflexible positions until it is assured that bonding has occurred and that the house and peers are of some value to the resident.

Another means of creating motivation when there are no goals is to focus on problems instead. Even if a resident wants to leave the halfway house, the worker can help her break down into steps the process of successfully doing so and help her work through the stages of leaving.

Pam had spent the last few years wandering, staying in various hotels, spending a small inheritance until it was gone. Then, actively psychotic and in need of hospitalization, she fell back upon the care of her family. She was 34 years old, cultured, well educated, and had held several jobs for sustained periods of a year at a time.

Pam was shocked at the realization that she was schizophrenic. She was embarrassed about her decompensation and hated the idea that she had to spend a period of time at a halfway house and attend day hospital. However, she did so because she had no money and no shelter. Pam spent seven months at the house and at her day program and at first continued a life pattern of aloofness from others. She had but one goal—to get out to her own apartment.

After staff in both locations had exhausted every means to persuade her to approach her rehabilitation period more positively, they set to work to help her achieve her goal. However, they helped her to address her rehabilitation by adding, with her involvement, the additional goal of acquiring whatever self-knowledge and living skills would help her, hopefully, never to have to reside in a halfway house or be in a day hospital again.

With this approach, Pam participated in planning her future, exploring her current functioning, and making some difficult changes. As she saw she needed better social skills in order to avoid isolation and the risk of decompensation again, she began to reach out a little to other residents. She improved her ability to maintain a support system, react more flexibly to stress, and adjust better to community life.

Successful work with many chronically ill residents can occur only when the mental health professional is able and willing to move into the world of the troubled person and help him find the means to reach his goals. This is precisely why the distant, reserved stance in therapy fails so often with this population (see Chapter 7). The therapist (worker, case manager, etc.) must be willing to suspend his own reality and enter selectively into the reality of the patient, understand and accept his dilemma, and gently persuade him to try and look at his situation in a slightly different way.

Ellen suffered from the delusion that she had no brain and therefore could not work. This in turn was so devastating to her that she periodically became suffused with suicidal thoughts, frightening staff and other residents with her obsessions of destroying herself. She had not been able to work since graduating from college and had had several hospitalizations.

Ellen had been at the halfway house for 10 months and her year was drawing to a close. Despite day hospital treatment, therapy, several consultations with the staff psychiatrist, and a number of attempts to work which had ended in quick frustration and failure, Ellen held to her delusion that she could not think and function.

Ellen had bonded well to the house and to other residents, had a good working relationship with her therapist, and despite occasional overtly paranoid, hypomanic episodes, had made a positive adjustment to the house and wanted to move to the supportive apartment.

Ellen's social worker decided to accept Ellen's stance that her brain no longer worked and after some deliberation, she and Ellen decided that Ellen could only survive in a job that required absolutely no thinking. Ellen found part-time paid work in a small family business stamping cartons with a label as they came off a line. Ellen did not enjoy this work, but found she could tolerate it and moved to the supportive apartment two months later.

Gradually, Ellen began to absorb other functions of the production process until she found she could stand in for family members when they were absent, including manning the cash register, a task that required her to think. She began to acknowledge the return of her mental capacities.

After a year, Ellen could no longer tolerate the boredom and low pay of her job. Over the year her self-esteem had improved and with a sense of expanded capacity, she began to do some writing, a skill that had earned her honors in college and that she felt she might be able to put to work for her. She obtained a part-time volunteer job editing for a public service agency.

The recognition she received for her work on this job provided the impetus for her to seek paid work on the staff of a magazine. She is now working full-time.

"One change at a time" is the standard of a good rehabilitation program and of the halfway house as people move their way through the year: "If you start a new job, don't break up with your boyfriend at the same time"; "If you're moving to the supportive apartment, don't do it just as your therapist is leaving on a three-week vacation"; "If you're having minor surgery this week, don't make any major decisions about your life." The emphasis is to push on limits in just one area at a time and then allow time for that change to consolidate and integrate before pushing in another direction.

One change at a time becomes part of a new life structure and of the developing identity of the recovering resident, giving him a sense that there are rules for living that will work for him. It is imperative that the worker contract with the resident to bring to session information about all potential changes on the horizon so that planning can keep apace. At first, this process is again one of worker lending resident his or her ego. As incorporation of the new planning structure occurs, the resident assumes more responsibility for this function, the worker remaining alert to potential problems. For those residents with affective cycles, it is *crucial* that worker, resident, and therapist plan changes that do not conflict with the cycle period. Ideally, the cycle season should be a calm, stable time in the resident's external life.

VOCATIONAL PLANNING

The goal in rehabilitation and at the community residence is for clients to achieve as much growth and independence as possible. For most, this goal encompasses paid employment. The esteem, confidence, sense of normalcy, and support system that grow in the individual and social arenas as described above fuel an accompanying desire for growth and risk taking in the vocational arena. Mastery achieved within the halfway house is gradually applied to endeavors in the wider community. Work and productivity reinforce all other rehabilitative efforts.

Most residents simultaneously enter a day hospital and the halfway house upon leaving the hospital. This is the first step in the journey toward vocational independence (see Chapter 7). While in day hospital, the resident addresses issues of emotional development and vocational readiness. Difficulties in concentration, working with peers and supervisors, assuming responsibility for one's actions, productivity, assertiveness, setting vocational goals, and so on are of daily concern depending on the degree of vocational emphasis at the program.

The move from day hospital to volunteer employment is an important advance in a resident's program as it offers him an opportunity to develop and strengthen his assets in an environment less stressful than he would experience in paid employment. It is essential that every rehabilitation service develop a network of sites that will accept volunteers with a history of emotional problems. Residents can thus enter into their first post-hospital work experience without having to conceal their past or worry that an anxious mood or a difficulty in concentrating will draw immediate criticism. An informed and supportive supervisor can make the difference between a successful and a destructive first job. Also, a volunteer job enables a resident to experiment with new work attitudes, develop new assets and skills, and perhaps enter a new field without the pressures of having to perform consistently at highest capacity in order to merit a salary.

The volunteer job can serve as a "most facilitative environment" (Anthony, Cohen, & Cohen, 1983, p. 75) for a resident whose functioning is enhanced under certain favorable conditions. The volunteer job, even if but a few hours a week, provides a work reference and a time filler on resumés, helping the resident to resolve the vexing problem of how to account for months lost due to hospitalization and recovery. Frequently, day programs help their patients accommodate a slowly increasing load from a brief part-time, inhospital volunteer job under controlled conditions to increasingly more demanding positions until discharge from day hospital occurs.

Often, the day program assists a patient to begin volunteer work as soon as he is ready so that he can be well settled into his work upon discharge from the day hospital. This smooths the transition, especially if the patient has had a day hospital staff person as his therapist and must begin with a new therapist as well. The halfway house social worker helps the resident arrange an increased program after day hospital terminates, including one or two volunteer jobs and/or school courses which maintain structure so that the resident is not left with long stretches of time to fill.

Some day hospitals offer longer tenures so that the patient can participate in the day program to some degree throughout the process of moving through volunteer work to paid employment. For the more chronic patient who needs more time and support, this continuity of care is extremely helpful. The transition from one program and/or therapist to another is often an anxious time accompanied by some regressive behavior. The resident usually asks for, and receives, additional support from halfway house staff and peers during this time.

Vocational counseling is crucial during this period to define whether and how long a resident should remain at each step in his rehabilitation program. Will the volunteer job be only a brief interlude before returning to paid employment? Does a particular resident need long periods of consolidation after each advance? Would a resident benefit from a period of sheltered work? Or perhaps sheltered or volunteer work is the best long-term plan for a particular person.

Not all who suffer emotional illnesses are able to return to active functioning in all areas. Some make significant progress in the social areas and cannot fully embrace work; others are able to support themselves financially, yet remain socially isolated.

Vocational counseling is helpful to residents at all levels of advancing from day hospital to paid work. Many residents secure this help from day program and outpatient clinic staff or from vocational counselors in private practice. Some halfway houses employ a part-time vocational counselor to guarantee assistance to all residents in need. This staff person may counsel residents on resumé preparation, job readiness, job search, and advancement. The vocational counselor may also develop job resources in the community, accompany a resident to interviews or the first day of work, and/or serve as liaison with an employer as a resident develops on the job. The latter can occur, of course, only if the resident wishes to reveal his circumstances to potential employers.

The Fairweather Lodge model (Fairweather, Sanders, & Maynard, 1969) (in which residents contract out as a group to perform jobs in the community) and the Fountain House Transitional Employment model (Fountain House, 1974) (in which members and staff, when necessary, interchange to work a specific job over time) are two variations which may be of interest to a vocationally oriented community residence.

Whatever the contact with vocational resources, community residence staff must frequently guide vocational counselors and employers to understand the particular strengths and vulnerabilities of the still emotionally sensitive resident. At times, the latter's equilibrium is so delicate that any new situation, especially a job interview or first days at work, even the first meeting with the Office of Vocational Rehabilitation worker, is very unsettling and the resident does not present himself at his best. OVR workers are often understandably hesitant to fund residents for training or refer them to jobs on the basis of their behavior or presentation at that first interview. It would be helpful to them and to the resident to arrange to see each other two or three times before vocational plans are made, as the resident may present a more valid picture of his functioning once he gets beyond the initial stressful moments. Also, many OVR workers are more knowledgeable and/or comfortable working with the physically handicapped than with those with emotional problems and the community residence staff may have to be quite active to interpret behavior and help the OVR worker understand the degree of sensitivity with which he/she is working.

At times, vocational counselors become frustrated with the resident's and social worker's requests for specialized types of positions, those best suited as a first working experience after hospitalization, i.e., the low-stress job with an accepting, low-key supervisor. Such jobs are available in the community but must be sought out. They may be positions as security guards, gardeners, data processors, ushers, and so forth. Depending on the amount of work required and the quality of supervision, they can be quite adequate starting positions which can be passed from one resident to another as the former gains in confidence to pursue a job more challenging or more in line with his/her particular interests and abilities.

The move from volunteer to paid position is perhaps the most significant risk that a resident takes while in the halfway house. Paid work so represents independence that it carries symbolic as well as concrete meaning. Time after time, when asked what is different about obtaining paid employment, residents raise the same issues: they are frightened that if they become functional to this extent, they will be expected to be functional in all respects, i.e., totally independent. To many residents, independence symbolizes absolute aloneness, abandonment and, thus, disintegration or death. Because they have "broken down" before, there is no assurance that they can succeed in holding the job or get along with the boss and coworkers, despite the support they are receiving now and the growth they have made. Therefore, they are faced with a terrifying split—either stay dependent forever or invite the abyss that comes with absolute aloneness.

In order to fuel and sustain a forward push through this crisis, staff and resident prepare in the following manner:

1. Months in advance, they begin to address the resident's cognitive misassumptions about work and independence—that independence means isolation and abandonment by those who care. Life in this respect will not change from what it has been; a supportive family will continue to be supportive even if the resident is earning his own money. Friends, lovers, and staff will still be there to offer support and to make demands. Independence is relative, not a polar split. It is any number of places along the continuum.

2. Staff charts carefully with the resident her progress so she can see she has more assets with which to enter the work force, be they improved concentration, greater social ease, less fear of authority, greater internal organization, the acquisition of a marketable skill, and so forth.

3. Staff makes the step to employment as attractive as possible. Besides more money for clothes, a car, or a college course, paid work can mean a move to the supportive apartment. Here there is more privacy and more latitude in exercising control over one's life. This incentive is most effective if the resident has been at the halfway house long enough and gained in functioning and confidence enough to feel constrained by the structure, rules, and regulations. If social skills are developing, the resident also sees the supportive apartment as a place where he can entertain socially with much more freedom.

4. All measures are taken to assure that the employment situation is as facilitative as possible of the resident's good functioning, that it meets his

needs in areas of interest, skills, and stress tolerance. This is a vital piece of ecosystem work on which resident and social worker, therapist, vocational counselor, day program, and so on can collaborate.

The route of choice for most residents as a first paid position is for the volunteer job to develop into a paying job. This obviates many obstacles and occurs frequently enough to be one consideration in volunteer job selection. In this way the resident can bypass the job hunt, the job interview, the need for a resumé that explains away long or numerous absences from the work force. This also eliminates the total change in work milieu when changes are so difficult for this population to accommodate, the "rejection" of not being hired, and the possibility of accepting a position which proves untenable for various reasons, leading to voluntary or involuntary departure.

A sheltered workshop may provide a positive transitional work experience for some residents who are too anxious to move into competitive employment or who require a period of on-site vocational evaluation and/or work skills training for such problems in functioning as tremors, difficulty in accepting supervision, chronic lateness, and so forth. The resident must be prepared very carefully for this experience as he or she may feel threatened by working in proximity with employees who are severely chronically ill, mentally retarded, or physically disabled. This situation will evoke all kinds of boundary issues in residents who have weak holds on their identities and feel themselves merging with those around them.

Mitchell was referred to a local sheltered workshop for a vocational evaluation period, after which the plan was for him to receive job placement services from the workshop and from OVR. Three weeks into the evaluation, Mitchell was arriving late to the workshop and appearing agitated around the house. Although he had participated in developing his plan, Mitchell reported that he was feeling depressed. He felt that he would never leave the workshop, that he was like most of the other workers who were there for a long term.

Mitchell found himself in a dilemma. At times he saw himself as quite ill and feared he would not be able to make it in the working world. It was safer, then, to let himself feel he would be sheltered forever. But this upset him as he also had several real strengths in addition to a desire to be like "normal people" and work to support himself. Staff continued to work with Mitchell on individuating and developing his own life plans regardless of what other people were doing. After some time, Mitchell could see clearly that he differed in some real respects from his coworkers, including that part of his ambivalence that hoped for independence. He began actively to monitor his performance and to push for job placement services.

For some, however, sheltered work is the most appropriate long-term plan. It is a legitimate work experience for many people who can thus be productive and earn an income.

Subsidized work is another employment option which falls between the sheltered workshop and the regular paying job. An employer on a work site receives monetary or other benefits to employ a worker who needs some special attention in the form of allowance for lower output, a special supervisory arrangement, a shorter workday, and so on. Thus, as in sheltered work, a person is productive, feels productive, earns money, and pays taxes. Since employers can rarely afford to initiate such a program on their own, subsidized work falls directly into the arena of governmental initiative, as in the form of affirmative action programs.

Frequently, in the anxiety that accompanies the job hunt, a resident looking for work on his own initiative will take one of the first available positions, exercising little judgment as to how this job suits him. If the job is too stressful or otherwise inappropriate, the resident leaves or is fired, and must begin the job hunt anew. This is disappointing and frustrating for everyone, but the resident should be encouraged to resume the job hunt as soon as possible, learning from, but not dwelling upon, his first experience. It is important for residents to be able to feel that mistakes or misjudgments are occasionally to be expected and are all right, especially if one can learn from them. But staff and peer support is crucial if these missteps are not to become "failures" and demoralize the resident just as he is expanding his horizons.

Flexibility of house structure is needed for the resident who is working and whose schedule may interfere with dinner hour, curfew, and so on. While some accommodations are made, the resident is expected to continue with responsibilities, such as chores and cooking dinner (which he may prepare the night before). The resident is encouraged to give himself a full month or two to adjust to the new job and routine. Once again, he should make no other changes while he is making this adjustment.

EVALUATION

As discussed in Chapter 6, the three-month evaluations are a mechanism to track the resident's progress and the effectiveness of his program in meeting his needs. The first evaluation focuses on the adjustment process of the first three months and sets some goals for the next time period in terms of both how the resident wishes to grow in skills and assets and how he wants to shape his environment best to facilitate his growth.

Second Evaluation

When resident and staff meet again around his sixth month in the house, they review his first evaluation, where he was then, the goals he set, and how he has grown since that time. The following format is useful:

1. Review first evaluation.
2. What progress have you made in:
   a. chores?
   b. staff relations?
   c. relations with residents?
3. What areas need further work to enable you to move comfortably back into the community?
4. What type of living arrangement do you envision yourself in?
5. What specific plans have you evolved to move back into the community?
6. How can the halfway house help you achieve these goals?

Current functioning is assessed with less emphasis on adjustment into the house and more attention to skills and tasks to be mastered. Once again, personal and program goals are set for the next time period. This same process is repeated for the third evaluation, which occurs at about the ninth month. While staff tries to keep to three-month periods, the evaluation schedule often varies because of events occurring in the house, the demands on staff, and the resident's progress at a given time. Staff tries to time evaluations so as to get the greatest positive momentum from them. There are usually some significant gains over this long period of time, often skewed, but enough to reinforce progress and renew energies to move forward, both for the resident and for staff. As the evaluations are recorded in some detail, growth and the lack of it are clearly noted.

Following are Pat Wilson's second and third evaluation sessions (refer to her first evaluation in Chapter 6). The second evaluation occurred five months after the first, somewhat late as Pat was involved in a chaotic love relationship which left her feeling angry and scattered and which absorbed much staff attention. Also, during this time, Pat's therapist referred her to day hospital because she was not functioning well in her volunteer job and was unable to mobilize herself to move to another position.

Pat Wilson's Second Evaluation

Present: Pat; the director; Cora, Pat's social worker; Inez, the counselor

I. Chores

Pat feels she has made progress in chores. She now gets satisfaction out of doing some chores she used to dislike. But she doesn't yet have a sense of totally putting a place together on her own. She feels she doesn't need supervision as she does her chore regularly on Sunday night. Inez has not heard any negatives about the chore responsibilities from the weekend staff.

Pat still is very disorganized in the kitchen. She feels she follows directions a bit better but agreed that she will begin working from a cookbook in order to become more independent.

Pat could also operate more independently and set some standards in her room. Pat doesn't feel her room looks that good. She considers it a functional place and she hasn't taken its appearance seriously. The director wondered why Pat's personal space, that area most hers, is not important to her. Pat agrees that a messy space reflects a mind that is not organized. She thinks that if she made it neater it might help her to be more organized. The director suggested that her room is like a microcosm of the apartment she may have on her own in the future. A helpful goal might be to start small and make her room now more pleasing to her. Inez will report to the director on progress.

Pat feels that a lot of her progress has been impeded because she has been obsessed since January with her relationship with David. Day hospital has helped her to focus on the fact that if she is to grow she will have to give less attention to that one relationship and more to other areas. Thus, in the last two weeks, Pat has made changes to lessen the intensity of the obsession. She recognizes that she has made no progress this winter on career goals and very little on developing social relationships with people other than David.

II. Relationships with Staff

Pat feels she has gotten to know staff better as people rather than as authority figures, especially since the period when Inez was monitoring her meds and she had that fight with her. Her awareness of Inez as a person has deepened. She's not so tense with Inez because she no longer sees Inez as a policewoman. She also sees the director more as a person, which is nice because there is less of a tendency to act out childish things around her as an authority figure. The director wondered why, then, is Pat so quiet in community meeting? Pat feels this is because she is thinking about David all the time, so tense over what he is thinking and how he is reacting. This is again an example of how Pat is so involved in one relationship that it blocks off other avenues.

Pat is now working with day hospital to devote more of her attention to work matters. She has just been placed on probation at her volunteer job. She needs to improve her performance on baseline things such as following through on directions, completing tasks, etc. Her vocational counselor has told her that she has to be able to perform and focus on a job before they can look at career planning. Pat is embarrassed to be on probation but she is trying to take responsibility for getting out of an antigrowth situation. Pat feels it has taken her so long to move away from her counterproductive relationship because she never had that kind of deep relationship or happiness before. The director suggested that usually a wholesome, happy relationship frees one to move into other areas. She wondered if Pat is equating happiness with dependency here.

III. What Expectations Do You Have for Yourself During the Rest of Your Stay Here?

Pat has been at the halfway house for nine months, by which time people are usually more advanced than she is in pursuing their goals. Pat wondered how this affects her status at the house. The director asked her what she thinks staff wants to see her doing. Pat feels that if she can show examples of what she can do, staff will have confidence in her ability to progress. The director suggested giving Pat three months to work on her goals. In September we shall meet again in evaluation to see what movement she has made.

Pat and staff agreed that the following areas are to be addressed:

1. Volunteer job—Pat should get herself off probation by attending to tasks assigned her, taking notes, making lists, doing whatever she needs to do there to make a contribution without her supervisor's having to expend so much time on her.
2. Attend to day hospital business while at day hospital: setting recreational, social, and vocational goals; finding ways to live so that a deep reaction to any occurrence doesn't take over her life.
3. Socialize with a broader group of people.
4. Work on personalizing and organizing her personal space at the halfway house.
5. Become more independent in the kitchen, following through on tasks, learning to use a cookbook, etc.
6. Sharing her ideas more at community meeting.

Staff feels that Pat has made growth in some areas, i.e., she doesn't need to be constantly reminded about chores any longer, nor does she have her former difficulty with getting out of the house by 9 A.M. Staff is trustful that Pat will use her support system to help her meet the goals she has set above.

Pat's third evaluation occurred four months later.

Pat Wilson's Third Evaluation

Present: Pat; the director; Cora, Pat's social worker

On reexamining prior evaluations, Pat was commenting on how she had worked to fulfill one goal of personalizing her room. She reported that she has enjoyed the pictures she has put up. Pat has not, however, completed the task of putting up the shelves which were procured for her. She described her fear of the new task, various obstacles which occurred, and her inability to see the task to completion. As each obstacle was discussed, it became clear that Pat lacked an organizing force, a certain assertiveness which would have stimulated her to proceed beyond the obstacle.

In discussing what Pat could have done to soften the fear of mastering a new skill, the director suggested that she might have asked either Ralph or Ron for guidance, for a lesson on how to work the drill, for instance. She then might have taken some time to practice on a board. Something stops Pat from using all of her resources. What can Pat do when something frightens her, seems new and strange? She might ask herself how she could make it easier, familiar, less strange. This is a microcosm of the kind of mastery Pat can feel in other areas also. It is important that Pat be aware of how she lets obstacles stop her when she is afraid so she can work on how to help herself. How she approaches new skills needs lots of attention.

Staff Relations—On the occasion of Inez's, the counselor, leaving the halfway house, Pat feels she has been overly critical of her. Inez has a solid, personal tie, Pat sees, to a lot of people at the house. Pat has made a date to see Inez and share some positive feelings with her.

Staff noted Pat's significant progress in the kitchen. She is now cooking quite competently as the result of working with the weekend counselors and day hospital staff on menu preparation, and of a real concern by Pat that she master this skill. On reflection, Pat feels that she acted like a helpless child in the kitchen when Inez was overbearing, so that Inez would take over. At the same time Pat became angry at Inez for doing so, for yielding to Pat's manipulation. The director remarked that it has become clear subsequently that Pat is *not* a helpless child in the kitchen. This helplessness was a *response* rather than really reflecting Pat, who is a capable woman. The director wondered if there is not also some hidden anger in Pat's abandoning the shelf project. Pat agreed there was some anger toward Ralph because he pressured about the drill. There has also been some anger at Cora when Pat wanted to tell her something in confidence and Cora advised that it might be information she would need to share with the team. The director remarked that in these instances Pat was aware that she was angry. Are there times she is angry and is not aware of it? Pat said that people have told her she has a lot of anger. The director said that it is clear that an authority figure can elicit that anger and then Pat begins to act like a child—with anger or fear or both.

Pat feels it is sometimes easier to act subservient to someone than to be angry at them. The director noted that Pat at times also finds it easier to be subservient than to be up front with people, to be clear about what she does or doesn't want. Pat feels it would be a goal for her to be clearer about resistances with people.

Volunteer Job—Pat reports she has performed adequately and was taken off probation after only a few weeks. Her supervisor was very pleased with her writing this summer. She is now looking for a less protective, more challenging volunteer job, but is waiting for affirmation on this next step from day hospital. With further discussion, it became clear that Pat has not really developed the volunteer job beyond what was asked of her. Again she took little initiative to make it more challenging or richer. She hangs back, waiting for other people to do, and then gets angry when nothing much happens.

Cora wondered what is the problem in asking people to teach her (Ralph with the drill, the supervisor with new tasks at the volunteer job). Is Pat unable to put herself in the less knowledgeable position? Pat states that she resists, she doubts her ability to learn a new skill, she never gets the knack of dealing with things when she doesn't have a lot going for her. The director noted this makes Pat either an expert or a nothing. Pat agreed, feeling that if she is ever going to succeed at a job she is going to have to work a lot on this extreme stance. She will have to change her view that the authority expects her to know everything when she's just starting. Pat feels a boss would expect her to be quick at what she does, knowledgeable, etc. The director agreed that that is what Pat *thinks*. In reality, bosses expect that there will be *errors* when people are learning in a new job. Pat stated that when she makes her first error, she decides that she can or can't do the job and if she "can't do it" she falls apart.

The director recommended that Pat use the volunteer job to address this issue—to say "I don't know" with new tasks and try to tolerate a step-by-step learning process. Can she trust that learning on the volunteer job is in her interest? Can she try not to hate herself immediately when she errs and then get mad at the person who is teaching her? Pat has observed that this step-by-step process works for others. Perhaps it can work for her. Perhaps she can tolerate not knowing in order to learn. By playing the incompetent child to the "mother," she takes the joy of mastery, strength, and control from herself.

Pat has been able to concentrate more at day hospital and use the program more effectively. She has been granted an extension in recognition of her progress so she can consolidate her gains and set up an appropriate postdischarge program for herself.

Pat set the following goals for herself for the next few months.

1. To ask for tasks to do at the volunteer job—opportunities to do new things.
2. To do more work on childlike behavior and resistance issues.
3. To request at day hospital an in-house volunteer job.
4. To take full responsibility for getting job information for herself, using the vocational group for help.

Relationships to Other Residents—Pat finds Terry still a thorn in her side, ever since she's been in the house. Pat's relationship with Edna has worked out much better than she expected. Edna has made an effort to have a relationship. The director asked what effort Pat has made with Edna. She asked Edna to go for a walk with her once. What has Pat done to make an effort in the relationship with Terry? Pat states she can't forgive Terry for certain acts of aggression. She finds her irresponsible and selfish. The director suggested Pat try, as an exercise, to find some way she and Terry could meet with common goals. Can they stop being antagonistic? Pat feels it is easier to see Terry negatively. The director agreed that it is easier but this is Pat's assignment—to find a piece of common ground so they can be amicable for Pat's sake. Pat could see that this exercise could be helpful to use in a job situation where there is animosity developing between her and another person.

Pat has broadened her social life to include a growing group of female friends with whom she has begun to socialize on a regular basis.

Pat will address herself to the above goals in the next three-month period. She has met the goals set with her in the last evaluation and will therefore be remaining at the halfway house.

As is clear from the varied use of staff at the halfway house and at day hospital, the help of a concerned therapist, and the support and caring of Pat's family and friends, Pat has required and used the input of many resources in her growth. The growth was reinforced by several well-considered cues from the various helping professionals suggesting that Pat must let go of some resistance and move to the next level of functioning or she would lose her housing and/or her day program, both of which she highly valued. Despite her strong regressive pulls, she was always able to take the risk of moving toward change, trusting her resources. Even when buffeted by strong emotions of fear, panic, and neediness, Pat's commitment to growth, and her intense desire to work and to love, was a great impetus to change. She has continued to reach for her potential and is now working in paid employment and has moved to a supportive apartment.

STAFF MEETING

The weekly staff meeting is tremendously valuable to staff for many reasons (see Chapter 6), but particularly as a forum for staff to discuss a resident's behavior or progress. Counselors who work directly on a daily basis with the resident, weekend counselors, the resident's social worker, the other workers who observe her at various times and have feedback to offer from what other residents say and feel about her, and the consulting psychiatrist, who can offer an objective view as he has no personal contact with the resident—all contribute information and suggestions about a resident's care. An action plan is instituted, with agreement as to what role each staff member will take. Details are then communicated to weekend counselors via the main counselors, by memo and by the director so that consistency is maintained. Staff can check with each other informally during the week as plans are carried through. Formal readdressing occurs at the next staff meeting where nuances in resident response are discussed and staff direction is reset.

Planning does go awry when all staff cannot meet personally to achieve consistency. The fact that such miscommunications occur in all organizations necessitates staff's alertness and the use of its meetings for constant reinforcement of consistency and effectiveness.

When a resident is called to staff meeting to address problems in functioning and it becomes clear that he is, in fact, decompensating, staff must decide if hospitalization is necessary. The most obvious indications for hospitalization occur when the patient is suicidal and he and staff fear that he may not be able to control his impulses; when the patient is so agitated and disruptive that he is a danger to himself or others; or when he is so depressed that he cannot function out of bed at all. In these instances, the consulting psychiatrist contacts the resident's therapist and/or day hospital and if there is no reason not to proceed, either party can arrange for admission to hospital.

PERIODS OF CRISIS

If the therapist or day hospital do not agree with hospitalization, community residence staff must determine if it is able to supervise the resident closely enough for a short period in hope that he may recompensate, perhaps with a medication change, reduced stress and/or increased supervision from counselors.

> Sue, age 26, worked full-time with a firm that held her bookkeeping position for her during her hospitalization. She had returned to work and gradually resumed full responsibilities until she had a serious battle with her mother which precipitated another episode of disorganization. The halfway house staff became a 24-hour support system in an attempt to keep Sue out of the hospital. Her social worker was in close contact with Sue's supervisor and with her therapist and, in turn, directed house staff in Sue's management. When Sue's agitation, confusion, and verbal ramblings precluded her going into work for two weeks, counselors, social workers, and clerical staff took turns through the day structuring her, assigning her tasks, and supervising her. She recompensated and returned to work.

The community residence is not a hospital and is not so staffed. It can offer close supervision for a limited time. The nights are long and lonely for one counselor to carry the responsibility for an actively psychotic or suicidal patient. When a resident decompensates in the evening, at night, or on the weekend when only the counselor is there to provide assistance, communication ensues among resident, social worker, the resident's therapist, the consulting psychiatrist, if necessary, the director, and the counselor to determine the course of action. If conditions warrant it, either the consulting psychiatrist or the therapist can hospitalize the resident. If, as on occasion occurs, no psychiatrist is presently available, a crisis team or the police can be summoned for assistance.

The crisis team is composed of mental health professionals, including a psychiatrist, usually based at the community hospital. The team travels to a location to render assistance to a person in emotional crisis. At times the crisis team can calm the agitated person and perhaps administer medications that will help him regain control. If necessary, the team can effect hospitalization.

There are occasions when the crisis team is unavailable and a counselor may be so struggling with an upset resident that staff must call in outside help in the form of the police. This is a last resort, as it is upsetting to the resident in question, other residents, staff, and neighbors. Most often, a resident who has lost control is frightened of his own impulses and will go willingly to the protection of the hospital structure.

When such a hospitalization occurs, staff is in ongoing contact with hospital and resident to ascertain if the resident will be returning to the house. Staff meetings are also utilized to consider requests for readmission by hospitalized residents. Staff is interested in learning more about the decompensation, its precipitators, its dynamics, and whether steps can be taken to prevent its recurrence. The hope is that the painful experience may become a source of growth, that the resident can learn something new about himself or the circumstances that stressed him to decompensation and thus alter his lifestyle, expectations, or environment. Halfway house staff ask to attend a hospital conference to ascertain the above information and to assure the readiness of the resident for discharge. There are occasions when readmission to the halfway house has been proposed prematurely, at times for the purpose of hospital utilization review. In these instances, when the resident has not been stable enough to return to house routine, readmission is delayed.

Knowing that the halfway house will want such a discharge conference, hospital staff who have systemic pressures for a speedy discharge are primed to work more closely with the patient on the dynamics of the decompensation, not solely on stabilizing him to return to the community. The resident is then asked to attend the halfway house staff meeting to convey to staff his or her understanding of the meaning of the decompensation and hospitalization. If it appears that there has been a precipitant potentially subject to the resident's control, staff wants to know if the resident is ready to make the growth to the next level of functioning. For instance, if the resident has been noncompliant with meds, is he now able to leave behind his denial and his anger at the illness and accept all of himself, including the part that must take medication? Consider the following two examples.

Alan was hospitalized twice in four months while at the house, each time in a hypomanic, agitated state. He was attending day hospital where his medications had been repeatedly adjusted in an attempt to find a satisfactory formula. It became clear that Alan was exquisitely sensitive to minor medication adjustments. Although it was suspected that there was some noncompliance due to grandiosity or confusion, staff at day hospital and halfway house agreed that the hospitalizations were necessary as part of the process to find an effective and comfortable regimen for Alan. Therefore, his readmissions to the halfway house were pretty routine, with some attention to the compliance issue.

In contrast, Barbara's second hospitalization, while a resident, followed the same course as her first—due in great part, staff felt, to

Barbara's unwillingness to address the emotional issues of separation from her parents. The parents lived in the area, but neither they nor Barbara could keep to structure around visits. Barbara kept returning home, conflicts about leaving the family home were rekindled and Barbara's functioning deteriorated. Staff disagreed with hospital thinking that Barbara should return to the halfway house but felt that she should be referred to a similar facility several hundred miles distant from her family where visits could be more structured.

Staff decided not to take Barbara back at this time and communicated with Barbara's social worker and her family that she might return in the future if she were to grow enough to be able to stay within the structure of the house in the areas noted above.

Suicide

Suicide is the most extreme behavior a rehabilitation facility is forced to confront. It leaves in its wake mounds of guilt, fear of loss of control over one's acts, insecurity, and hopelessness among the other residents. "Can this staff keep us safe?" is a recurrent question for which there is no firm answer.

Any group is tragically affected by a suicide. In a therapeutic community, one in which members struggle daily with vast physical, emotional, and intellectual losses and in which there can be the temptation to resolve the unresolvable by suicide, the impact is deeper, more disruptive, and more terrifying. It erodes confidence in the rehabilitation effort. Many residents come with histories of hospitalization occurring either in the wake of an actual suicide attempt or in search of a safe haven until the impulse to find a quick and permanent way out of recurrent miseries has subsided. The sudden suicide of a friend or associate, especially if he lives in a rehabilitation facility, reactivates these terrifying impulses which may have been arrested by hard work and by confidence in the program endorsed by hospital staff, family, and therapists. It erodes trust that the rehabilitation philosophy of the halfway house and staff can provide the needed safe harbor. Belief in the possibility of one's own recovery sags. In addition, there is always the added possibility that one suicide in a facility can cause a chain reaction, triggering others to carry out often-present suicidal impulses which had been suppressed with such difficulty.

The United States has witnessed an unprecedented growth in the suicide rate among young people. Suicides in the years 1950 to 1980 have surpassed those in Japan and Sweden, who formerly ranked highest in the world. Cotton, Drake, and Gates (1985) have developed a profile of schizophrenic patients who commit suicide. The patient, around 30 years of age, had suffered his illness from five to 10 years. During this time he had experienced recurrent bouts which hospitalized him an average of six times. Sixty percent of the suicides were male, unemployed at the time of the completed act and frequently living alone. Before the onset of the illness, the patient progressed well in school or work and had satisfactory social relationships. The drop in functioning accompanying his illness, however, remained unacceptable to him. With early aspirations shattered, the ill person may have held tightly to one intact aspect of his life which fed his self-esteem. This could have been a prized relationship (perhaps with a young child or a family member or therapist) or a job or a status possession such as a home. Loss of the valued relationship or possession could have triggered the suicide. The depressed schizophrenic is at his highest risk for suicide during nonpsychotic periods. At such times, he is painfully aware of his inability to achieve his former high aspirations.

Minkoff et al. (1973), in their studies of suicidal intent among patients diagnosed as depressed, noted a strong correlation between the seriousness of the suicidal urge and feelings of hopelessness about the future. Roose et al. (1983) found that, in a wide spectrum of diagnoses, depressed persons who were also delusional were five times more likely to kill themselves than depressed persons without delusions.

A caring therapist and a supportive living arrangement may reduce the despair and hopelessness a chronic relapsing illness imprints on a person. Empathy for his despair while he is rebuilding mastery of essential life tasks may repair lost self-esteem.

Family members or an available support team become essential lifelines for an ill person. Often, he projects responsibility onto them for his stabilization. When an environmental change or separation upsets the status quo, a suicide attempt may represent an effort to regain control over his parents' lives through his own death, as is shown in this example.

Hilary had been a natural leader in the community. Her wit, flamboyant looks, and dress, unimpaired intellectual ability, and excellent organizational powers combined to make her a role model for many in the group. During the period of her residence, she struggled with innumerable real or fantasized somatic complaints which, one by one, were eliminated.

Prior to the onset of her illness, she had entertained ambitions to embark upon a political career. Because she was unable to work, she expended her considerable energies trying to exert control over her parents' lives. She could involve them but she could not keep their failing marriage together. Once they separated, she could not prevent her mother from simplifying her life and finances through the rental of the luxurious family home, replete with tennis court.

Hilary's loss of control of her family, of the family home, and the loss of her obsessional somatic complaints, which she needed as a defense to bind up her anxieties, may have shattered her fantasy that she could control some aspect of her universe, thereby leaving her prey to her overwhelming anxieties. One morning, in a wooded grove of her favorite park, she ingested a handful of lethal pills. Her death jarred the entire house. If Hilary, who had so many assets, had failed, how could anyone else recover? Why had staff not tuned in more finely to her distress to prevent her from destroying her life?

The facility met this catastrophe by assembling the residents as a group to hear about Hilary's death. Staff hoped to convey the feeling that the community had built-in supports and strengths to deal with the tragedy, to cry about it, and to comfort each other. The loss of a cherished member was acknowledged and openly mourned. Each member of the group was given an opportunity to express grief, sense of loss, remembrance of Hilary, and anger at Hilary's betrayal of what each one had been attempting to achieve. All were encouraged to confront administration for its inability to be more powerful or all-wise.

Staff, too, openly recognized their feelings of anger at the act and their own feelings of loss. But beyond the expression of deep emotional reactions, staff reiterated the firm conviction that the facility remained a place for hope and unremitting effort and that finding alternatives other than suicide was the essence of life. The themes of courage and rededication and constant staff availability when anyone was in crisis were symbolized through holding of hands.

Together, staff and residents attended Hilary's funeral and comforted her grieving family. After the service, the entire group lunched together. Repeated reactions to the funeral sermon and to Hilary's death surfaced during the trip and the meal and for weeks thereafter. Several individuals expressed their guilt over small negative encounters they had experienced with her. Each one was reassured that no one incident leads a person to the decision to end his life.

For many days, the facility was subdued. Staff not only repeatedly stated, "Life goes on," but underscored that message by initiating plans for diverting activities such as barbeques in the park, attendance at "Y" discos, and so forth. Members of the house further confronted their angry reactions by taking issue with the newspaper article describing Hilary's death. The newspaper headline read, "Mentally Ill Person Suicides." Residents objected to the labeling. They mobilized their frustration and anger by laboring over a response to the article, thus reasserting a measure of control over life events which Hilary's sudden death had shattered. Fortunately, their reply was published. The reporter who prepared the article met with the group at a community meeting. He apologized for the emphasis in his story. Slowly life restabilized.

Ordinarily, persons contemplating suicide consider the impact on their friends and seek a location other than the halfway house for their self-destructive acts. Most difficult to handle is an in-house suicide.

His roommate discovered Sonny, in bed, gasping for breath. He had spent his birthday with his family enjoying the celebration in his honor and swimming at the local club. As he returned to the residence, one of the men reminded him that he had neglected his chore of defrosting the refrigerator. He reacted with explosive anger and commented, "I don't have to pay attention to your criticisms any longer!" He dashed into his bedroom, swallowed innumerable pills, and climbed into bed. His irregular breathing brought a cry for help from his roommate, but emergency treatment came too late.

Such an event left an unforgettable scar on the entire house. Although staff utilized efforts akin to those outlined above to mourn the loss of a loved friend and to express anger and frustration at the disruption of life in the house, the horror was deeper because the death was witnessed, the fear of loss of control greater, and the individual sense of guilt more pervasive. Confidence in the step-by-step progression toward health was shattered and healing was more protracted. Sonny's roommate could not feel safe in the residence. He moved back to his family's home. The room was left vacant until the mattress was changed. Although new residents were admitted as quickly as possible thereafter to normalize the atmosphere, repercussions continued. One young man became so stressed he needed a brief hospitalization. It was not until everyone who witnessed this tragedy had moved on to other housing that the impact on residents subsided. On staff, it never did. Events such as these are fortunately rare.

In essence, the way to react to tragedy is to pause, to acknowledge it and honor the dead, and then to underscore staff's constant availability when pain is acute and anyone is in crisis and to ask house members to rededicate themselves and their efforts to life. After a reasonable interval, staff discourages further reflection about the event, usually by providing diversion. Some halfway houses or day hospitals take minimal time out of program to dwell on the tragic event. They quickly move the attention of the group to more rehabilitative pathways.

MEDICATIONS

As most halfway house residents are prescribed medications by their therapists or physicians, medication management is a crucial area for residents and staff. The variety and amount of medications on the premises of a community residence are staggering, ranging through all the neuroleptics, antidepressants, sedative hypnotics, and lithium. For everyone's safety, especially for those who may suffer periods of suicidal ideation or despair, a community residence must adopt a strict policy regulating the administration and storage of these drugs.

Some halfway houses take possession of all medications upon admission and issue daily dosages to each resident. The advantages of this system are that all medications are under lock and key and staff is aware daily that each resident is issued the proper amount to take (this becomes helpful when a resident is confused or begins to decompensate). The disadvantage of this regimen is that it takes from the resident the responsibility of managing a vital part of his daily routine in a setting that encourages such responsibility in other areas.

If the house policy is for residents to manage their own medications, each resident can be provided with a locked metal box in which to keep them. Counselors must make daily checks to ensure that the boxes are secure and there must be sanctions for failure to keep them locked. Medications cannot be left loose on bureau tops or in medicine cabinets. Some residents will, out of curiosity, experiment with others' medications or borrow them if they run out. For obvious reasons, all interchange of medications should be discouraged. If a resident runs out of his own meds and has failed to renew the prescriptions, the consulting psychiatrist can issue a one- or two-day prescription if necessary. It is also helpful for staff to know the closest pharmacy that accepts Medicaid funding.

It is vital that the social work staff have a good working knowledge of medications, their effects, and side effects. Program directors should provide periodic education to all staff and can make creative use of the consulting psychiatrist to this end. Although counselors and other residents are often the first to notice subtle changes in a resident's behavior which may signal problems with medications, these sources report such observations directly to the social worker, who calls the therapist or the medicating physician. Often, it is the social worker's intimate knowledge of the resident's functioning which, when communicated to the therapist, directs the adjustment of the medications.

During the course of his time at the halfway house and supportive apartments, Reed had several manic episodes. Normally on a maintenance dose of lithium, Reed was prescribed a major tranquilizer by his therapist during the manic periods. Although the therapist saw Reed each week during these four- to six-week episodes, Reed's worker spoke with the therapist every two or three days by phone so that she could communicate shifts in Reed's functioning and request medication adjustments. Worker and therapist developed an alliance which enabled the latter to be much more responsive to Reed's course during episodes. This important alliance, as well as the other supports available to Reed within the community residence, enabled him to avoid hospitalization and to address the issue of his control over the stresses that precipitated his manic episodes.

Because of the fragility of the population in community residences, staff is frequently confronted with the task of evaluating suicide risk. Since many commonly used medications are potentially lethal, it is essential that staff develop protocols for immediate response to suicidal thinking or behavior. In addition, staff should attune itself to the areas of client functioning that may be jeopardized by the sedative effect of some medications (Matorin & DeChillo, 1984) or the tremors, blurred vision, and so forth, which accompany the use of other medications.

In a halfway house where group meals are prepared, residents who are taking MAO Inhibitors will need to help plan menus that can accommodate their diet. This is an opportunity for staff to help a resident focus on taking special care of her own needs rather than relying on others to do this for her.

Needless to say, all of this knowledge and effort are useless if the halfway house staff is not notified of medication changes by the prescribing physician. Some psychiatrists are not accustomed to, or are resistant to, sharing management of their patient with another resource. Others forget to make the communication. Some residents are quite reliable about informing their workers of medication changes, others are not. Inevitably, the staff social worker must take responsibility for contacting the prescribing physician regularly for written medication updates.

Medication noncompliance is a constant issue confronting halfway house staff. As stated earlier, many residents retain components of denial of or anger about their illness and therefore may forget or refuse to take their medication appropriately. Noncompliance usually is not apparent until decompensation is underway and then it may be too late to restabilize the resident even if medication resumes and is monitored. If noncompliance is acknowledged or suspected, staff can monitor meds at each dosage by having the resident bring his meds each time to the counselor or by having the counselor hold the meds (in cases of concern about suicide potential). At times, counselors may need to verify compliance by making sure that meds are not hidden in the hand or mouth rather than ingested.

Whenever there is noncompliance, it naturally becomes a treatment issue and one on which continued residence in the house is dependent. Staff can monitor medications to various degrees for short periods of time, but eventually the resident must resume this responsibility if he or she is to continue to move toward independence.

Finally, drug holidays, whether related to research, tardive dyskinesia, or the desire to keep a patient as drug-free as possible, present understandable concerns about decompensation. Particularly close communications are necessary between treating physician and halfway house staff during such periods.

SUSPENSIONS AND EXPULSIONS

As discussed in Chapter 3, staff considers suspension or expulsion as consequences for certain severe breaches of house protocol, particularly when a resident endangers his or others' lives or safety. Engaging in alcohol or drug abuse, physical abuse of staff or other residents, destruction of property, or public disturbance which threatens the existence of the house in the neighborhood is all so dangerous to self or to others that the house must take serious action. The resident may be suspended to the family home, respite shelter, or motel room, depending on the resident's strengths and resources. Whether the penalty is suspension or expulsion, the resident's treatment team, day hospital, and/or outside therapist are made aware of staff's thinking, their input is considered, and the resident is given time and assistance in making the necessary plans for alternative housing. Suspensions focus in on a specific problem behavior and, in the great majority of cases, work to make the behavior ego-alien or provide the stimulus for the individual to exercise more control. Residents may be suspended from one housing unit to another if the behavior in the first unit is unacceptable. Once again, suspension is more effective as an intervention if bonding has occurred.

ECOSYSTEM

Interaction with all facets of the resident's ecosystem continues throughout his or her stay in the halfway house. As he becomes more functional, the resident can cope with a continually more challenging world, socially, vocationally, and recreationally. Chapter 7 focused on this interaction with treatment facilities, and we have discussed above the interaction of worker with family and with vocational resources. Staff should be equally cognizant of other resources in the community and how the resident can connect with them, continually updating planning with the resident and considering which resources will facilitate his growth and functioning.

AUTHORITY ISSUES

Life in the halfway house provides many opportunities for authority issues to surface in relation to staff and structure. The transference to most staff, especially to older members, is, of course, as if to parents. Residents relate to each other as with siblings in opposition to staff and structure or in competition with each other for staff attention.

For treatment purposes, the opportunity to observe residents in daily life gives clear and rich pictures of the permutations of their difficulties with authority and presents helpful material for work with residents around problems with parents, teachers, bosses, siblings, and work-mates. This valuable information is available, then, to therapists.

Most residents are quite frightened of authority figures and the latter's real and imagined power vis-à-vis the vulnerable resident. Their defensive behaviors around the core fear range from overcompliance, lack of assertion, and passive resistance, to rebellion, antagonism, and overt hostility. Staff works to help the resident deal more openly with her fears, let go of the more destructive, extreme reactions, and increase the repertoire of constructive, modulated responses to those in positions of power. Staff also presents a consistent, benevolent authority, to contrast with more negative experiences residents may have had in their lives.

As the resident's own self-esteem and sense of personal strength grows, so, of course, grows his ability to deal more directly and less emotionally with those in authority and to use his new skills with greater confidence.

Martin, early in residency, described his feelings when confronted by anyone with actual or ascribed authority. "It's like I'm one lone soldier with a rusty, broken-down weapon, my back against a wall, facing a whole army with all the most modern guns and tanks pointing right at me." Three years later, after moving from the supportive apartment, he described with wonder the vastly improved relationship he now had with his parents. "It's like I was always running away from them and all the destructiveness. I had to get away for my life, and finally my mother would come swooping down and gather me up and bring me back home. And I would run away again and again my mother would come and gather me up. I had to get away but I loved it when my mother brought me back, even though I fought it. I needed both. Finally, when I went to the halfway house, I thought I was leaving them for good. 'F_____ you,' I sneered at them in my mind. 'You'll never see me again.' But now it's different. It's funny, how as you become a separate person from your family, as you get stronger and learn the skills of taking care of yourself, you can actually be closer with them in a very nice way. Coming to the halfway house was an essential amino acid in the protein framework of my family."

EATING DISORDERS

As noted in Chapter 2, eating disorders warrant special attention because of the management challenge they present to community residence staff and because of an increasing number of such referrals to halfway houses. Very often, concerned staff find themselves falling into control battles when confronted with an anorexic who will not eat, a bulimic who binges, or the ritualistic behaviors around food that are peculiar to those who suffer from these syndromes.

Some of the most recent recommendations of those who treat anorexics and bulimics are:

1. that patients should not return home to their families where issues of control or denial have become so intense as to undermine the patient's progress;
2. that patients are most helped in a structured environment where issues of separation, self-esteem, and female identity (the overwhelming majority of those suffering from eating disorders are female) can be addressed.

For these reasons, referrals to community residences will continue to rise.

Current thinking recommends a split of the outpatient psychotherapy of the anorexic or bulimic from the medical management. The latter should be handled by an internist who can be objective and firm about the weight limits that are initially contracted by therapist, patient, and internist. A minimal weight level is set for the anorexic at which point she will be hospitalized. The internist weighs her each month and reports the weight to the therapist. Likewise, the internist administers monthly blood tests to the bulimic which alert the physician if purging activities are reaching dangerous levels. This information is also reported to the therapist. The therapist need not then get involved in manipulations around the weight or degree of purging but only act on what the physician is reporting. The limits are medical and graphic and hospitalization occurs when those limits are exceeded.*

Such a clear treatment regimen would be helpful to the halfway house so it, too, can stay clear of the emotional conflicts around food. Only a few clear guidelines apply at the house:

1. The therapist-internist team make the decision about hospitalization, if necessary.
2. The resident must be present at the required number of dinners per week.
3. She may eat or not eat as she wishes, but she may eat only the food prepared—she may not prepare special foods for herself.
4. She cannot binge on house foods so that it reflects in the budget. She must binge outside if she is going to do so. (As most bulimics prefer to binge privately, such activity is usually self-restricted in view of the limited privacy in the house.)

Staff can expect a fair number of rehospitalizations of residents with eating disorders as treatment outcome with this group is similar to that of the schizophrenias: one-third recover, one-third stay the same, and one-third get worse.* The residence may want to set a limit on the degree of symptom severity and on the number of bulimics and anorexics it will accept at any one time so as to keep a balanced population in the house.

DISCHARGE

Residents enter and leave the halfway house in a staggered fashion. A newcomer has apartment mates who are at various stages in their lives and in their tenure at the house. Residents learn from their therapists

---

*From seminar given at New York Hospital-Cornell University Medical Center/Westchester Division, 4/11/85, by Lisa Kinigstein, Social Work Services.

and from staff, and from each other—from the experience of living together. The time comes, though, when they must turn their attention to discharge, to moving on. They have grown in sense of self and in functioning and they begin to feel the structure of the house as confining and infantilizing rather than as helpful and supportive. The world of independence beckons.

CHAPTER 9

Discharge Planning: The Last Three Months

The last three months of a resident's stay in the halfway house focus on the consolidation of gains and on preparation for the move to the next living situation. It is a time of ambivalence for many residents for, as they take pleasure and pride in the growth they have made and look forward to more independence and opportunity, they also greatly fear the challenge that that opportunity presents. They wonder if they will be able to sustain the new level of functioning at the new level of independence and stress.

FINAL EVALUATION

Staff and residents devote much of the last three months to securing and polishing the skills that will be needed after leaving the halfway house, selecting and obtaining the environment that for each resident will best facilitate good functioning, and addressing the emotional issues around the move. A final evaluation session, as illustrated below, is geared to these issues, to set the specific goals for this time period.

Final evaluation: Donald R.

Present: Donald R., Sarah, the Director, Donald's social worker, and his counselor

Don feels he is friendly or not, depending on the mood he's in. If he's feeling well, he can relate to anyone. If he's feeling down, he can relate only to someone similar to him or who complements him. His basic problem, as he sees it, is how to regulate his mood, to bring it up; otherwise he cuts himself off from people, loses his self-confidence, interest, and energy. When he's down, he doesn't feel safe, gets hypersensitive, and is unable to converse. He spends a lot of time with Carol, his girlfriend, as she seems comfortable with his quieter self.

Don thinks his present situation deflates his mood. He is not working or living in his own place and he fears the future. Sarah wondered what comes first—the negative feelings or the reasons he has cited for them. Don thinks that his new volunteer job will lift his mood because he is busy and not preoccupied all day with his thoughts. This had happened when he was working at his day hospital volunteer job.

However, his interview at the Office of Vocational Rehabilitation this morning left him depressed. He wants to be a writer, for which he needs a college degree (he has one to two years to finish). But OVR will not fund him for that as it was at college that he had his decompensations. Don feels they were related more to smoking marijuana and not taking his meds and since this has changed, he would be more stable at school. He has enough funds for one course next semester, which he is looking into. His time at the halfway house ends soon and he needs a job, but with a spotty resumé and no degree, can he sell himself as a writer? Sarah suggested we go on to other areas and return to this one later in the evaluation.

Don has not progressed much in his relationships with counselors. Again, because of his mood, he doesn't converse much with people. It is better at the volunteer job as his boss is very social and he can respond well to her. He is meeting other people there, mainly older women, but he is better at rising above his mood and functioning in a structured situation like that. He doesn't get into his emotions that much at work, whereas he does when he is socializing without work as the core.

Sarah suggested that there are many levels of social interchange where emotions don't have to play a large part—talking about the weather, cultural events, politics, etc. Don finds it hard to stay outside of the emotional area when talking about music or a film, for instance. Then he sounds depressed and this is a downer for people, although he can fake it a little which helps break the mood, but only temporarily. Also, after therapy and sessions with his social worker, he feels more positive, but again, he has a hard time holding on to this. Sarah agreed that the mood seems to be the greatest problem area now. Don said again that he is not sure how much it is related to the fact that he is not working and is not where he wants to be in life.

Sarah suggested that there may be more than one route by

which Don can get back to work in his preferred area. Could he
work six months at any job and save enough to return to school on
his own? He would need a certain amount of money for a semester
at the state college. This is another reason Don is depressed. He
used to take care of his affairs better. Four times he returned to
school after hospitalizations but now he just doesn't have the
drive. He *wants* the things he's talking about but he doesn't take
the time to even secure the information he needs to get them. *This*
is what scares him. He knows that if his mood weren't so down, he
could work at something to save money and be patient.

Sarah agreed that there are many ways to achieve what Don
wants and one year is not so long in the course of a career. Also, a
college degree is not the only route to become a writer. He can hone
his skills at the volunteer job and develop a good recommendation
there, too. He is making progress just being at a job. Don is concentrating on where he is behind, not where he is ahead. He is
frustrated because he feels he isn't doing anything, but in reality,
he is.

Don continued to be concerned about his lack of motivation that
prevents him from moving ahead. He feels he spends too much
time with Carol instead of using that time for other pursuits. Sarah
suggested that he use the help of his social worker and his therapist
to structure himself so that he sets aside time for socialization,
Carol, self-development, chores, etc. Don feels that taking a course
now might also help to strengthen his motivation and offer him
more structure. Upon reflection, he feels it would be best to take a
writing course. Next year Don will probably be able to go to school
free as he will have been independent from his parents for two
years. This is a further indication that OVR is not the only route
available to Don. He can enrich his life this year with experience in
his field, either volunteer or paid, and return to school when it is
financially feasible.

Don stated that he has trouble remembering what the opportunities of his situation are and for some reason he focuses on the
limitations. This is not the way he used to be. Sarah noted the
importance of Don's reminding himself of the positives again, even
if he has to write them down on a list in his pocket to remember
them. Don recognized that he is creating his own block and reassessed the importance of using people around him to help him
hold a steady course.

Sarah wondered how Don functions even when he's feeling low.
Don feels he maintains his chore responsibilities and his own cleanliness, and the counselor's report confirms that he performs his
responsibilities consistently. Don also feels that the volunteer position is the best job he could have right now and he is making more
efforts to talk to people, probably because he has left day hospital.
So his next task is to schedule himself for the other things he needs

to do, one of which is to edit the new halfway house brochure. If he does this, the halfway house can also provide a reference for him and he will have another publication for his portfolio. The latter is something Don can construct which may have more impact on a job interview than whether or not he has the college degree.

Don would like to move on to a supportive apartment and is aware that he needs either to be working in paid employment or to be enrolled in school courses. His halfway house anniversary occurs in March so Don has some time to work on a program for the supportives, which would include the areas discussed above:

1. structure his time (not just "hanging out" on Sundays but using his time to do specific social, vocational, or individual activities);
2. develop a specific social network to carry with him to the supportive apartment;
3. build a portfolio—look at Alex's (another resident) portfolio, for guidance;
4. arrange exploratory interviews with people in his field;
5. take a course.

Don agrees that he has to stop being so dazed by everything. His future is unclear and unstructured and he ends up confused. Sarah recommended that the first thing Don should do is to structure that future—set up a plan and he will feel less confused. Make the next three months a creative time and use people to help him as there is a good chance there will be a supportive apartment available in March. Don may have to force himself to act at first, as with an exercise plan, to go through the pain of starting until, with time and activity, he begins to feel better. Don agreed that he may not be attacking his low mood vigorously enough and it was agreed that he would spend the next month preparing his plan for the Spring so that he will have sufficient time to activate it.

Resident and staff plan together the program and housing situation which best will meet the resident's needs after discharge. This molding of the ecosystem is a critical element in the resident's continuing recovery and for the achievement of more independent functioning.

Personal care, household management, and organization issues are of key importance in moving to a living situation where there will not be a live-in counselor to set the structure and assure that basic needs are met. A resident who has been progressing slowly and steadily may need only to concentrate energies on a few areas for fine tuning before the move: Has he been shopping regularly with the counselor and does he have a working knowledge of food values, use of coupons, and so on? Is he able to prepare at least five different meals in the kitchen? Has he been able to personalize his room, make it a piece of home for himself? Is his personal hygiene of an acceptable standard?

Of equal importance is the development of a viable and supportive social network. Social isolation undermines adjustment into the community as it intensifies the sense of aloneness which makes burdens seem heavier and stress more noxious. While the development of social relationships has been a priority during the tenure at the halfway house, in this last period a resident must seriously consider who will constitute his network after he leaves. Whom will he call to invite to his new apartment, dorm, movies, coffee, and so on? If the resident has been moving slowly, the prospect of leaving the easily available group at the halfway house is an incentive to become more socially active in, and outside of, the house.

The resident's daily program is also a focus of attention during the last few months before discharge. Again, his adaptation to community life will be more comfortable and complete if his program is well set. Any final changes in program are planned to occur at least a month or two prior to or after the move from the halfway house so as not to have two major changes at the same time.

Finally, the living arrangement itself must be chosen. For instance, will the resident move to a supportive apartment, his own apartment (alone or with a roommate), back to college dorm, or in with family? If available, most residents choose to move to a supportive apartment as it helps the resident push toward his or her potential, offers support from a trusted source, yet does not infantilize the resident.

DESTINATIONS

Supportive Apartment

Halfway houses differ in their admissions criteria for supportive apartments. For some, good household functioning is sufficient. Others set program criteria, i.e., the resident must be in substantial paid employment (20 plus hours of work a week) or in school (two or more courses) to qualify to move. The latter criteria can serve as incentives to help the resident make the difficult and often frightening final steps back to work or to school. The supportive apartment becomes a reward for taking risks, for pushing limits. The timing must be carefully planned by staff and resident, however, so that the risks are appropriate to the resident's strengths.

If a supportive apartment is unavailable, or if admissions criteria cannot be met by a specific resident, other living alternatives are considered. If a resident needs extended supervised housing, he can transfer to a long-term halfway house or adult home. If his daily living skills are good, he might qualify for a supportive apartment in a facility which does not have program requirements specific to this move.

Community

Some residents prefer to bypass the supportive apartment and return directly to the community to live with a friend or a lover, to move to the college dormitory, or to secure a room or apartment of his or her own. In each of these circumstances, the resident, social worker, and therapist weigh the demands and rewards of the alternatives vis-à-vis the resident's needs and strengths; the resident then chooses that arrangement which best facilitates his functioning and does not exacerbate his vulnerabilities.

Joseph had obtained a paying job in preparation for moving out of the halfway house. Although a supportive apartment vacancy was available, Joseph rejected that course, feeling he wanted to move away from the world of the "mentally ill" and live more independently. Staff did not try to persuade Joseph to move to the supportive apartment as Joseph had required the counselor's intervention many times during disputes with staff and fellow residents and staff was concerned that he might not be able to get along with two roommates where group interaction was required.

However, Joseph could not afford an apartment of his own. He looked for a situation where he could have his own room with a roommate who could tolerate distance and where interaction would be at a minimum. The apartment had to be near a bus line for transportation to work and in a community which had a Gambler's Anonymous chapter so that Joseph could continue attending daily support meetings.

After a search, Joseph found the right apartment with an undemanding roommate, which was near the halfway house main office and he kept in touch by calls and visits. He used agency support to help him during some rough times but has maintained himself in this setting.

Family

Some residents choose to return to the family home to live. This is happening more frequently as apartments are becoming less affordable. Naturally, one of the concerns with such a move is the quality of the parent–adult child relationship. If there has been excessive dependency and/or hostility in the past, have enough separation and maturing occurred on both sides to permit a peaceful coexistence? Will there be regression to former levels of behavior?

Often, returning to family can work if the resident, especially, can relate to his parents from a position of greater independence. As Martin stated in Chapter 8 (pp. 156–157), he was able to experience his parents in a different way once he no longer needed them for so much of his own sustenance. He was able to move back home in order to save money to return to college. When his parents do or say something that would have made him frightened or angry in the past, or that is destructive, he is more able to leave these problems behind and go on his way.

Martin hopes his college degree will help him move toward a career that will provide income and status important to his sense of identity. He plans to move on afterwards to his own living arrangements. Some ex-residents, however, feel safer and more settled when near their families. They are more independent now than before, but the tie to family continues to be a source of strength and sustenance. Mental health professionals are now recognizing that the family, aided by expanded learning about mental illness and its continuing and unpredictable effects, is an excellent support. This is a model for support in living that ex-residents are developing. The chances of its working successfully improve if the part of the home that the adult child occupies is somewhat demarcated from the rest of the family. This physical separation—by a separate entrance or floor—creates a distance and a recognition of the ex-resident's adult status.

STEPS TOWARD DISCHARGE

In recognition of the resident's growth, some structure is relaxed toward the end of his stay. He or she may take extra overnights, be excused from curfew to attend events in the community, and so forth. Structure is not so relaxed, however, that the resident becomes too comfortable at the halfway house. Were this to happen, he might lose incentive to make the difficult move out. Staff is pleased to see some impatience with structure as evidence of a resident's readiness for more self-direction and control.

The move out is planned to occur over a transitional period to decrease the stress of the actual exit and the feeling of abrupt change. The resident is encouraged to take several overnights in his new domicile and slowly transfer his belongings. Whenever a resident makes a one-step move without such preparation, there is likely to be a more severe reaction. If the move is to the supportive apartment, it is paced to the resident's needs so long as there are not administrative problems that interfere. The resident attends several supportive apartment group meetings in advance of moving so that he or she can gradually enter the world of the future roommates. These meetings address the expectations each roommate will have of the other, how to cooperate around community issues, and how to give each other sufficient space. They also establish the rights of the newcomer to participate fully in the new setting while respecting some rights of seniority. Furthermore, at these meetings the prospective resident can plan his overnight visits at such times when the current residents will be present in the apartment.

In the resident's last week at the halfway house, she is the focus of the community meeting. She is given recognition for her progress and readiness to move to the next level in an air of celebration complete with cake, music, and so forth. The departing person is asked to speak to the group about her experience at the house and to articulate what kept her moving toward her goals. For those still struggling, this resident has "made it" and serves as a role model. It is at this time that the emerging altruism is so evident. Most of those who are leaving really want to help those following and speak quite thoughtfully to the group of what has most helped them to become more independent.

Dolf was scheduled to move to the supportive apartment on Saturday, so Tuesday night's community meeting was his. After several residents and staff expressed congratulations for his progress and feelings about how he would be missed in the halfway house, Dolf was asked what thoughts he would like to leave with the group. Dolf said he was conflicted. He was scared about leaving the halfway house, not sure he was ready to live more independently in the supportive apartment. Staff felt he was ready though, and he had to trust their judgment. On the other hand, he felt encouraged to be at this point. He had had many struggles in the halfway house, resistances that he had to overcome, risks he had to take, and he could see his growth over time.

Dolf felt lucky to have had the opportunity to be at the house, to get the support of staff, but more important, of his fellow residents. Although he hoped eventually to be working in a job that was satisfying to him, the greatest value of the house had been in the friendships he has made. He came to the house 18 months before, isolated, without friends, and was leaving now with a support system that was the most important thing in his life. He recognized the challenge now to keep this going once he moved and hoped he could do so. He urged the other residents not to let pass this opportunity to make relationships with people who will matter in their lives.

All residents, regardless of the setting to which they move, are invited to return to dinners at the house during the first month away. Again, this softens the impact of the move.

TRANSITION—PREDICTABLE BEHAVIORS

Staff must be prepared for some regression accompanying the move out, no matter how carefully planned. This usually becomes evident in the weeks prior to the move and continues for one to three months afterward. Patterns of behavior long since left behind reappear and more recent growth is temporarily lost. Residents are frightened and anxious at leaving staff, structure, and peers, very significant sources of growth, esteem, and support for the past year or more.

It is most helpful to residents for staff to discuss the regression matter-of-factly as a normal piece of the process of moving. Residents know when they are regressing and are quite dismayed and frightened to experience the return of a behavior they worked so hard to put behind them. They fear that the backsliding is permanent. Calm, firm reassurance that the regression will lift when they are settled at the next level is comforting when it comes from a trusted source. This stance by staff is very helpful later, too, when the regression has gone on long enough and the worker can suggest to her resident, "Enough, already. Time to move on." The worker, who knows the resident through all manner of stress, is frequently able to intuit the appropriate time to call a halt to the adjustment period and ask for progress once again.

Often, the first signs of regression in a resident who is preparing to move from the halfway house show themselves in the form of personal disarray. Perhaps there is a falling off from usual standards of personal hygiene, the level of performance at household tasks decreases, appointments are forgotten, and so on. Occasionally, the regressive acting out is serious enough to warrant delaying the move.

Sean was called to staff meeting as his acting out was not responding to interventions by staff or therapist. Sean appeared nervous. He reported that he hadn't been doing very well—that he drank too much a couple of times and made some upsetting announcements. Two months ago he had told another resident that he was suicidal and more recently he had told several people that he was gay. Dr. Moore indicated that the timing of Sean's announcements (just as he is to be moving into the supportive apartment) is what staff is concerned about. Sean continued stating that he was drinking because he had wanted to socialize at the bar. Presently, when he goes to the bar he drinks club soda. He added that last week he ran out of medication and experienced sleepwalking as a result.

Sean felt that his therapy was not going well. He explained that his doctor is against his gay lifestyle and tells Sean that when he talks about it publicly he is ruining his reputation. Sean stated that he would like to change therapists but he does not want to do anything presently which might delay any further his moving into the supportive apartment. He explained that he had chosen his doctor in January because he had been helped by the medication that the doctor had prescribed for him while at day hospital.

Discussing his move into the supportive apartment, Sean felt that his announcement of being gay was indeed poorly timed because now the men who will be his roommates are afraid of him. He guessed that they are afraid that he'll do something crazy like walk in his sleep again.

Dr. Moore reviewed all of the things that are happening to Sean at this time when he is getting ready to move out of the halfway house. He added that it sounds as though Sean does not want to leave. Sean argued that the poor behavior all occurred outside of his control, either when he had been sleepwalking or drinking. Dr. Moore suggested that Sean is hiding behind a wall of ignorance, claiming that he is not in control of his behavior. He told Sean that until Sean's behavior demonstrates that he is in control, he cannot move into the supportive apartment.

Some residents find it so difficult to make the move from the halfway house that they can leave only in a burst of anger, camouflaging the pain and the fear of separation, as in the following example.

Jennifer had worked very hard in the halfway house to stay drug-free and to complete a computer programming course of study without the traumatic interruptions that had plagued her in the past. She was functioning well in the halfway house and, even though there were still many interpersonal issues that needed work, she and staff agreed that she was ready to move to a supportive apartment. She waited impatiently for four months for a vacancy to occur, but when a place suddenly became available, she asserted that she was not ready. As preparations for her move began, she started to skip dinners at the halfway house and neglect responsibilities, upsetting other residents and the counselor.

Some of this behavior frequently occurs as residents begin to withdraw their attention from the house and start the separation process. When this happens, staff asks the resident to continue to focus some attention on the house routine despite the concentration on the move. Many residents are able to do so. In the case of Jennifer, however, she became angry at the requests of staff and the anger escalated as staff considered with her delaying her move until her behavior improved. But it became clear that Jennifer was not able to tolerate her ambivalence about the move. The anger continued and was upsetting to the whole house. When anger is used by the resident as a cover for her ambivalence, as a means of helping her to separate, and so forth, staff must evaluate whether the resident can work through the anger and deal with the real issues. Staff did not feel that Jennifer could do so at this time and, in the interest of house harmony, proceeded with the move. Jennifer calmed quickly in the new apartment.

As in Jennifer's case, house considerations may affect the process of a move. If there are applicants waiting to enter the halfway house who must be discharged from hospital or whose living situation is extremely noxious, the resident may be asked to speed up his move. If this is necessary, staff does try to provide compensatory supports to assure that the move is successful.

For those residents who are not moving to the supportive apartment, the halfway house offers aftercare services geared toward supporting their adjustment into the community. These services are discussed in Chapter 11.

Hopefully, through the process of examination and evaluation as described above, the halfway house resident readies himself to move back to the community or on to the next level of care. When that next level is the supportive apartment, the resident commits himself to a new experience, a new set of challenges, a new set of goals, and a new level of involvement with staff.

CHAPTER 10
Supportive Apartments

The myth that custodially oriented state hospitals are necessary for a large portion of the mentally disabled must not be replaced by an equally fallacious myth that the vast majority of outpatients can be housed in independent settings without supportive services. The failure of such laissez-faire deinstitutionalization has become quite apparent (GAO, 1977). A continuum of residential alternatives, including cooperative apartments, may be seen not as a panacea, but as a viable option to counter both these myths (Carling, 1978, p. 60).

For many residents, a one-year stay in the halfway house is not sufficient time to effect and reinforce adequate and lasting rehabilitation and modification of behavior and self-image. Yet residents can progress to the extent that they no longer need the 24-hour supervision or intensive structure of the halfway house. In fact, as research indicates (Test & Stein, 1977), further growth is often enhanced in an environment that offers opportunity to assume greater responsibility for daily living and that does not overprovide services.

Living arrangements with varying degrees of structure, supervision, and lengths of stay provide the kind of environmental differentiation that compensates for many deficits in autonomous functioning. They offer periods of successful adjustment at different levels of care which raise self-esteem and confidence and set a tone, an expectation, of future success. Such housing alternatives "address the total spectrum of clients' various levels of functioning, and . . . allow clients to move freely to a more or a less structured setting as their functional capacity progresses or fluctuates" (Pepper, 1985, p. 2).

Pepper recommends "the development and maintenance of several different housing programs in different locations in the same general community . . . that would include three or six different levels of care at different sites, embracing a total bed capacity of 40–80 residents" (Pepper, 1985, p. 2). Such a diverse program allows for personal, noninstitutional care as well as for economic efficiency. Pepper (1985) recommends the following levels of care:

1. A crisis residence of about 10 beds for short stays to avoid hospitalization;
2. A supervised residence of 14 beds for highly symptomatic persons;
3. A supervised residence of 14 beds for those less symptomatic who can utilize a more highly developed rehabilitation program;
4. A supportive residence of 14 beds, with less supervision (under 24-hours), geared for persons who are actively engaged in outside daily programs;
5. Supervised apartments (14 beds) with daily staff visits and monitoring of functioning;
6. Supportive apartments (14 beds) with semi-weekly staff visits to residents who are at a high level of functioning both in the apartment and in the community.

Pepper (1985) also describes the RCCA (Resident Congregate Care for Adults), 50–200 bed, highly supervised facilities now being developed in New York State for those chronic persons who can leave the hospital but are unable to utilize a daily program. These residences will probably be located on the grounds of the large institutions and thus will not be included for discussion among the community residences.

Carling (1978) also describes a comprehensive residential program which includes the crisis hostel for psychiatric emergencies, transitional halfway houses, and various apartment options. His Horizon House model describes, in addition, the cooperative apartment leased by clients who may continue to receive from the agency residential and rehabilitation services which fluctuate according to changing client need. (See also Zanditon & Hellman [1981] for technical information on establishing residential alternatives under the auspices of HUD sections 8 and 202.) Preliminary research conducted at Horizon House Residential Programs indicated that when the combination of rehabilitation and residential services was offered within the setting of various apartment options as opposed to only halfway house services, the proportion of clients "requiring rehospitalization or a more structured setting decreased by half" (Carling, 1978, p. 60).

Other researchers have reported similar findings. Tomlinson and Cumming (1976) report on a supportive apartment program in Canada and conclude that, economically and socially, this living arrangement is preferable for the former patient to other more institutional alternatives. Therapists reported "significant changes in residents' ability to socialize and meet others with a greater degree of self-confidence" (p. 26) and residents reported that they were "visiting the outpatient services less often, and some were having their medications reduced" (p. 26).

Gomez (1978) reports that after hospital discharge patients who shared small supportive apartments scored higher than patients living alone on measurements of post-hospital adjustment, self-responsibility, employment, reduced readmission to hospital, and subsequent time spent in hospital. This study illustrates "the importance of the development of small residential systems of mutual support in which the disabilities of one patient can be compensated by the strengths of another" (p. 216).

Lamb (1976), in advocating graduated residential alternatives for the mentally ill, recommends that for the group of people who cannot, for the long term, live independently, satellite, scattered housing is more normative and therefore more desirable than are halfway houses.

Campbell (1981) notes that quality rehabilitative work with psychotic clients in remission can continue, with great cost reduction, in supportive apartment settings. In this alternative to highly structured settings such as halfway houses, clients can assume more responsibility for directing and maintaining their personal lives.

LEVELS OF SUPPORTIVE LIVING

The supportive apartment is an important facet of the resident's ecosystem. It should therefore be located near to the resident's other supports (his therapist, CSS worker, job, etc.) and to the halfway house or agency offices from which it is supervised. It is helpful for residents to feel that staff is close by and accessible and it is helpful for staff to have quick access to the apartment in case of emergency. Since most supportive apartment residents are only newly employed or are in school or training programs and are likely not to own cars, it is essential that the apartments be located near main lines of transportation.

Ideally, the supportive apartment houses a small group of two to four people, each having his or her own bedroom. The privacy and normalcy of this arrangement offers the supportive apartment resident a concrete reinforcement of his mature, adult status. It provides an incentive to those who live in the dormitory atmosphere of the halfway house to push to become eligible to move to the next level.

In the more intensely supervised apartments, staff is on site briefly for a set period of time each day, and thus assures that the residents are up and caring for themselves or off to program and that the premises are properly maintained. The residents return to the halfway house for meals and perhaps for some social activity but do not need 24-hour supervision.

More advanced supportives operate more independently. Residents are responsible for cooking for themselves, shopping, setting up and maintaining a chore schedule, dealing with the superintendent about minor repairs, putting up their own shelves, getting the blinds refurbished at the local hardware store, and so on. A social worker attends a weekly apartment meeting to supervise maintenance and to help the residents work out their own solutions to management and interpersonal problems. (Supervisory requirements vary from state to state.) Each resident learns how to handle every aspect of apartment living in preparation for assuming more complete responsibility for his later care.

The resident continues to see his or her social worker for ongoing planning and coordination of his total program, but now there is the additional focus on the new challenges of apartment living. A resident who has adjusted well into the supportive apartment, is in control of his program, and has a good relationship with his therapist may decide with his social worker to meet only every other week. Thus continues a weaning process as the resident needs less supervision and also has more time available for his expanding social and work life.

At times, however, residents have problem areas that continue to warrant weekly sessions with the worker.

Morgan moved to a supportive apartment a month or two after beginning a year-long training program in business machine skills. He adjusted well into the apartment but was quite anxious about his ability to complete the training program and he continued to have only minimal social contacts. In addition, because of administrative problems at his clinic, he had to change therapists. Morgan asked for continued weekly sessions and his social worker agreed that he could use the added support for a time, as well as the further attention to socialization issues which he was neglecting in order to concentrate on his courses. He saw his worker weekly until he was more settled in his program and with his new therapist.

As in the halfway house, the supportive apartment resident is required to see his or her outside therapist weekly. When the resident functions at increasingly higher levels, the contact between the therapist and the resident's social worker usually decreases, to revive if and when the need arises. However, the worker's attention to the resident's needs vis-à-vis community resources does not diminish. The social worker continually assesses with the resident his use of his ecosystem. Are his needs for support gradually decreasing? Is he able to assume all or more responsibility for seeing after his own needs in the community? Will he eventually be moving out of the supportive apartment and, if so, what environment will best facilitate his functioning?

Although the amount of supportive external structure available to the resident decreases in the move from the halfway house to the supportive apartment, certain carefully designed pieces of structure remain. The weekly or semiweekly sessions with the social worker and the weekly group meetings with the supportive apartment worker are the two most significant agency supports and are the vehicles by which the additional structure—the routines of daily living—is maintained. The long-term goal, as in the halfway house, is that such structure will be internalized and become the resident's own.

ADJUSTING TO THE MOVE INTO THE SUPPORTIVE APARTMENT

The underlying assumption in the supportive apartment is that each resident is there to continue his work toward more independent functioning and to be of support to his apartment mates in their similar efforts. This double emphasis, on mastering living skills and on developing a caring relationship with others, is reflected in the preparative counseling each resident receives as he plans his move to the apartment.

Residents move into the supportives as vacancies occur. Occasionally, it is possible for two residents to move together and the company of a friend always somewhat diminishes the sense of loneliness and the stress of the move for each. Although the newest apartment resident usually knows the persons he is joining from having lived with them earlier at the halfway house, there is a certain amount of reacquainting to do, which is begun during the group meetings and the overnights the new resident spends at the apartment prior to the move.

There are always major adjustments for everyone when a resident moves out of the supportives and a new one moves in. Established routines are disrupted, new ones are set, territories are renegotiated. After a more senior resident has moved out, often one or both present occupants move to the more spacious rooms so that everyone is unsettled for a while. The supportive apartment social worker helps everyone to weather this adjustment period—the senior members to accommodate to the fact that what has worked well for them must now change, and the newest member to voice his concerns about being an invasive force and perhaps feeling outnumbered and fearful that the senior residents will not make room for him and accept his ideas.

Sometimes a resident is hesitant to express such feelings at the supportive group meeting but ventilates them freely in individual sessions with her ongoing social worker. This worker can encourage the resident to be more assertive in the group, role play with her and serve as a source of tension release, while she also communicates with the supportive worker who then can be aware of undercurrents and seek to ease their expression in his meetings. The resident takes part in deciding what shall be communicated to the supportive apartment worker and understands that the worker will be supportive when the resident eventually is able to express herself more freely in the group.

It is wise for the agency to plan moves with residents' personalities in mind. Individual residents' adjustments into the supportives can be enhanced or jeopardized by the amount of stress they experience in living with a particular person. Residents have been willing to move from one supportive apartment to another at a time when they could join or leave a specific person in order to achieve a better roommate match.

It sometimes takes the new resident several months to adjust and feel at home in the supportive apartment. The change from the busy, bustling halfway house, where there is always someone around for company, as well as a counselor for security and for setting structure, to the quiet, comparatively empty supportive apartment, where roommates may be preoccupied with their own already established routines, feels quite major. What if the roommates are away all weekend? What if a plan made to fill the space of Saturday is suddenly cancelled? What if the resident gets into a heated argument with an apartment mate? Who will prevent it from coming to blows? What if a pipe bursts when the resident is home alone? What if it feels too close to be living with one or two other people with no buffers to the intimacy?

Such fears and concerns can preoccupy a new resident and retard his adjustment into the apartment. Staff, aware that such concerns are a part of the move for most residents, anticipates them, watches for their signs (failure to unpack completely, tendency to stay out of the apartment for long periods, etc.), and encourages the resident to explore them in session during the months after the move. If the resident does not respond to this intervention, if he seems to be taking an overly long time to settle in, or if a regression does not eventually begin to lift, the resident may be asked to come to staff meeting to address these issues and look for additional help in resolving them.

Gert characteristically exhibited great resistance to major change, simultaneously desiring and fearing it. She was asked to come to staff meetings as she had not been functioning well in the supportive apartment. She had moved three months ago to join Nell and Marsha. She and Nell have gotten along all right but she and Marsha have been in verbal hostilities since a month after the move, perhaps a continuation of some problems they were having when both were at the halfway house. Both young women are very bright, competitive, and narcissistic.

Gert had a very difficult time separating from home and adjusting into the halfway house and it was anticipated that she would find the move to the supportive apartment disruptive. She insists she has felt pretty good about the move but her functioning has suffered. Both Nell and Marsha complain that Gert does not do her chores, especially a problem when she doesn't clean the bathroom she shares with Marsha, leaves dirty dishes, and doesn't clean up after she prepares food for herself. Marsha complains that Gert has used her hairspray from the beginning without replacing it and both women are very upset that Gert doesn't want to acknowledge her responsibility to her roommates, and is only now willing to change her behavior because she's been told by staff that she'll have to move out if she doesn't improve.

Gert's social worker and the apartment worker have been trying to address this problem for weeks individually and in the group, but Gert's behavior has not changed. Therefore, Gert's worker told her last week that she would have to move back to the halfway house in one week if she continued in her resistant stance, as there are two other women who are eligible and wish to move to the supportive apartment. Gert said she would change immediately as she highly valued the supportive apartment. She recognized that she has been refusing to cooperate because she feels Marsha has been obnoxious in the way she has been handling the situation. She agreed to cook the community meal for group on the next Tuesday. Then staff learned, however, that Gert had baited Marsha in a hostile way after the Tuesday night meeting. As a result, she was called to staff meeting where she and staff examined her attitudes and behaviors and the meaning of the supportive apartment to her.

After this meeting Gert's behavior changed significantly. She became a more active member of the apartment as she was able to de-emotionalize her responsibilities there. Both she and Marsha (who was being helped by her worker to assess her contributions to the hostilities) were able to relate more constructively and to begin to get pleasure and companionship from each other.

The intervention described above was successful because staff knew Gert well from having worked with her for 18 months at the halfway house. Staff knew her patterns and what measures finally would help her leave her resistance behind. It is recommended that residents spend a period of time at the halfway house before moving to a supportive apartment even if they are highly functional and otherwise eligible. Staff can then be more confident of its ability to interpret behavior, effect change, and assure, to the degree possible, the safety of each resident.

SKILLS OF SUPPORTIVE LIVING

The social and functional skills of apartment living receive equal attention in the group and individual sessions. Skills of living that were developed in the halfway house are refined and more completely internalized in the apartments. Peers demand that chores be done. A resident on a tight budget hones his food-shopping skills. Because residents tend to eat alone and fast-food style in the supportives, they are required, for social and nutritional reasons, to cook and eat together at least one meal per week. When this is not a piece of structure, it does not occur. When it is required once a week, it frequently happens more often.

There are living skills particular to the supportive apartment. Residents have more responsibility for household maintenance, from changing light bulbs, to exterminating roaches, to assuring that the smoke alarms are operative. They measure for blinds and learn how to deal with a superintendent. As Joelle once remarked, "I have learned that with this super it is best to alert him to a problem and then wait. He will eventually get to it. Yelling at him as Maura did last week only irritates him and then things take longer to get fixed." Residents are encouraged to tackle maintenance problems themselves or to consult with staff, but only receive staff help and involvement if there are complications beyond the capacity of residents to handle.

The social learning that occurs in the supportives is broad. Apartment mates (especially the women) quickly learn to be aware of each other's routines and whereabouts. Four weeks after Risa moved into the apartment, her unexplained overnight absence so concerned her roommates that it became an issue and was raised at the next group meeting. Risa, who felt socially distant and unnoticed, was surprised and touched by everyone's worry and need to know that she was safe. Each apartment decides how it will handle this piece of social responsibility, but each resident learns to live within a system where she is considered valuable.

When supportive apartments are located close enough to each other, frequent meetings of all the supportives encourages greater interaction and comfort among the apartments. Only when this is fostered can the apartment residents truly be supportive of each other in time of need.

Supportive Group Meetings

At the weekly group meetings, the experience of self-expression, hearing others, negotiating solutions, and arguing nonviolently offers a working model for residents to emulate elsewhere in their lives. It gradually becomes clear how compromise—with everyone's getting something and no one getting everything—can be carried over from the halfway house as a tool to resolve conflict. Sharing of time, space, and control becomes the value which is articulated at the meetings and is the framework for addressing issues.

The following group meeting occurred after Dara, the group worker, and Sandra, Brett's individual worker, had been trying for several weeks to help Brett express, in group, concerns he had about the behavior of his apartment mate, Tom.

Brett had told Sandra in their individual sessions these past few weeks that he was at his wit's end in trying to deal with Tom's anger and need for attention in the apartment. Yet when asked to confront and deal with these issues in group where he would have the help of staff to work them out with Tom, Brett has chosen to retreat and state that "everything is fine now." This was the same pattern that took place between Brett and his former roommate, Mark, until a few months ago when Mark began acting out in psychotic ways. After Mark moved out, Brett finally broke his silence and disclosed in the meeting how much of a problem Mark had been to him for many months.

Sandra and Dara agreed that it might help if Sandra joined the men's meeting, as her support might encourage Brett to speak more freely. She had gotten his somewhat reluctant permission to attend. In fact, he went so far as to say that all the problems were solved, which is what he said the week before when encouraged to confront the issues at the group meeting.

Dara: How is everything tonight?
Men: Fine. (*Everyone looked uneasy.*)
Dara: Tom, Brett, Stuart, I believe you knew Sandra would be joining us tonight. (*They shake their heads in agreement.*) Stuart, Sandra is new at the agency and was interested in seeing as much of

our supportives as she could. She was interested, too, in seeing how we run our meeting here and felt she'd like to join in tonight and be a part of it. Does everyone feel OK about that?

(The men nod their assent, looking more relaxed.)

Dara: How have things been going in the apartment? Is there anything we need to bring up?

Tom: Yes. Well, there have been some arguments in the apartment but all of us . . . Stuart and I just had one . . . but we worked it out.

Stuart:Yeah. You know sometimes tensions get to all of us . . . in one way or another all of us have tension, things that get to us, and sometimes we fight about it.

Dara: Can you share with us the argument that you and Stuart had and how you worked it out?

Tom: Sure . . . well . . . it seems like nothing now but it had to do with just being irritable and how we could say things in a way that didn't come off real hostile, just say what we felt.

Stuart: Yeah . . . it was no big thing but we talked about it and it got worked out just fine.

Dara: Brett, you seem quiet tonight. What do you feel about what's been going on in the apartment?

Brett: It's no problem. (*Little affect*)

Dara: Well, do you have any feelings about some of the arguments that have been going on in the apartment?

Brett: No. No . . . (*Looking upset*)

Sandra: Do you feel uncomfortable or concerned when the arguments go on?

Brett: No, not really. (*Looking upset*)

Dara: Have the arguments not included you in them? I thought I had heard Tom say last week that the arguments were between all of you from time to time.

Tom: Oh, yeah, Brett's been annoyed by things.

Stuart: Yeah. Brett's been in the arguments too.

Dara: Wouldn't you care to talk about what you've been feeling about this, how it's affected you?

Brett: No. And I really don't like being put on the spot! (*Looking very red in the face, full of rage, talking very loudly, especially for Brett who speaks so softly*)

Dara: Does it feel like I'm putting you on the spot?

Brett: Yes it does. And I really don't like it!

Sandra: Brett, we're trying to help. It really can be helpful to talk about your feelings and this is a good place for that. If there are any problems in the apartment between you and the men, this would be the time and place to bring them up and try to work things out.

Brett: I've handled the problems. There's nothing to talk about. (*Brett gets up from the chair near the window and walks across the room—takes a seat by the dining room table and lights up a cigarette. The seat he took is behind Dara, out of her view.*)
Dara: Is there anything else that's come up that we need to talk about tonight? (*She moves her chair so that she can see Brett.*)

(Tom and Stuart begin talking about some of the things they feel they need in the apartment. Tom asked about a device to suck in the cigarette smoke. The men want a scale, a bulletin board like the one at the halfway house, and give Dara a list of some other things. Dara said she would discuss these needs at the office to see what is feasible to purchase now.)

Dara: Brett, is there anything you feel we need to add to the list?
Brett: No. I think everyone has covered it.
Sandra: How are you feeling, Brett?
Brett: OK.
Sandra: Why are you sitting way over there?
Brett: Oh. Well, I sit here when I smoke so as not to bother Tom with the smoke. (*Looking uneasy*)
Sandra: I thought you might be upset.
Brett: No. It's not because of that but, yeah, sure I'm upset. I didn't like Dara's putting me on the spot. (*Looking very angry*)
Dara: Brett, I can understand that. It felt like being put on the spot and it was uncomfortable but I'd like to tell you what I was hoping to do. Most of the time you are quiet at these meetings and the other men pretty much take the time of the meeting to ask their questions and get their help. They are very verbal and really use the time to get what they need from it. But it's like you're cheating yourself. Each person here should be getting one-third of the time to use for himself. Instead, because you don't take the time for yourself, the other men get 50% apiece and you get none. I don't like that. It makes me feel something is really wrong with that. I don't want you not to have your share. This time is for all of you. It's like wanting to give you a gift. Something I have to offer. Something we can offer to each other and you won't take it. So tonight I was trying again to offer you this gift, and you didn't take it again. It's very frustrating to see you cheating yourself of what the other men give to themselves. Now, you don't have to do anything with this tonight, Brett, but I really hope you will think about it and maybe there will be a time when you will decide to accept your share, OK?
Brett: (*Smiling*) OK.
Dara: Is there anything else?

(Tom talked a bit about his job training coming to a close. He and Sandra talk about this for a few minutes. Then, as it is time for the meeting to end, people start saying their goodbyes.)

Brett: Dara, I'd like to bring something up now.
Dara: Sure Brett.

(Brett began to talk about some of the times he felt annoyed because Tom came on too strong, that Tom got upset because Brett and Stuart talked about their parents in a very positive way. Tom doesn't have a good relationship with his family and he often feels the pain of that when the men talk a lot about their parents. Sandra and Dara opened up a discussion. The men first were going to put restrictions on what they could talk about, but then decided they could be more flexible. If on a particular day Tom was feeling very sensitive about the parent issue, he could tell Stuart and Brett and then they could moderate their conversation. This would then not entirely eliminate talking about parents, which seemed, after discussion, to be a harsh alternative. The men all agreed to be flexible and more sensitive to each other's feelings.)

Brett's beginning ability to speak out for himself in this meeting reflects months of work in individual sessions on this skill as well as good communication between group and individual social workers.

Establishing and maintaining boundaries among roommates in the supportive apartments is a recurring issue which necessitates concentrated work in the group meetings. In the following vignette, several meetings had focused on a resident's resistance to apartment routines and her inability to respect the property of her roommates.

Dara, the group worker, discussed various activities that she will be able to get free tickets for and the women suggested others in which they might be interested. Mary will take the TV and sewing machine in to be serviced.

Dara noted that Winnie wasn't looking so well and Winnie admitted she wasn't doing very well. She was in the process of changing therapists, but didn't want to discuss what was going on with her.

Mary then expressed her anger and frustration about Winnie's recent behavior in the apartment. This had included leaving her clothes strewn around, leaving dishes in the sink, and not cleaning up after herself, as well as not contributing her share of money for apartment items. Mary felt that she has been put in the role of "babysitter," which she doesn't like, by Winnie's irresponsibility.

Jenny was furious because Winnie was going through her possessions again and had borrowed her bicycle without asking. Jenny felt she had made it perfectly clear to Winnie how upsetting it was to have her things taken and that Winnie had violated their agreement that she would stop.

Mary and Jenny felt that Winnie doesn't ask for help when she needs it. She had refused an opportunity at last week's meeting to discuss the problems she was having, which might have headed off some of this acting out. Jenny felt she would have trouble being able to trust Winnie again. She felt she had come to terms with living in the same apartment with Winnie, and that they had all been getting along better lately. She didn't want to have to put a lock on her bicycle.

Both Jenny and Mary had already confronted Winnie about her behavior on Sunday night, including giving her a written list of their grievances. Dara asked Winnie to respond to what her roommates were saying. Winnie was aware that she had been having problems in all three major areas of her life—apartment, school, and work. She was beginning to see that she did things that created the situation she was in. She had made arrangements to see her social worker twice a week and was talking to her new therapist about her problems. She felt she would do most of the work on these problems in her therapy sessions.

Dara pointed out that although Winnie would be talking and understanding her behavior in her sessions, the real work would be to change how she acted in the apartment. She would need to make specific plans for change that her roommates would find acceptable. Winnie again was very vague in how she planned to correct the situation. She felt it wouldn't help just to say what she planned to do, because no one would believe her anyway. Mary and Jenny disagreed, and said that it was important to them to have her state her goals.

Winnie said that she planned to keep a journal and write in it what she was experiencing whenever she felt like using something that wasn't hers. Dara asked her to be more specific. Then they went through a list of Jenny's and Mary's complaints and discussed how Winnie would remedy each one.

Dara suggested that Winnie make a record specifying what chores, etc., she was to do, with a place to check off everyday when a task was completed. The group discussed this at length, including Winnie's resistance to having her performance so openly visible. The group also suggested a graph to note Winnie's daily progress and be an indicator to her when she was beginning to slack off and needed to ask for help.

Winnie actually became quite excited with the idea, and felt that it would really help her structure herself. It seemed an appropriate solution since Winnie seems to get vague and confused about what is expected of her. Mary and Jennie will also prepare a chart for the apartment that will include weekly contributions for shared items.

Both Jenny and Mary were helpful and supportive, although they were clear about their anger in regard to Winnie's recent behavior. Dara underscored to Winnie that she was at risk at the house and needed to satisfy her roommates with responsible behavior. Dara agreed to take the information back to staff for discussion at the next meeting and to review Winnie's chart on a weekly basis. Jenny and Mary agreed to help Winnie with the list of what would be included on the chart, but that Winnie would draw it up herself. Jenny and Mary felt that the chart would provide Winnie with a much needed structure and would satisfy their needs, too.

Developing Self-Concept

Once new skills have been attempted, then mastered, then made consistent features of the resident's functioning, they must be integrated into the resident's self-concept in order for self-esteem to grow, for the resident to feel fuller, richer, more powerful. There is always a lag between the mastering of a skill and its integration into self-concept. The resident's worker functions in the capacity of assessor to help the resident keep step with his growth. This is particularly important in the supportive apartments where gains may be less dramatic than those made earlier in the halfway house and where the emphasis may be on more subtle changes and on consolidation.

Developing a Social Network

In the supportive apartment, staff is attentive to the continuing development of the resident's social network. Residents become aware that they impact on their neighbors. They learn lease requirements and neighbors' tastes regarding the volume of the television set at night and the way garbage is bagged and disposed of. They are encouraged to make relationships with neighbors, socialize, and "borrow sugar" from these people who are potential members of their social support system.

As noted earlier, the resident must now become more active in making arrangements to meet with friends. He is encouraged to invite them to the apartment and to meet them in the community. Each time a new resident moves into an apartment, funds are provided by the agency for a housewarming party. Residents are expected to invite other agency residents to this event and may invite any outside friends they wish.

Residents who are now further along in their programs are usually interacting with people in the community, in school or at work who do not know of their histories. Their social circles are widening and their activities are moving outside of the "mental health system." Frequently, because of their fear of the stigma of mental illness, residents constrict their lives. They don't invite friends to the halfway house or to the supportive apartments. They don't attend certain support groups available to them. They don't obtain reduced-price transportation passes from the Office for the Handicapped, even during periods when they are on limited budgets. Although some are afraid to go outside of the mental health system for socialization for fear that they will not be able to keep up with or to interest "normal" people, others devalue fellow residents and once out of the halfway house have little or no contact with their former peers.

Thus does the stigma of mental illness pervade the lives of its victims. Throughout the years in the halfway house and the supportive apartment, staff helps each resident, both individually and in groups, to wrestle with her feelings about where she stands on this issue. Naturally, such feelings run deep—from concerns of identity and self-worth to concerns about social network. As each resident is able to lighten this burden, so is she able to experience life more broadly.

Crises

During the time in the supportive apartment, some residents are able to make the transition from a "sick" to a "well" identity. With each advance in growth, the fear of decompensation gradually diminishes. Many residents have left the supportives, despite some continuing symptoms, confident that they will not again experience a psychiatric hospitalization.

For those residents who suffer from a more chronic illness, for whom, because of continuing vulnerability to stress, it may be unrealistic to expect no future episodes of illness or decompensations, staff and resident continue in the supportive apartment to develop coping mechanisms and to manipulate the environment to be as conducive as possible to good functioning. They look together at which stresses to avoid, how to buffer those remaining, how to handle the onset of symptoms and to temper the episode itself, and how to regard oneself in this context.

When Chris decided to withdraw from the relationship with her abusive boyfriend, her worker began to consider how Chris was likely to handle this stress and what the possibilities were of muting the strength and effects of the episode of illness that was likely to follow. The worker then learned that Chris had not been taking her medications regularly since she began the breakup. Chris felt tremendous anger and then showed beginning signs of depression. As soon as she knew of the lack of medication compliance, the worker contacted the therapist to gain her support and to advise that staff would be monitoring the medications. The worker recontacted the therapist when the depression began and as it developed in order to keep her advised of the symptomatology so that medications could be properly adjusted. Chris's therapist began seeing her an additional session each week.

Chris seemed able to limit her symptoms at her college classes but did decide to drop one course to lighten her schedule. However, at the supportive apartment, Chris was weepy, clingy, and spent long periods in bed. Although she tried to control these symptoms, her roommates were feeling quite stressed. Chris spent several respite periods at the halfway house to give her more structure and to relieve the roommates.

Chris allied herself with staff in an effort to limit her decompensation. She felt then and later that she had a choice: to let go and yield to her mood or to hold on wherever she could and structure her day. She was thus able to ride out her depression and gradually regain her equilibrium.

This was the second episode of illness Chris had experienced while in the community residence. She had had less control during the first, had completely dropped her school program, but had at least been able to stay out of the hospital. As this time she had been able to continue at school, Chris began to feel more confidence in her ability to control her illness. She more vigorously addressed the self-destructive behavior that had precipitated this episode—allowing herself to be abused in her former relationship, not taking her medication properly, and so forth. She saw that if she could minimize this kind of trauma in her life, she could decrease the threat of decompensation. Chris is now actively planning with her worker measures to take to prepare for the time of year when she traditionally cycles into a depression: She has prophylactic medications available, is planning no major changes, and is trying to be self-caring.

Chris's self-image, as it changes from that of a negative, self-deprecating victim to a more positive, hopeful, competent person who can act to shape her life in constructive ways, will have a major effect on the course of her illness. Once again, the work of the community residence staff and the work of the outside therapist continually reinforce each other to help Chris in her growth.

Supportive apartments may be used creatively by agencies in many capacities. Just as residents who need the structure of the halfway house during crises can return there briefly for respite, so can the halfway house use a supportive apartment vacancy to shelter temporarily a prospective halfway house resident until there is a vacancy in that facility. Also, if the two or three supportive apartment residents are in need of long-term or permanent housing in a supportive setting, the agency can consider transferring the lease to the residents, along with supplying some continuing aftercare services. This step presupposes that the agency is able to replace the apartment it thus loses. However, most agencies in saturated housing areas have experienced great difficulty obtaining apartments and know they cannot replace stock so easily. The high rent such areas command is an ancillary problem for agency and for clients. Residents who are working part-time and/or in entry-level or low-stress positions cannot afford to pay the competitive rents. Agencies therefore operate these apartments at a loss unless there are public or private funding sources to cover the deficit.

MOVEMENT TOWARD DISCHARGE

The majority of community residences place a time limit on the length of stay permitted in the supportive apartment, usually about two years. Residents may leave earlier if they prefer and they may sometimes stay longer if a few more months in residence would appear to contribute constructively to the resident's life (i.e., if the resident is in mid-term at school, or if he is in crisis).

Planning a move from the supportive apartment into the community involves all the dynamics discussed in Chapter 9 around discharge from the halfway house. Staff and resident plan the move carefully to capitalize on the resident's strengths, compensate for his vulnerabilities, and support his highest level of functioning.

Some residents seek to live alone for a while—to have their own rooms or apartments and to experience as much independence as they can. Others want or need roommates for social or financial reasons, but wish to move into a "normal" situation outside of the mental health circle so they can test their wings socially with a new group of people who have no knowledge of their history. Others plan to move with supportive apartment roommates or to join alumni of the community residence, day hospital, and so on, and very much want the support of living with people who know them well and can accept whatever symptomatology the persons may carry with them, such as tremors or compulsive rituals. Still others have been able to strike a good balance in their relationships with family and decide to move home.

Whatever the circumstances of the move, the process varies only by degree. There is always some anxiety about the move, an evaluation period to assess current level of functioning and to determine what skills need to be sharpened, and usually some regression. Adequate time to plan, efforts to moderate other stresses during this time period and, again, steps to select the most facilitative environment into which to move are in order. The resident is reminded of his last move (from halfway house to supportive apartment), can see his patterns, make the move slowly, and take some comfort in the knowledge that he can survive the anxiety of the move and will feel more comfortable once he has adjusted to his new home.

Always, the agency is "with" the resident during and after his move to offer supportive aftercare services, which we shall explore in Chapter 11.

Some chronically ill adults are so sensitive to stress or so vulnerable to isolation and deterioration that they are in need of permanent supportive housing. They are unable to live independently for long periods of time without putting some part of their life situation into jeopardy— medication compliance, job, treatment program, income, or housing, itself. All these community services and activities tend to wash out when this group does not have an appropriately structured and supportive living arrangement to anchor their lives. The very fact of living in a community residence keeps this population concretely connected to a support system which provides them with such a basic stability and stress-regulating resource that they are able to function more consistently in the other areas of their lives.

Many of this group have been able to stretch their limits and increase their functioning. Some are in competitive paid employment, or in sheltered workshops, or have returned to college or vocational training. Many have established kinship systems which provide them with friendship and support, and look to be doing well. However, many of these residents would put their growth and stability in jeopardy were they to attempt to live independently in the community. They are people whose illness is truly chronic—who have persistent deficits of functioning for which the supportive residence and its services compensate, or whose course of illness runs an insidious cycle of episodes and remissions. During episodes, the resident requires periods of more intensive support—perhaps more sessions with agency personnel, perhaps a respite period back with the supervision of the halfway house, perhaps a period of medication monitoring. These periodic surges of support enable the resident to keep his job, stay in school, or stay out of the hospital. Any comprehensive residential program should provide a number of permanent supportive units for this group of residents.

If the residents in a particular supportive apartment will be moving on eventually to independent life in the community, it is important not to provide *such* comfort in the apartment structure or setting that the motivation to move is compromised. The few rules that make the residents chafe also stimulate them to reach for independence. If, however, the apartment will be a permanent or long-term residence, it should be designed to be as much like home as possible. Residents are more likely to be committed to such an apartment as home, maintain it as such, and settle into their building and their neighborhood, making long-term relationships (if they know this is where they will stay) and establish their roots.

Community residence staff, having lived with residents through the highs and lows of mental illness and recovery, establish a bond which, if ex-residents wish, can extend for many years. It may be part professional, part friend, part family, and can serve as support for as long as the former resident desires, providing the foundation for the aftercare program.

CHAPTER 11
Aftercare

Ex-residents return in a variety of circumstances and conditions to refuel with the care and concern of staff and peers. The contacts can be formal or drop-in, group or individual, brief or protracted. A former resident may want help in finding or keeping a job, locating an apartment, working out trouble with a roommate or family, keeping to a budget, selecting a new therapist, finding a lost friend, recovering from a broken romance, or surviving the reemergence of symptomatology.

Aftercare begins with the move from the halfway house or the supportive apartment. The ex-resident is offered a number of formal, follow-up sessions with his social worker to help in the adjustment to the new living situation. Most ex-residents accept and continue the sessions until the stress of the move subsides. Some ex-residents are so frightened of independence that they wish to continue the sessions for a longer period—at first weekly or semimonthly, then gradually decreasing in frequency. It is preferable to permit ex-residents to wean themselves off at their own pace, which they eventually do when they are ready and able.

The agency also offers its graduates a few meals at the residence during the adjustment period to ease the transition, as well as the option of returning to the house to sleep for a few nights if they so desire. They are encouraged to maintain contact with counselor and peers at the house and at the supportive apartments.

As discussed earlier (Chapter 10), community residence staff, in some circumstances, continue to offer full agency services to ex-residents who have secured their own apartments in the community. This occurs, for instance, when agency supportive apartments are filled but residents who have become capable of more independence must leave the halfway house to provide space for less functional applicants. If it is agency policy to relate to such an apartment in essence as a supportive apartment, such services technically qualify as aftercare. In addition, to help residents to move into the community when ready, such direct concrete aid as furniture seed money or funds for a security deposit might be included in the aftercare budget, if such funds exist. The importance of this assistance has not been reflected in the budgets of state-funded halfway houses. In not-for-profit agencies, boards of directors can establish such funding to provide the essential bridge to independence.

A formal aftercare group for ex-residents, which meets regularly, serves the purpose of maintaining a supportive agency contact as well as of reinforcing the members' social networks and providing for an exchange of information about jobs, apartments, and so on. So, too, do formal agency activities for graduates such as parties, trips to the beach, the open annual meeting of the Board of Directors, and gatherings around the holidays, especially when the ex-resident's natural family is deceased, alienated, or absent.

> In April, staff sent out invitations to alumni to attend a Spring luncheon. The majority of those who came were ex-residents of the last five years, but one man in his mid-30s, who had resided at the halfway house before the others and knew none of them, came alone. During the course of the afternoon, this articulate young man spoke of his pride at having been able to hold a job now for almost a year after many years of brief work experiences. He was also pleased that this job paid decently and allowed him to support himself reasonably well. He was anxious, though, that he would "blow it," become self-destructive, and somehow manage to quit or lose the job. Three or four of the others responded positively to Earl and engaged in conversations, exchanging information and support. They invited him out with them after the party. Six months later, Earl continues to be a member of this particularly supportive social group.

Most ex-residents maintain an informal contact with the transitional house. They call for an occasional appointment, meet a staff member for lunch, or drop in to chat with the counselor. This usually continues as long as staff remain who were employed during the ex-resident's tenure in the house, or if there are enough formal aftercare events (usually at agency's cost) to encourage contact with new staff members.

There are occasions when an ex-resident is in real crisis and turns to the agency for assistance with a significant problem, as in the following example.

Ann had been a halfway house and supportive apartment resident who then obtained her own apartment and was working steadily in an almost full-time job as a secretary. She had several friends who were ex-residents and two friends not related to her halfway house experience. She had no living family, however, and because she was a dependent and needy person, she continued sessions with her social worker, first weekly, then less often until, two years after leaving the supportive apartment, she was seeing the worker every eight weeks.

Ann experienced several episodes of illness per year during which she had frightening paranoid symptoms, became impulsive, and alienated her friends. She would then maintain regular contact with her halfway house social worker for the several days or weeks until the symptoms subsided. She saw a psychiatrist regularly for supportive therapy and medication supervision. This therapist changed yearly, as Ann attended a training clinic which rotated its staff. Her attachment to her therapy fluctuated to the degree to which she liked her therapist and felt his or her empathy.

Another significant support in Ann's life was her community support system case manager who saw Ann every four to six weeks, and from whom Ann felt much warmth, concern, and support. After several years, however, the Community Support System (CSS) terminated service with Ann as she was seen as less needy than other clients who were waiting for care.

Shortly thereafter, during the season when Ann historically experienced an exacerbation of her symptoms, a close friend committed suicide, an event which so stressed Ann that it precipitated a particularly severe episode of illness. Ann secluded herself in her apartment and lost her job. Ann's social worker, therapist, and friends were in continuous contact with each other trying to offer enough support to help her remain in the community.

In a final move to avoid hospitalization, Ann's therapist asked if Ann could stay at the halfway house for a time to reduce her stress and give her structure and support. The agency agreed to this plan and Ann stayed 10 days at the halfway house in the respite bed. She calmed somewhat and though still paranoid in a fixed area, she sought and obtained part-time work. She soon felt life would be simpler for her back in her own apartment and she returned home.

This appeared to be the turning point for Ann. She began to make a slow recovery from her episode. She continued to see her halfway house worker through this period while her therapist rotated out of the clinic and another was assigned. Also through efforts of the halfway house worker, Ann was reassigned a temporary CSS worker who proved most supportive over the next few months of Ann's recovery.

In essence, while the other mental health personnel in Ann's life changed, her halfway house supports, as well as her peer network, remained steady through several years. She also made some new peer contacts during her brief respite period at the house.

Agency follow-up services, besides providing various forms of direct support, nurture the ex-resident's social support system. A stronger peer network, lower rehospitalization rates, briefer length of time in hospital, and higher levels of community adjustment are variables positively related to formal and informal aftercare contact with the community residence.

Research clearly indicates that ex-residents of transitional houses choose in great number to maintain contact with the residence after discharge and to participate in aftercare programs if such programs exist (Budson, Grob, & Singer, 1977; Lynch, Budson, & Jolley, 1977). They select housing in the vicinity of the transitional house in order to continue the formal and informal supportive relationships that were established during residency (Berman & Hoppe, 1976).

Further research indicates that those ex-residents or ex-patients who maintain contact with a caring facility after discharge have a lower rehospitalization rate (Alpert et al., 1971; Vermont Longitudinal Study, 1984). Other studies show a highly positive relationship between continuing contacts with the transitional house and the level of adjustment in the community (Budson, 1978; Holman & Shore, 1978; Landy & Greenblatt, 1965). There is also a correlation between the existence of a psychosocial support network and successful tenure in the community (Lynch, Budson, & Jolley, 1977).

Budson et al. (1977) stress that continued halfway house contact with ex-residents supports further growth of adaptive strengths at the same time as it fosters a social connectedness among present and former residents.

> The authors believe that too often it is thought that the halfway house residential experience is itself the final rehabilitative measure. We strongly believe, however, that it is only one stage leading ultimately to the establishment of a social network into which the former resident enters. He then continues in the community in this network, living in clusters, relating less and less directly to the house—but always using it if a crisis arises. Through this continued availability of the house and maintenance of social network the community experience of the formerly hospitalized patient is supported and enhanced. (p. 128)

Holman and Shore (1978) stress in their study that the optimum aftercare program does not foster unhealthy dependency, but encourages self-sufficiency and productive functioning while offering "(e)nduring contacts and supports" (p. 128). As an agency plans its aftercare services, it must take care, as it does in the residential program, not to support regressive functioning.

> Harry had been seeing his former social worker at the halfway house as he had had some financial reverses resulting from a recent resurgence of his illness and was trying to establish a budget for himself. His worker saw him in biweekly sessions immediately after he received his paycheck to help him set budget priorities for the next two-week period and to decide which bills to pay. However, after four or five sessions, it became clear that Harry was not interested in logging his expenses and foregoing some luxuries in order to gain control over his spending. At one point, he called to tell his worker that he had spent all the funds which were to last him the 10 more days until his next payday, but he could not account for where the money had gone. He was asking to eat a few meals at the halfway house as he had no food in his apartment and had already eaten several meals at friends'. He complained that he was starving, penniless, and had no place to turn.
>
> The worker felt that to feed Harry directly at this time would be regressive, that it would be more helpful for Harry to experience the consequences of his carelessness. He was referred to a local foodbank where he could go through the process of applying for and receiving assistance. Even though this procedure was distasteful to Harry, it did not deter him from continuing to utilize the services of the halfway house appropriately.

During halfway house residency, staff provides case management services to each resident, freeing CSS case managers to work with other clients who are living in the community. Even when ex-residents are eligible for and accept CSS case management services, they can positively utilize the transitional residence's aftercare program. Despite the growth in functional skills attained while in the community residence and the careful discharge planning which facilitates a living and work environment most conducive to the former resident's good functioning, the nature of his illness—its chronicity, its episodic upheavals, and the lack of certain life supports in his ecosystem—may be such that the ex-resident requires the contacts with the transitional residence as one of several supports in his ecosystem.

This is especially so with an ex-resident like Ann (see above), who is very dependent, without family resources, and impulsive and explosive enough that during episodes of illness she needs more support than her CSS worker, her therapist, and her peers can provide. Once again, staff has, in effect, joined "the extended psychosocial kinship system of the patient and his family . . . (and) made a significant and vital shift. They have moved from conceiving of themselves as remote, professional, singular bestowers of health, treating the stigmatized sick, to aspiring to be skilled, caring people who have entered their clients' world to assist them in healthy living . . ." (Budson & Jolley, 1978, p. 611).

Occasionally, when an ex-resident who chooses to continue contacts with her halfway house social worker begins treatment with a new therapist, the latter encourages the ex-resident to discontinue such contact. The therapist is usually concerned that the ex-resident is too dependent and/or that the contact with the worker will dilute or interfere with the relationship with the therapist. This response frequently occurs when the ex-resident is seeing a therapist who has been educated in a traditional psychoanalytic mode, or is still in training with an institution of like orientation (refer to Chapter 7).

The therapist who has experienced some years of work with chronically mentally ill patients usually welcomes and is welcomed by other professional supports in the patient's life. The therapist recognizes that the problem of exhausting resources and of staff, family, and peer burnout is a serious one for the patient and for the support system. Long-term work with such patients living in the community takes on the nature of an orchestration. The patient and one or two special members of the support team—perhaps the therapist, the CSS worker, or a family member—are responsible for calling in the services of other members of the team when appropriate.

The clinical efficacy of aftercare services has been well researched and documented. These services are also clearly cost-effective. In the case of Ann, cited earlier, the services rendered in one month encompassed several individual sessions with the agency social worker, a number of telephone contacts with Ann, her therapist, her CSS worker, her friends, and her place of employment, 10 days of respite bed care and a small financial grant in aid, and agency staff conference time. The cost to the agency of these services for one month was approximately $700. Ann would surely have been hospitalized had the respite bed not been provided her. At current local hospital rates of $300–$400 per day, the cost of Ann's 10-day hospitalization alone would have reached about $4,000 at public expense.

This is a stunning statistic of cost comparison, but in reality most agencies are not reimbursed for aftercare expenses. Agencies may indeed be discouraged from offering them at all by public funding sources who see only today's saving and lose sight of tomorrow's expense.

The success of a program for mentally ill persons should not necessarily be defined in terms of the client's eventual total independence from community care. If some persons can adapt outside of the hospital only with the continuing assistance of various levels of community support systems, then the provision of such services represents not only concrete savings to the community, but also an essential predictor of more positive community adjustment for those who are chronically psychiatrically impaired.

CHAPTER 12
The Staff

The concept of a halfway house is still in its evolutionary stages. It can be defined merely as housing, but a creative board and staff can mold this service into a highly productive source of healthier functioning for its inhabitants. The house can be a microcosm which evolves its own values and standards, preferably values and standards that will mesh with those outside its walls. Thus, if the resident internalizes them, he is halfway across the bridge to the outside world. The players in this orchestration are the staff. They create the atmosphere of warmth, of acceptance of the individual with all his drawbacks, of understanding of the pain of past defeats, and of sustained expectation that continued efforts with reachable goals will produce growth.

The halfway house is one of the frontiers of professional freedom, an arena in which staff can stretch the limits of their ability, experiment with new rehabilitation pathways, and create an atmosphere that fosters growth while utilizing all their professional training and personal background to help others. The sense of flexibility, balanced by freedom to experiment and be a full person, not merely a professional persona, evolves from the director down to every member of the staff. This freedom must, of course, be tempered with responsibility and accountability, but opportunity for professional growth is unlimited.

Not surprisingly, many of the tenets of effective business management practices, which Peters and Waterman describe in their book *In Search of Excellence* (1982), apply directly to the successful running of a halfway house. Their study found that success flows from "a culture that encourages action, experiments, repeated tries" (p. 114). Outstanding corporations would have their people believe that they are employed by the best corporation in the country, one that invites innovation and accepts failure as inherent in experimentation. Innovation is not reserved for top staff alone but is encouraged throughout the entire organization. Constant staff interchange is fostered in every way, even using coffee breaks as a device for keeping abreast of new developments. Informal communication creates the concept of being one big family. No cumbersome chain of command holds up decisions, thus "encouraging maximum fluidity and flexibility" (p. 287). Of paramount importance in these effective companies is the value system established by top executives. They generate excitement and enthusiasm through deeds rather than words.

The management of a halfway house falls squarely within these precepts. The optimism, the vision of change, and the stimulus to experiment create an environment in which residents can again feel hopeful about themselves and begin to risk new behaviors. Peters and Waterman (1982) believe that "clarifying the value system and breathing life into it are the greatest contribution a leader can make" (p. 291). In a halfway house, the director, social workers, and counselors "prod, challenge, and stimulate the resident to scale new heights" (Budson, 1978, p. 175) but if he falters, are ready to stand by him and "to support and nurture him" (p. 175) until he can risk another attempt.

THE DIRECTOR

When halfway houses arose in response to needs within a community, they were frequently administered by a professional organization with an outside consulting psychiatrist. A house manager, with perhaps no professional credentials, would implement administrative directives. "In contrast to the nonprofessional management in which life within the house is seen as somewhat peripheral to change in the residents, the professionally managed house tends to view its structure as playing a fundamental part in effecting change" (Raush & Raush, 1968, p. 97). In professionally managed houses, directors vary in background and skills. The psychiatric, social work, or nursing fields have supplied many excellent administrators who have created the harmonious environment which rehabilitation of this population demands. If the director possesses clinical skills and programmatic expertise, the halfway house can indeed evolve into a rehabilitative setting which extends the work of the therapist, the day hospital, and other rehabilitation agencies. With current complexities of budgeting, fund raising, staff recruitment, training, and deployment, a director's background should include administrative experience to ensure a high level of service delivery.

Because most halfway houses are small, self-contained units, the director may be available to supervise staff directly, to provide a non-threatening, listening ear, and to help all levels of personnel identify problems at their inception, before they loom so large that the entire house is involved or staff members leave, burnt out and in despair. She should also relate personally to the problems of management of the daily lives of the residents, sample the foods cooked by them, or be involved with the decor in the bedrooms in addition to dealing with the state bureaucracy, the fire and health departments, or laboring over the ever-growing deficit in the budget.

A congenial, harmonious staff is the building block of the therapeutic milieu. Tension, rivalry, and favoritism resound throughout the residence creating anxiety within staff which inevitably is transmitted to the residents.

Since he or she hires, trains, and supervises most of the staff, the director becomes the mechanism for forging a smoothly functioning team, an absolutely basic ingredient for the creative and careful management of the facility.

Although staff members may come from widely different educational and cultural backgrounds, the director binds them together via common goals to foster an upbeat spirit, creating the comfortable cocoon in which residents can grow and finally outgrow.

When the director has recruited dedicated persons who can identify with the aims of the house, who can develop in their ability to understand the intricacies of the illnesses despite their complexities, and who succeed in promoting changed behavior, their continuity as employees must be her prime concern. Peters and Waterman (1982) studied companies that outproduced others in their field. Those that were most effective cared deeply about their employees. Similarly, in halfway houses, salaries and working conditions deserve personal attention. Are there comfortable quarters, sufficient privacy, soundproof rooms to ensure a measure of separation from residents, opportunities for professional realization, sufficient support when residents are in crisis?

A caring administration reacts sensitively to events and holidays that have particular significance to employees. Not only should substitutes be recruited to relieve staff members for family events or personal crises, but achievements such as the acquisition of a degree, the purchase of a new car or the celebration of birthdays or anniversaries should be joyfully noted to promote a sense of kinship or bonding. Interpretation of these needs to boards, budget departments, or community groups are the director's responsibility if she is to maintain a smoothly functioning team without constant turnover.

A director represents authority not only to staff members but to residents. As a component of their illnesses, residents may suffer from exaggerated ideas of authority or unrealistic fears of it. It is therapeutic, therefore, for the director to be an approachable, visible source of caring, day-to-day prosaic interaction.

One technique a director can utilize to maintain regular interaction with all the residents is the weekly community meeting attended by residents and clinical and counseling staff. At this meeting, she samples the cooking, notices the housekeeping, hears about unmet household needs or frustrations (such as a nightly accumulation of dirty cups in the kitchen), and discusses plans for celebrating holidays and reactions to possible new arrivals or to residents who are planning new steps in their rehabilitation programs. Again, Peters and Waterman (1982) underscore that "management by wandering around" (p. 289) is one of the approved ways to evaluate effectiveness of a program, to uncover problems in the social system that need attention, or to modify an aspect of structure for the benefit of the group.

The basic tool a staff member can acquire from a director—and the most difficult to impart—is to learn to empathize with a resident. Trop (1984) has described this concept as "a particular way of trying to understand and listen to a patient" (p. 293). Ornstein (1979) states, "Empathy leads us to comprehend complex feelings and thoughts (needs, wishes, conflicts, fantasies, etc.) from the vantage point of the patient's own inner experience, as contrasted with the vantage point of an external observer and that of a particular theory" (p. 99).

Whether a resident feels understood, cared for, calm, and relaxed depends upon the empathic responses of staff members. Differences in expectations, lifestyle or life cycle, ethnicity, or social class can diminish a staff member's ability to experience empathy for a resident and can impose barriers between the resident and the counselor and/or social worker (Gitterman, 1983). An overly intellectual response by staff, which does not tune in sensitively to feelings, merely serves to increase a resident's anxiety, fragmentation, and instability. Pat solutions to problems are experienced by residents, particularly at times when they are not in good contact with reality, as not hearing the depth of the feeling. "The empathic vantage point is not external but rather is achieved by understanding what the patient feels from his own subjective experience. . . . The more important focus should be on the patient's internal experience as it relates to feelings of vulnerability and lack of self-confidence and self-cohesion" (Trop, 1984, p. 300). When he feels that a staff member relates to his concerns as he experiences them, the resident can more readily calm himself, strengthen his sense of inner security, and move on to an outer reality. The director who communicates this all-important concept to every staff member has gone a long way in creating a therapeutic environment.

ADMINISTRATIVE SUPPORT STAFF

If the director has administrative support staff which may include an assistant administrator, a secretary, a bookkeeper, and an accountant, he can be more available to devote his major efforts to staff development and to the utilization of the outside community to further the agency's goals. Relieved of the burden of responding to an endless stream of state forms, billing the residents for their monthly rents, collecting these fees, keeping records of all day-to-day financial activities of the agency and the board, hiring and supervising the many repairmen necessary for the upkeep of the premises, tracking the details of fund raising, he has time to promote helpful relations with cooperating day hospitals and vocational rehabilitation agencies or to interpret the illnesses of the residents to selected members of the business community in an effort to overcome prejudice in employing and housing mentally ill persons who are in remission. Administrative staff usually are thoroughly familiar with each resident, interact briefly with them when they come to pay rents, ask for special favors, or simply drop in to discuss a movie, report a change in status, or ask for extra support. Office staff, too, frequently become part of the extended kinship group or support system for some residents in crisis.

SOCIAL WORK STAFF

Many halfway houses operate with the assistance of only one trained social worker for intake and discharge planning. They utilize counselors with varied training to perform all other functions. At these houses, the main thrust of rehabilitation management comes from the outside ecosystem. A halfway house, however, is indeed fortunate when it employs a corps of trained, skilled clinical social workers to interact closely with each resident, tracking his first timid approaches at intake and his hesitant or resistant entrance, as well as his subsequent adjustment to the life and structure of the house, to the other residents, to his day hospital program, and to the total ecosystem. Managing severely ill people who "daily struggle with the shame and stigma of being 'crazy' and the despair of being chronic . . . " (Minkoff & Stern, 1985, p. 863) is an exhausting, frustrating operation. Staff disappointment and burnout (which includes anxiety, irritation, depression, and low self-esteem) are all too frequently the human reactions which strong administrative support may help avert. If psychological aspects of helping are separated from day-to-day supervision of food procurement, medication compliance, and chore detail, the group can be more adequately served.

A halfway house demands of its social work staff a unique blend of skills to operate effectively in its casual, intimate, family-like setting where there is much informal relating outside of each client's weekly session. Residents may be fragile, fearful, or working out authority issues in which there is testing, anger, or seductive behavior. Yet almost all transactions between the worker and resident offer the opportunities for therapeutic intervention provided the workers are mature and knowledgeable about the people served. The worker must be confident and flexible enough to sustain an attitude of relaxed professionalism despite the fact that he is on a first name basis with the client and carries no visible insignia to establish resident–social worker boundaries.

Finely tuned clinical skills, eclectically derived from analytic, cognitive, behavioral, rational-emotive, or family systems modalities, are called into selective use daily in rehabilitation work with this fragile population. The social worker must sensitively determine whether a resident possesses sufficient stability and bonding to explore if there were familial interactions which might have contributed to present-day dependencies or developmental lags. When anxieties are immobilizing a resident, supportive skills may become "central to the worker's effectiveness" (Shulman, 1979, p. 58). At other times the worker may adhere rigidly to basic structure, rewarding a resident with greater freedom or privacy as he modifies his impulses or takes on more responsibility. The social worker establishes goals with each resident under his supervision and contracts with him how to reach them on a step-by-step basis. This contract is the centerboard for the hard work ahead. It is the guide delineating the essential work to be done, when this work is avoided, and when it is completed. Clinical skills dictate when support is the basic approach and/or confrontation, behavioral techniques, or careful dissection of cognitive processes (see Chapter 3). Whatever the techniques, goals and objectives must at all times be mutually agreed upon by resident and social worker and, once established, consistently maintained. With growth in a resident's adaptation to his disability, new goals for the improvement of his daily life or reducing his symptoms may evolve.

In addition to having a melange of clinical skills, social workers attached to a halfway house must engage in "old-fashioned" social work. They must be ready to serve as a resident's advocate with the public assistance systems or the Social Security Administration. Case management, central to helping an ill person reestablish himself in the community, is most effectively achieved by a skilled person who understands and has formed empathic bonds with that client. First steps require a careful assessment of a resident's abilities and limitations to perform simple tasks. What can he take care of on his own? Where does he need reminders or outright assistance? If a resident does not feel confident to present his financial needs to the funding agencies, a social worker can choose from a number of options: explore the resident's resistance; assist him to confront his fear or anger at his financial dependency; accompany him to the interview to support his efforts; or, if the system is treating him unfairly for any reason, including ineptitude of its employees, the worker can utilize his knowledge of that agency's hierarchy or its rules to press an appeal. When a program does not meet a resident's needs or aspirations or terminates him because of its funding pattern or his non-compliance, his social worker becomes his compass, assisting him to discover alternate routes which are constructive or goal-directed.

Although rehabilitation agencies address the vocational needs of a recovering mentally ill person, their efforts are sometimes narrowly directed. An inhouse social worker who relates closely to a resident's deep-seated fears about independence or failure may more sensitively engage and support his faltering efforts to reenter the world of work and lend him, as an auxiliary ego, her sense of confidence when he feels bereft of his own.

In addition to addressing anxieties which may in this population trigger decompensation, the social worker offers such directed aid as helping a resident tailor a resumé to account for his period of unemployment, evaluating with him how he presents himself physically (a fresh haircut, slacks, not jeans), role playing the interview or even accompanying him there, and encouraging him throughout the first anxious weeks of employment. In all these efforts, the social worker's positive expectations of a successful outcome sustain attenuated motivation.

The social worker is the link between the family that may be either nervous about the decision to separate from its ill member or angry at all past defeats and failed efforts. Understanding the illness, the difficulty in treating it, the importance of medication, and the value of individuation for any adult are areas of concern which the social worker can interpret and sort out. She can help families achieve some comfort and perhaps free them to pursue their own lives with reduced guilt.

Complexities of the Social Work Role

Frequently inexperienced workers are so related to internal dynamics that they tend to overlook or ignore the physical manifestations of unsatisfactory functioning. They may be alert to reactivations of sibling rivalries but fail to notice that no one defrosted the refrigerator, cleaned the kitchen floor, or scrubbed the bathroom. Their idealized professional images prevent them from opening a cupboard to observe the mountainous accumulation of unreturned deposit bottles. As they grow professionally, they learn that such interventions are clinically sound. In structuring domestic responsibilities, they perform a rehabilitation function.

Although "one change at a time" is an echoed and reechoed principle, an enthusiastic social worker may at times generate too many premature initiatives in approaching a problem with a resident, ignoring the biological and functional fact that aggressive planning and movement are not options for a resident directly after his hospitalization. He must yield clues that he is ready for some shift in motivation.

Casework performed in a halfway house with its warm yet relatively undefined structure demands that the social worker be sufficiently mature and well enough integrated to organize his time to encompass all his responsibilities to the residents, their families, and the cooperating agencies. Nevertheless, he must still find time in a busy schedule to listen to rock music with a group, eat a meal with a unit, or accompany a resident on a shopping expedition to ensure suitable attire for an employment interview or appropriate drapes for the supportive apartment. The social worker is frequently required to take up the slack in those areas in which the supporting ecosystem has either thrown up its hands or simply has not worked a problem to a satisfactory conclusion. Difficult or impossible as such a commitment seems, it represents an excellent potential for evolving innovative or ingenious solutions for unremitting problems not resolved by other cooperating agencies.

Max, an intelligent, highly impulsive young man, had inordinate needs to control the world around him. This drive naturally attached itself to the work scene. He tried a variety of jobs, the details of which he readily mastered but he was repeatedly fired because he chronically created head-on collisions with his employers, who became parental equivalents. His day hospital program of six months attempted to address his negative interactions, but his discharge occurred before he was able to alter his behavior. His vocational rehabilitation worker who placed him in various jobs soon became discouraged with the repeated firings. Exploration of the inner dynamics which spurred his volatile behavior ran counter to that agency's function.

During the remainder of his stay at the halfway house, Max probed his power struggles from a family dynamics viewpoint both in sessions with his therapist and with his halfway house social worker since issues similar to family-related ones frequently arose within the halfway house setting. Max developed new insights and tried to modify his impulsivity. With the realization that he might spend the next several years restructuring his characterological problems with his therapist, he devised with his worker's help a work plan whereby he could utilize his excellent skills as a landscaper and gardener. He capitalized on his friendly initial affability to develop his own clientele whom he would service on a per-job basis. He printed and distributed cards. His clientele slowly grew because of his superior abilities. Within a short time, he was able to open his own business, hiring some halfway house residents to assist him.

Teamwork is the crucible in which the efforts of a halfway house staff simmer as they attempt to reshape the quality of the lives of its inhabitants. There should be no territorial feelings or favorites among the varied staff members. If Paul, whose female social worker had helped him evolve from a highly delusional young man to an excellent accountant, decides that he needs the male worker on the staff with whom to discuss his car repair or his dates, such free movement is accepted with the assurance that this is not reflective of professional inadequacies but of the fact that each staff member offers different avenues for growth. In Paul's case, he had moved to independent quarters and needed to define his growth by a change in social workers for aftercare services.

Social workers, as in most social agencies, have individual responsibilities for a number of residents, but in a halfway house they are at liberty to form ad hoc groups to address specific problems that develop. For example, three couples became romantically involved with each other. These romances, in a confined society where bedrooms are shared, became a threat to those residents who could not find partners and restrictive to the involved couples. The ad hoc group of enmeshed couples considered these problems and explored ways of interacting which would not disrupt the house. Because the agency was small and flexible, no elaborate administrative machinery was necessary to organize this group. The regularly scheduled sessions immediately reduced pressures in the house.

Other ad hoc groups have been formed to concentrate on problems of discharge or return to work. The leader of one group helped three residents, who could not find or finance an apartment, band together to look jointly for suitable lodgings. How to approach landlords or superintendents, obtain fair rentals, read leases, and select furnishings became the focus of this subgroup.

Since most halfway houses are small units, none of its operations remain mysteries. Staff is aware of and lives closely to the vagaries of the budget, or interacts personally with all cooperating agencies. Staff members mingle with board members at annual meetings, agency parties, or case presentations. Every member of the social work staff can handle the collection of the rent, make out rent receipts, or represent the agency at hospital rounds to discuss the translation of psychiatric diagnosis into a daily routine geared toward helping a resident overcome deficits.

In addition to the director, staff social workers are effective trainers of counselors who change frequently because of a minimal career ladder and sleep-in demands. Training is informal, nonthreatening, on a case-by-case basis, and usually in response to a felt need of the counselor. An understanding of dynamics deepens significantly if a counselor reports freely to another associate, the social worker, that he had a rough weekend with Kenny, for instance, who was overly demanding. Hearing that "Kenny has no boundaries of his own and needs your firmness and limit setting" comes as a relief to the harassed counselor and offers the social worker an opportunity to train staff and to define the illness.

Staff members are frequently advocates for residents. They know the impact that changes in state or federal regulations or funding has on the lives of the people they serve. In one halfway house, a position paper on the disincentives of social security income was prepared by one staff member, while another wrote a paper advocating for aftercare funding.

Halfway house staff develop and utilize not only professional skills but their own selected personal goals as well to motivate residents. A staff member shared her struggles to learn to play the trumpet. She carefully prepared several simple carols which she executed at a Christmas party. She discussed the trials and errors of learning, thus encouraging those who were afraid of risking new learning for fear of failure. In such efforts the staff member and the residents experience new avenues for growth, creative solutions for problems and freedom to experiment.

COUNSELORS

The counselor is the team member who lives with the residents, often on a 24-hour basis; who gives shape and meaning to the basic structure of each day; who relates with warmth, support, and direction to all residents and helps them surmount a crisis; who is perceptive of changed nuances in behavior which signal an incipient manic episode or a possible decompensation; and who recognizes a lapse in medication adherence and reports such behavior to the social worker, therapist, or director for immediate attention.

A counselor was described by one resident as the "backbone of the facility." It is he who shepherds the group through every aspect of the day. He helps the residents negotiate the hassles of daily living, which Tolman and Rose (1985) found "are more closely linked to and may have greater effect on moods and health than major undesirable events" (p.

151). The ordinary daily tasks of personal hygiene, food preparation, or keeping on a schedule constitute major challenges for the recovering emotionally ill person.

The counselor procures the food, at times accompanied by residents; oversees the menus, food preparation, and cleanup; supervises chores; deals with the janitor or handyman; plans outings; discusses the aftermath of a family visit; and celebrates the acquisition of a new friend. He is the eyes and ears of administration and an all-weather friend to the resident. He walks the tightrope of being a peer and yet he must constantly remember that he represents administration, its structure, and policies and that he cannot burden any resident with his own problems or hang-ups.

Because the counselor's role has such great impact, it is of paramount importance that residents who are the consumers of services accept him as a leader. A component of the hiring process, therefore, is an evaluation by the group, who meet the applicant at dinner and have an opportunity to talk to him and to evaluate his suitability. Before making the final decision on hiring new staff, administration asks for resident input. This evaluation continues during the first days of employment. If residents have strong negative reactions about behaviors or attitudes that are not readily solvable through supervision, then the new recruit may be summarily released.

Developing and maintaining a dedicated, well-balanced counseling staff is one of the challenging aspects of managing a halfway house. Since many counselors work part-time or on weekends, persons are recruited who often have other career goals. The training of new staff members, a continuous function of the director, must be specific and comprehensible, provide shape to a counselor's day, and develop attitudes of acceptance for the illnesses served as well as for a variety of behaviors. Training cannot be achieved in big gulps. The process calls for monitoring and feedback. Ideas or prejudicial attitudes which need dissection and remodification surface slowly. Directors and supervisors will constantly be startled by inappropriate reactions or activities of newly hired staff. Whether the counselor is asked to leave or to work to change nonconstructive attitudes will largely depend on the employee's willingness to explore the roots of his prejudices, on his eagerness to learn and on his acceptance of supervision.

Halfway houses differ widely in their counselor staffing. Some utilize a wife-and-husband team who live at the house, with respite days provided by relief staff. Other houses provide more personnel for shorter cycles. The number of persons required for adequate coverage at any time naturally depends on the level of functioning of the residents. Houses with more regressed persons may utilize richer staffing to teach basic survival skills, whereas other houses with more functional residents may utilize only one counselor on a shift to supervise as many as nine residents who can cook meals and sanitize the bathroom but might disintegrate at the possibility of returning to work or making a decision as to whether or not to accept a date.

No matter what the staffing pattern, the morale of staff and their readiness to connect empathically with residents and to accept their disabilities while helping them take small steps toward change are essential ingredients delineating the effectiveness of the program. Counselors are the role models residents emulate most frequently. They are the staff members who engage (or discourage) the new arrival to confront his fears or resistances and to establish roots in the house. They provide the welcome and acceptance the frightened newcomer sorely needs.

Length of stay in a halfway house has been found to correlate positively with staff acceptance; inversely, staff satisfaction is tied to longevity of residents' stay. If staff perceives the new admission in a negative way, an early departure of the new arrival can be anticipated (Velleman, 1984). With adverse reactions, staff distance themselves from the newcomer. Consequently, they are not sensitive to the resident's growing dissatisfactions with life at the house. If ongoing negative feelings toward residents exist, outlets such as sensitivity groups, strong staff support, or increased supervision are needed. Counselors frequently are "notoriously undersupported and isolated with high caseloads." Without continued training and support, dissatisfied "staff members discharge their negative feelings covertly toward the residents and so become part of the negative system that they should be seeking to change" (Velleman, 1984, p. 257). Good relationships with counselors and clear rehabilitation goals are more important to resident longevity in the halfway house than whether or not other residents like the newcomer.

Solomon and Solomon (1982) regard counselors as "models for maturity in friendship" and as "therapists in a therapeutic family" who "offer the residents opportunities for learning the self-healing skills they need to grow beyond their emotional barriers" (p. 55). With skillful selection and training, counselors can become adept at responding to and strengthening reactions that foster growth rather than pathology. Initially, the counselor performs a parental role but, unlike natural parents, he is not burdened by past defeats.

It is essential that a director explore an applicant's motivation to become a counselor. Is he merely a rolling stone who has exhausted all his short-lived efforts at work, who is easily bored or unable to accept any authority? Naturally, such an applicant cannot serve as a role model for disorganized individuals. Does he see himself as a rescuer who will lead the weak to a sunny future? Such an attitude indicates inexperience and a degree of naiveté or grandiosity which might lead to overinvolvement and eventually to deep frustrations when his charges do not progress. Is the applicant seeking an experience which will provide some answers as to whether or not he wishes to work in the human relations field? Such a person may be ready to develop his own personality and his ability to accept a variety of atypical behaviors. Graduate students in the field of human relations are often excellent relief counselors. A counselor who "wants personal growth provides residents with a natural role model of continuing efforts toward self-improvement" (Budson, 1979, p. 50). Glasscote et al. (1971) spoke of recruiting mental health workers among "people discontented with the traditions of their disciplines." These authors felt that such workers could more readily kick "over the traces of traditional services in favor of something with more compatible goals and modes of operation" (p. 194).

Whatever the motivations for pursuing this work, each staff member must be sensitive, but not overly, to behavior that may be inappropriate, resistant, unmotivated, or exasperating. He must possess an ability to ignore many undesirable responses, electing to intervene only in those incidents in which there is a likelihood of improving the resident's quality of life or his relationship to the entire group.

What assets equip a person to become a rehabilitation counselor? Since a halfway house is a round-the-clock operation, its counseling staff must be relatively free of family responsibilities so that they can leave home for extended periods without undue concern or distraction. Unless a married couple is employed, recruitment tends to be of single persons or those who are separated, divorced, or widowed. It is critical that the latter have ended mourning for losses lest they utilize the group for adjustment to pain instead of vice versa. Careful screening of applicants can establish emotional availability. Middle-aged or older adults who have successfully reared a family, whose members are now independent, can become good candidates offering accepting, parental models.

An educational background in some phase of the social sciences is an asset, but lack of a college degree should not preclude hiring a person who is outgoing, open, easy in his ability to form healthy relationships, and who can be a pillar of strength to fragile others in a crisis. In one halfway house a particularly dedicated counselor was a woman of grade school education who had reared her own six children into adulthood, who had strength yet compassion for her own alcoholic son, and who was available to relate with equal-handed warmth and acceptance to others who needed assistance in daily functioning. Supervision provided her with a knowledge base about the residents' illnesses.

Every member of the staff must accept the daily routines of cleaning, shopping, laundering, and cooking as not demeaning to anyone but as absolutely essential to good functioning and to growth. In addition, performance of chores can be viewed as tension reducing and as preparation for more taxing tasks ahead. Residents progress more smoothly with staff who have control over the activities of the house; who spell out clearly what is expected of each resident; what will, or will not, be tolerated; and who make certain that assigned chores are completed or contracts kept. Every staff member must be prepared to demonstrate what he teaches. This clarity of expectation operates most effectively if it is underscored by the director.

Other requirements of a counselor include excellent physical health and high levels of energy combined with resilient spirits. A counselor must be able to survive monitoring a depressed resident at 2 A.M. and still arise at 7 A.M. to assist the entire house to awaken, breakfast, and leave on time to catch a bus for program. A ready smile and a fresh feeling for life are welcome. A counselor must be able to handle intense feelings but always with a clear definition of his own boundaries. Because a group home is an intimate setting, the counselor must satisfy his personal needs elsewhere. Screening for such criteria is, at best, difficult.

The effective counselor has empathy for those who function marginally and in a low-key style, sets small reachable goals which he applauds when achieved, and remotivates when goals are not reached. It is he who establishes the relaxed encouraging atmosphere in the house which permits individuals to progress at their own pace. He needs to generate that degree of intimacy and concern for the welfare of each individual which never becomes intrusive or pressuring. Counselors represent the authority of the agency and, without being authoritative and without the obvious signs of authority, must establish a positive identification with administration. If the counselor makes such a connection, if he understands the rehabilitative aspect of the structure, then the flow of events in a unit moves smoothly. If he is not clear, his management of a group may become antiproductive. The following vignette exemplifies an imperfect understanding and implementation of a rule designed to quiet the house at curfew.

Ada, the counselor, tried to uphold the curfew on telephone calls. Peggy, who had recently moved to a supportive apartment and was not adjusted to life without set limits, called her friend who resided in the halfway house after curfew, thus disturbing all who had gone to sleep. Ada intercepted the call to inform Peggy and her friend that a curfew was in effect. However, in so doing, she permitted Peggy to involve her for the next hour in the problem that motivated the call. She innocently undid the structure she tried to uphold, namely to make certain that the house quieted down so as to encourage a regular sleep-wake cycle.

Although spontaneity is a valued trait in a staff member, emotions must be tempered despite negative interactions or upsetting events. Residents lean heavily on the stability and predictability established by the counselor. In Chapters 2 and 3, the effect of expressed emotion (low or high EE) was explored as it colors the atmosphere of the house. The counselor's reactions can calm a situation or escalate it.

The counselor's low-keyed responses can lighten a depressed reaction which might, if unaddressed, promote decompensation. The resident, returning at night after a discouraging weekend with his family, can be helped considerably over a cup of tea when some positive aspects of the visit can be identified so that the canvas is not all black. ("Your brother did make a 50-mile trip to see you. It is true he has a MBA and you are struggling to finish college, but he must care about you to travel so far.")

If, however, the counselor feels his authority threatened and overreacts, a light-hearted event can quickly escalate, causing massive disruption to the entire household, as the next example demonstrates.

Morris, at curfew, thought a noxious odor emanated from the hall refrigerator adjacent to his bedroom. He involved several men in diagnosing the odor and in speculation about its probable cause. The banter denigrated the housekeeping efforts of the group but remained good-natured. Ede, the counselor, appeared. She reminded the group that the hour was late and some men were already asleep. When the levity continued despite her admonition, she became authoritative and confrontational.

Morris, at this juncture, insisted that the counselor had upset him so gravely he needed a group discussion to examine the event. Feeling her loss of control and the threat to her authority, Ede again reasserted her position in a dogmatic, emotional manner. Morris became angered at Ede's stance. Once Morris's anger started, it became uncontrollable. No man slept that night and many started to feel insecure in the setting. If Ede had not entered into a power struggle with Morris, if she had treated the breaking of the curfew with a sense of humor or made some suggestion which could have put closure on this minor attempt to bend the rules, she might have quickly calmed the group. The agency curfew could have been bent in the service of joining with the men to avoid a no-win tug-of-war.

Because managing a group in a halfway house mimics a new family system, it allows for a variety of personal styles, as evidenced in the following vignette.

> Jennie's style as counselor was clear and precise, with every chore spelled out in detail. She demanded compliance or else readily imposed consequences. Yet she was fair, available when someone needed her, and conscientious about her responsibilities to the group. Enoch fell apart when she left. He missed her meticulous limit setting, which helped organize his anxiety. He could not adjust to Benno, the new counselor's laid-back, softly spoken directions. Whereas Enoch felt alone and isolated in the less directive atmosphere, William blossomed in this more relaxed setting. He had felt that important nuances of his behavior had never been appreciated by Jennie who looked at performance as either acceptable or non-acceptable.
>
> For the entire group, the transition from the rigid, meticulously enunciated program to the permissive one created a brief period of upheaval until a sense of predictability about ongoing expectations could be established in the more tolerant, yet caring management style. Support by the entire staff was called into play to reassure the group during the transition.

Supervision must differentiate between a counselor's permissive style and areas of inexperience or insecurity which training or reframing can alter.

> Residents informed the director that Enoch had slammed a bathroom door four times and kicked at the walls after Benno reminded him that his chores were not done. Since Benno was relatively new to the staff, the director explained to him the importance of sharing such information quickly. Enoch's therapist and the day hospital had to be apprised of such behavior to evaluate whether Enoch was indeed decompensating and should be hospitalized quickly or whether increased medications and exploration of his stress could reduce his angry feelings.
>
> Benno reflected upon the reason he did not spontaneously share his observations. He stated that he had an emotionally ill brother and was perhaps too empathic. He had recognized a few days ago that Enoch was under a great deal of tension. He did not report his observations because he did not feel much could be done to help the young man.
>
> The director emphasized that Enoch was not his brother who was not helped. Moreover, sharing observations did not diminish his ability to manage the unit. She pointed out that the entire staff was available to assist him with Enoch's, or the other men's, reac-

tions to changed supervision. Upset responses from the group were expected whenever staff members were changed. Benno realized how the atmosphere had altered when Jennie left, and recognized that his predecessor had been a strong presence. He was encouraged to be clear in his expectations of the men, to reveal more of his personality.

The director clarified that she did not expect or want him to duplicate Jennie's style. His assets were discussed: his experience with animals, his somewhat different cultural background, and his genuine concern for each resident. The supervisory session further clarified that he and all the residents had a right to be protected from unleashed psychotic behavior and that the sooner such behavior was addressed by Enoch's treatment team, the sooner all would be protected. Such incidents, handled with care, support, and discussion of the dynamics of the illness, provide growth and build a unified team.

Sometimes the strong bond a counselor establishes with a resident also blurs his objectivity in evaluating changed behavior.

Counselor Rena related warmly to Janet, a resident whose sunny, good-natured disposition was a welcome relief to the withdrawal or negativism of others in the group. Janet regularly shared all her romantic misadventures. The interchange was warm and friendly. When Janet stopped taking medications because their ingestion interrupted menses and consequently made her feel unfeminine, Rena could not recognize that Janet was not following conversations, was snapping at others, and had changed her eating and sleeping habits. Fortunately, Janet's roommate shared such observations and concern with the director who alerted Janet's clinical team.

Counselors who are relatively inexperienced frequently feel impelled to discuss in a personal way such inappropriate questions from residents as, "What is your sex life like?" or "Do you enjoy sex?" The resident may be grappling with an emerging interest in such activities. The experienced person can deftly universalize such a question and avoid revealing personal information.

Counselors occasionally do not recognize how desperately residents struggle to determine what is real and what ideas arise from their own confused thoughts. Any mysticism expressed by a counselor, who is an authority figure, can upset the fragile sense of reality of a resident. For example, Cora, a resident who struggled with haunting hallucinations, became frightened when her counselor produced a deck of Tarot cards and proceeded to predict her future.

"Inappropriate and maladaptive staff responses to a specific client are more likely in a halfway house in view of the egalitarian aspect of the program and the sustained proximity of staff to the clients" (Budson, 1979, p. 56). It is a vastly easier task for the professional who sees a resident once or twice a week, for an hour, to accept those who are wearing or excessively demanding. For a live-in counselor, some behaviors may be overly difficult to tolerate. Hence, during the intake process a counselor's negative reaction to a potential resident must be evaluated carefully for possible later impact. Will the counselor consciously or unconsciously be tolerant of a new resident's nonconformance, which may be symptomatic of insecurity in a strange environment? Will she minimize or ignore faltering efforts to adjust or be impatient with acting-out behavior? As mentioned above, these are critical interactions. Difficult as the rehabilitation process is, it is even more an uphill struggle if the counseling staff does not have some measure of sympathy for the underlying pain a resident experiences, even though his method of handling this inner turmoil is self-defeating.

The problem in retaining staff with mixed virtues is great and dependent upon the relationship with the director. Can she help the staff member tolerate infantile or inappropriate behavior without contempt for the negative symptoms of the illness? If the staff member cannot grow with the proffered supervision, she must be asked to leave.

Many halfway houses are strong advocates for the employment within the community of persons who are recovering from a psychiatric illness. Some group homes themselves employ, as counselors, former residents who have been stable for at least three years, who are functional and committed to a career in human services. Such persons frequently bring to the position an extraordinary tolerance, understanding, and acceptance of pathology, and offer deeply felt empathy and patience. Graduates implicitly underscore the philosophy of the agency that progress can be made, even if the pace is slow.

Selected sharing of problems a counselor has surmounted can be utilized to encourage a young person to persist in his efforts to improve his functioning. Such communications must be made with sensitivity and appropriateness lest the residents feel that the counselor is so laden with his own problems that he is not available to tune in to the needs of his charges.

Seven days a week coverage inevitably means that several persons will supervise a unit. Management must ensure that important pieces of structure are known and adhered to by regular and relief staff lest the gains of the week be obliterated on the weekend.

Long weekends often offer temptation to staff to invite their own friends into the house. Here, too, residents frequently feel pushed aside, whether they actually are ignored or not, and resent such persons as intruders.

Agencies that staff their residences more richly may avoid some of the above problems, but may find that the counselors either spend a great deal of time with each other or develop antagonisms. No system employing humans can ever be problem-free, but quick and direct confrontation can minimize undesirable behavior. Most agencies opt for shifts which overlap so that outgoing counselors can report to incoming personnel the special needs of residents and any unanticipated problem or piece of structure which should be encouraged. A well-maintained log which reports activities, moods, and methods of handling a group is an essential tool in providing a sense of continuity to the management of the house.

Volunteers

Some halfway houses have not used volunteers to augment staff, partially because of the resistance of residents who categorically state that the presence of volunteers is too reminiscent of hospital wards. A prime unmet need residents experience—the lack of suburban transportation on weekends—is a service that few volunteers are available to offer. Volunteers are often deemphasized for the additional reason that residents are encouraged to perform as many activities as they can and to utilize as many outside resources as needed to reestablish links to the community and to take increased responsibility for their own actions. Volunteers with such specific skills as bread baking or indoor gardening can be invited to a community meeting to demonstrate techniques.

CONSULTING PSYCHIATRIST

If a halfway house has a strong rehabilitation program, a consulting psychiatrist with his expertise in diagnosing and treating the psychiatrically disabled assists in assessing the more troubled applicant, in tracking the progress of residents in the facility, and in evolving their individualized programs. He meets weekly or biweekly with staff, evaluates residents who are in crisis (see evaluation of Beth, Chapter 6) and acts as a neutral but sympathetic force in examining staff impasses with residents or other staff members. In addition, he serves as a resource person for learning about various medical facilities, acts as an educator in teaching clinical skills and group dynamics or deepening staff's perception of the illnesses served by the house, and shares his knowledge and understanding of prescribed medications and their impact on client behavior.

He is an excellent sounding board for ideas or new directions in rehabilitation initiated by any staff member. He further has the authority to hospitalize a decompensating resident when all other resources fail and the safety of the individual or the security of the group is at risk. Finally, he helps staff with their morale when they are frustrated, angry, or devastated by the suicide of a resident.

STAFF MEETING

Individual supervision and the staff meeting are the ongoing vehicles for training staff and updating knowledge of the field. One problem frequently encountered by agencies is the inability of relief or weekend staff to make themselves available for such sessions so that they, too, can secure support needed to surmount problems and be briefed on planning or new programs. Frequently, part-time personnel are engaged in other employment or school programs which bar regular participation in meetings. Offering compensation for the time spent in staff meetings sometimes brings selected relief workers to such meetings. Those who have tight schedules, however, may never be able to attend.

Minutes of staff meetings distributed to all relief staff, special memoranda on sensitive issues, or designated times for direct supervision become the substitute methods of ensuring communication to absent staff. Thus, they can become aware of changed programs or individualized planning to engage a resident, to move him to a higher level of functioning, or to assist someone who is either in crisis or who could profit from firm adherence to structure.

The meeting is also an excellent time to give plaudits to staff when residents progress or to empathize with frustrations that arise from problems with residents or community agencies. It is also a time to evaluate whether or not the structure or procedures of the facility basically serve the agency's function or its changing needs. It is an opportunity to share information, to problem solve in a group, to air viewpoints and collaborate in programming, to foster staff unity, and to avoid splitting. "Team planning for a client enables staff to guide his move through an increasingly more difficult hierarchy of assignments" (Carling, 1978, p. 56).

The team meeting provides a locus to explore the guilt of staff members which surfaces at those rare times when there is a suicide. The group can help resolve such feelings as, "Could I have done or said anything to have averted this tragedy?" "What clues did I miss?" On other occasions the meeting provides an opportunity for laughter at each other's foibles or at resistant facility dilemmas. Staff meetings may be preceded by luncheon, at which time each participant has an opportunity to share personal happenings, to joke or to enjoy each other's basic humanity.

It is a time to express the deep disappointments a colleague may feel when he has invested heavily for months to promote progress and has achieved some success with a resident only to find that when that person seemed well launched he stumbled, fragmenting all hopes and reverting to helpless dependency. Such volcanic upheavals make staff empathic to the repeated efforts of families who similarly have invested heavily in their ill member's rehabilitation only to find that regression, not progress, was their reward. This is the occasion for all to pull together, to remind the colleague in pain that his clinical skills have been a source of strength and movement to many. It is a time to remind the depressed staff member that "the mere existence of a caring person can become for . . . (the resident) an escape from total despair and any shared closeness a first step toward further progress" (Minkoff & Stern, 1985, p. 864). Such reframing of a setback may prevent the disillusioned staff person from distancing himself emotionally, thus increasing the resident's sense of hopelessness. The presence of a supportive team operates to prevent burnout, the bogey of all intense programs.

Staff growth is a continuous process. Workshops, attendance at grand rounds at local psychiatric hospitals, conferences at day hospitals, case presentations at board meetings, and interaction with board members at annual meetings provide opportunities to expand knowledge, or offer new approaches to daily problems.

A halfway house setting usually attracts persons who have strong feelings for the sufferings of others and for whom gratification and a sense of achievement come from participating in the process by which people grow and move away from pain. The following statement, made by an ex-resident after he had completed his interrupted college degree, summarizes the importance of staff commitment:

> Staff members always had time for me. When you are ill, you feel an urgency about discussing things that concern you. I was never turned away. There was a strong feeling of staff being on my side, rooting for me, as when I was able to be off medication. I felt that people were saying, "That's the way to go!" If the staff were just people doing their job and not into it with their hearts, I might not have gotten better.

CHAPTER 13

The Board of Directors

Halfway houses are usually "begun by organizations which sought out individuals to carry through and staff a project conceptualized by the organization's leaders" (Raush & Raush, 1968, p. 51). An alternative format is for local mental health associations, rehabilitation organizations, or a consortium of several social agencies to found halfway houses to service a local region.

A board of directors is given the "legal, corporate authority and responsibility for an organization's institutionalization and operation, for its stability, and for provision of systematic linkages with other organizations and parts of the social system" (Guide for Board Organization in Social Agencies, 1975, p. 1). A board functions as a final authority in an agency and as a policymaker which establishes the direction, growth, and target group served. It "assigns priorities and ensures the agency's capability of carrying out the program by continually reviewing the work of the agency" (p. 3). Every board must be accountable to the people it serves, its funding sources, and the community. It should always reflect current needs and operate as spokesmen for its clientele. It must, therefore, provide for continuing evaluation of the agency's effectiveness, efficiency, and achievement under the leadership of the director it selects and to whom it delegates the responsibility for carrying out general policy directives, hiring, training, and supervising staff.

The present era is one of escalating litigation when private, not-for-profit agencies have lost their time-honored "charitable immunity" and, along with pediatricians, orthopedists, and other professional groups, are targeted for legal damages in the event of financial losses, injuries, or suicides. It is more important than ever that "board members . . . insist on being fully briefed, both orally and in writing, regarding the requirements of their position" (Zelman, 1977, p. 271). Board members must set aside sufficient time to attend board meetings so that they are active and aware of all important decisions. In the event that they oppose a course of action, they must make a record of such disagreement. The greater legal vulnerability of board members may mean that, in the future, boards of directors will define very precisely the exact scope of a director's authority and will hold executive officers accountable for performing delegated duties only as defined. In addition, boards will insist that these officers not exceed their authority.

To be duly diligent, board members will be required to read carefully all minutes of meetings they did not attend and not merely file such documents away as they did when not-for-profit agencies enjoyed "special status" as charitable agencies immune to litigation. Financial statements, contracts with state or county governments, leases, and personnel policies must be understood and thoroughly scrutinized, since members of the board can be held liable for any financial irregularities or unfulfilled obligations.

Since the courts have chipped away at the concept of "charitable immunity," board members must now become more involved in day-to-day operations of their agencies, an area in which they may have had little previous experience. "This, of course, will greatly affect the individual social worker, whose practices will come under increasing scrutiny" (Zelman, 1977, p. 273). Aside from due diligence and prudence in exercising duties, boards of directors are purchasing liability insurance and are seeking "legal advice whenever they are doubtful about the legal ramifications of their actions" (p. 274). This extension of responsibility has made it increasingly more difficult to recruit competent persons to serve on boards. As a response to broadened responsibility and escalating insurance costs, one state (New York) added a new section 720-a to chapter 220 of the Not-For-Profit Corporation Law. This section grants immunity for officers and directors of not-for-profit corporations holding operating certificates from the Office of Mental Health, provided such officers and directors serve without compensation and act within the scope of their duties. The law does not exempt from liability conduct that constitutes "gross negligence" or actions which cause "intentional infliction of harm."

Since the board is expected to provide adequate funding for its program, it recruits members who can "bring influence and affluence to insure that the agencies . . . are adequately funded" (Guide for Board Organization in Social Agencies, 1975, p. VIII) and who can interpret to the community the nature and effect of services and act as advocates for the unmet needs of those served. Boards should represent all strata of society and should reflect a diversity of professions, interests, and skills. Nominating committees usually try to incorporate a cross-section of such technically skilled persons as accountants, engineers, lawyers, and doctors to serve either as board members or as consultants for specific problem areas. Expertise within the board in several key areas can reduce the cost of needed services or, if these are too time-consuming, board members can act as resource persons for the procurement of specialists.

Recent philosophy has evolved a strong argument for representation of consumers on the board. The inclusion of recovered former residents or family members of ill persons often meets this standard. But the presence of staff members on the board of directors raises many questions: "In general, if the board is to act objectively, it must be shielded from constituency pressures. Boards must be assured that their members have no personal stake in the outcome of decisions, are free from conflict of interest, are impartial, and have as their only concern the overall interests of the agency" (Guide for Board Organization in Social Agencies, 1975, p. X). For special circumstances, staff members often serve jointly with board members on ad hoc committee assignments which call for close collaboration.

In addition to policy formation, fund raising, and fiscal management, the board of directors serves as an important interpreter of the functioning, needs, achievement, and philosophy of its agency. The more effective its outreach in telling and retelling the story of its efforts to provide a normal environment for its recovering residents, the more effective it may be in opening up employment possibilities and housing opportunities, in raising funds, or in dispelling stigma in the community, especially in the workplace and the housing market.

Frequent meetings between the board president and director of the agency are essential to maintain channels of communication about goals of the agency and their translation into daily practice. Board members can plan visits to the facility, eat an occasional meal there, or meet with the residents at community meetings. Residents in halfway houses are curious about board members, eager to interact with them and to discuss their struggles with the community or their employment dilemmas. Many residents, as they grow healthier, are eager to make contributions to the board and to society at large. Often "graduates" of a halfway house volunteer to utilize their contacts or skills to assist in fund-raising campaigns. Residents also volunteer to address local civic groups for such purposes. Others, recovered sufficiently to be employed, contribute small amounts of money, anonymously, to the agency.

Early in the history of the halfway house movement, an aura of disgrace clung to those who suffered from mental illness. Consequently, board members understandably were concerned that persons served by the halfway house remain anonymous to all in the community, including the board. With more acceptance and wider knowledge of mental illness and with intense efforts of advocacy leagues and family members to interpret the misconception that violent or criminal behavior constantly lurks in the shadows, such impressions have been somewhat dispelled. As bias has slowly eroded, more interchange has transpired between board members and residents in some halfway houses. When residents interchange with board members, such contacts have been beneficial both to board members who have learned by direct contact that their efforts and policies produce results and to residents who form new linkages to a caring group.

The time-honored case presentation by staff is another method of systematically providing dialogue between staff and board and introducing them to each other. Such interchanges ensure that board members, especially new recruits, are knowledgeable about the illnesses the agency serves and are fully aware of the vicissitudes of rehabilitation efforts experienced daily by staff. Some presentations focus on the new resident's lengthy process of adjustment to the house; others chart the stages of a resident's growth from the transitional house to the supportive apartments and out into the community at large.

New members of a board are routinely briefed by the director on the organization of the halfway house, its staff, its goals, its fiscal responsibilities, and community problems. They are invited to tour the facility, usually when the residents are engaged in their outside programs. They are offered an opportunity to meet the residents at a community meeting. Some board members accept these invitations to exchange information about the board organization and personnel and in turn hear firsthand accounts about residents' problems in reentering the community. Others have described interesting trips to foreign countries or halfway houses visited elsewhere. All such interaction serves to reduce the mystique of mental illness so that the board members can more effectively advocate for the population they serve.

Many states dictate that community advisory boards be established in each area in which a facility is located. These boards are recruited from local officials, tradesmen, and neighborhood residents. Such groups, when thoroughly briefed about the work of the organization, can become powerful interpreters to skeptics about the impact of a facility on the life of the neighborhood. When a new site in a resistant area is targeted for the establishment of a halfway house, the advisory committee is frequently the vehicle for promoting a forum for discussion, or arranging open houses to answer questions or to alleviate doubts about possible deterioration of real estate values or danger to the neighborhood. On an ongoing basis, advisory boards have used their knowledge of local resources to channel residents to the friendly druggist for prescriptions, to provide free passes to theaters, concerts, and recreational facilities, or to reassure concerned neighbors about their safety.

At the time of salary negotiations, it is the task of the director to inform and educate the board, via the personnel committee, as to the importance of an agency's staff to the ongoing effectiveness and tranquility of life in a residence. Board must be aware that staff morale depends upon many factors, such as size of caseloads, opportunities for growth, working conditions and, most important, adequate, competitive compensation for educational qualifications, skills, and years of service. Members of the board have the duty, and should have the commitment, to learn how draining a decompensating person can become, especially for that staff member who is kept up late at night or is aroused at 3 A.M. The staff member is expected to keep the resident community calm and summon needed help or resources for the ill person while remaining composed and reassuring.

Good practice dictates that a staff member, well versed in the ongoing program and sufficiently secure in his ability to interchange with authority, serve on a personnel committee as a spokesman for his fellow employees. The director and staff member should be equipped to provide the committee with comparable salary scales of selected agencies performing similar functions so that staff's agenda may be viewed in broad context. Negotiations are best resolved when the board is convinced of the staff's identification with the objectives of the program, and of their professional expertise. Providing for stability and growth of staff must be a board concern if it is to maintain and improve the quality of service. In some areas of the country, the higher salary scale of the state employee is an ever-present threat to the longevity of personnel in the not-for-profit agency and this differential must be dealt with in state-approved and mandated budgets if rehabilitation in small, not-for-profit agencies is to be effective and the agencies themselves are to survive.

Long-range community focused planning naturally rests with an informed board which remains active and alert through participation in local political and social organizations. Board members must sensitively tune into unmet, shifting community needs to assess whether change or additional programs should be developed.

CHAPTER 14
Conclusion

The developmental/rehabilitative community residence model as described in these pages is highly flexible. It can serve populations with a broad spectrum of disabilities and maturational lags, from the client who needs help getting out of bed in the morning to the person who has tremendous drive but little ability to harness or direct it. The residence program can be grossly modified for higher- or lower-functioning groups of residents or finely tuned to respond to differences in functioning within a client group. Its program can be as intensely applied as that of a residential treatment center, using the broad ecosystem as an integral part of the milieu, or it can be simply a structure and support—a warm place to live with a new kinship group—if such is the need of a particular resident.

It is this flexibility that makes the community residence model so uniquely responsive to the needs of an individual resident and to the treatment plan of that resident's therapist. The expertise of the community residence staff not only reinforces the thrust of the therapy but, as stated earlier, can add immensely to the therapist's knowledge of his patient's functioning and of the patient's responses to stress and change.

As indicated in research cited in prior chapters, those persons who live in community residences experience fewer and briefer rehospitalizations and more positive adjustments to community life in human and economic terms than do those persons who are discharged from psychiatric hospitals directly back into the community. These positive outcomes carry over through the supportive apartment program, through the aftercare program and beyond, as ex-residents use their new or renewed skills of living and working and the social networks they develop in the residence program to improve their lives in the community. Therefore, the community and the individual patient are best served if there is transitional housing available to those with all degrees of psychiatric disabilities, acute and chronic.

The community residence model presented here has been tailored to the higher-functioning patient who may go on to vocational training and then to employment, or who may be able eventually to move on to independent living. (Yet, as noted above, this model is flexible enough to accommodate to those persons whose illness takes a more chronic course while in residence.) However, this is not the model that is presently being promoted both politically and in the mental health field.

In the political spectrum, the most visible problem tends to create the most pressure for change. In the last two decades, effort has appropriately, although never adequately, been directed toward helping the chronically ill move from long-term care in the state hospital to life in the community. This effort continues as seen in the recent thrust to develop the RCCA (Resident Congregate Care for Adults) facilities in New York State. However, the RCCA may not offer a quality of life substantially different than its future residents are now experiencing in the state hospital, and may be less richly staffed. Whether the RCCA can motivate its residents to better functioning any more successfully than has the state hospital is still an open question.

The numbers of homeless in the United States will continue to grow in response to current social, economic, and political forces. Neighborhood gentrification and reduced government support for new and rehabilitated housing have greatly diminished housing stock for the poor and disabled. Cutbacks in social programs, which had provided food and financial and medical benefits, coupled with pressures resulting from economic recessions and industrial shutdowns, have pulled remaining supports from under marginal populations, many of whom have dropped into the ranks of the homeless. The crisis of the homeless warrants all the attention and resources being directed to its relief and begs for new and creative approaches to resolve these problems.

In an effort to provide solutions to the pressing problems of the institutionalized and homeless chronically ill, however, legislators and administrators are failing to note and evaluate the implications of the buildup of another pressure—those psychiatrically ill who appear to be higher-functioning and who may have some capacities and support system, but who flounder because of their inability to use these assets. This group is in danger of losing its residential supports and of falling, therefore, deeper into psychological and social maladaptation. It is essential that community residences be available as well for the higher-functioning acute and/or chronically psychiatrically disabled in order to prevent or diminish the scope of a downward spiral in functioning which, if untreated, may eventually end in institutionalization or homelessness. Each episode of illness, each breakdown, each loss of job, of relationships, and of continuity, each hospitalization takes a toll. The ill person suffers a loss of energy, esteem, and resilience with each episode and finds it more difficult to recover to previous levels of functioning, to begin life again.

When research clearly indicates the efficacy of community residential care in preventing or decreasing the episodes of illness and in improving the quality of life in the community, of functioning and of self-esteem, it is foolish, expensive, and tantamount to mental health malpractice for legislators and administrators to direct all community residence efforts to the care of only the low-functioning and minimal effort or resources to preventive and restorative care for the higher-functioning mentally ill. This latter group, if appropriately treated, has the potential to achieve full employment and to be economically self-supporting instead of living a lifetime on SSI (Supplementary Security Income).

Leighton (1982) notes that, historically, efforts to treat and prevent mental illness have been plagued by inadequate staffing and insufficient funding, conditions that still prevail and probably always will. For this reason, Leighton recommends developing "priorities based on such criteria as those diagnostic categories which are the most treatable, those which are most disabling, and those which have the highest rate of prevalence. In this way, it should be possible to ensure that treatable conditions get treated, particularly those which are disabling, and that persons with severe chronic disturbances that respond little to treatment nevertheless get the social supports which would serve to moderate their sufferings and the difficulties faced by their families and others around them" (p. 5).

An example of the insufficiency and irrationality of funding for the mentally ill is the Supplemental Security Income (SSI) classification placing transitional rehabilitative housing in the same Level II category as adult homes "that are custodial-care facilities with different needs, philosophy, requirements, and therapeutic goals. This fundamental act has seriously damaged the proper development of community residences, since the funding is inadequate" (Easton, 1978, p. 921).

Most not-for-profit community residences operate on prohibitively restrictive budgets and are frequently allocated lower amounts for staffing and capital expenses than are state-operated facilities. Not-for-profit agencies are thus at a competitive disadvantage in attracting and keeping competent staff, and are not able to provide adequate supportive housing to residents once they leave the halfway house. Innovative housing initiatives are needed for the chronically ill homeless and for those adults who are moving out of halfway houses and supportive apartments, but who are unable to afford or find adequate housing.

Housing insurance, organized on the principal of health insurance, may be one alternative funding resource for the disabled. Another initiative is the requirement that developers allocate apartments for the handicapped in every building constructed with the aid of state or federal funding. This second requirement has provided only a small number of units, however, in these years of shrinking federal involvement in new building.

The collaboration of small not-for-profit agencies with local, state, and federal government funding offices has provided the most creative recent housing innovations. Westhab, a Hartsdale, New York-based housing and development agency, has combined funds from the New York State Homeless Housing Assistance Program and private resources to renovate and refurbish buildings for homeless tenants (McCoy, 1985). Westhab has also joined with the Westchester County Social Services Department to establish emergency housing apartments in a unique arrangement by which the building's landlord receives higher-than-market rents to reserve apartments for homeless tenants but agrees to use the extra income for building repairs, and to continue to rent to such tenants for a specified time period after the repairs are completed (McCoy, 1985).

The City of Portland, Oregon, has used U.S. Department of Housing and Urban Development "Section 8" funds in combination with state, city, and private resources to rehabilitate old SRO hotels into safe and supportive shelters for homeless, alcoholic, and mentally ill Portlanders. As of November, 1985, 114 emergency cots and 917 SRO rooms were in use at a fraction of the usual cost of HUD rehabilitation. This "hierarchy of SROs, from the emergency shelter up to beautifully painted and maintained facilities" (Pierce, 1985, p. A12), enables people to move to more desirable housing as their functioning improves. Moreover, this project has also provided paid employment to those tenants who are interested and able to work as facility managers.

As noted in Chapter 1, the recent federal efforts to conserve funds expended on the inpatient care of the physically and mentally ill, as represented by DRG and PRO utilization review strategies, will inevitably hasten the trend toward briefer psychiatric hospitalizations. These developments increase the need for transitional housing for those unable to return to their former living situations. They also exacerbate the noxious revolving-door syndrome experienced by so many patients who barely reach stability in the hospital and are discharged, only to return quickly, when unable to accommodate to the community.

Young adult chronic patients who suffer from major psychiatric illness and/or severe personality disorders and/or substance abuse are a group who experience the revolving-door syndrome, not only in hospitalizations but also in movement from one community program to another—day hospitals, vocational rehabilitation agencies, and so forth. This is the group described in earlier chapters whose growth process has been interrupted by their illnesses, whose development is slowed, and who lack essential interpersonal skills. These young people require a stable, supportive environment in which to continue their growth, learn the skills which will enable them to interact positively with others at home and at work, tolerate frustration, and resolve conflict around issues of autonomy and authority, and so forth. But the young chronic patient is often "an elusive and therefore service-deprived person" (Pepper & Ryglewicz, 1985a, p. 3) who needs "programs—both treatment and residential—that have a dynamic developmental thrust appropriate to their age and adaptive to their hopes and goals. If there is one key to the failure thus far of most treatment as well as residential programs to engage and maintain these younger clients as effectively as desired, that key is the lack until recently of recognition of the age-appropriate and age-related characteristics, needs and interests of this younger client population" (Pepper & Ryglewicz, 1985a, p. 1). Comprehensive developmental and rehabilitative residential care is a vital resource to anchor this young, mobile adult population to their community treatment programs and to assist their therapists in treatment.

We repeat here some key principles which would distinguish a superior residential system of care for the mentally ill:

1. A multilevel residential spectrum to service all degrees of illness from the severely chronic to the high-functioning, those who need long-term or permanent care and those who need a brief, transitional program.
2. Several levels of care within the same residential facility, enabling the client to move from greater to lesser degrees of care and the reverse, as needed. Each residence is small, familylike, and supportive of some degree of social intimacy: halfway houses accommodating ideally six to eight residents but no more than 15, and supportive apartments no more than three or four.
3. It appears helpful to residents to encourage a mix of personalities, levels of development, types of behavioral, social, vocational difficulties. The mixture of more active and less active, compliant and assertive, makes for richer complementary interaction in a setting where residents can contrast their assets and deficits with those of their peers and offer help and support to each other.

However, if the range of functional capacity is too broad, the group tends to be pulled to the lowest denominator, sapping the ability of the higher functioning to propel themselves forward. Normalization is enhanced when attention is given to grouping residents within a prescribed range of functioning.

4. Each residence is to offer a developmental, rehabilitative program working in cooperation with all facets of the residents' ecosystems—therapists, day treatment centers, clinics, vocational and recreational resources, etc. As noted earlier, the number of rehabilitative skills taught in the residence should be limited; otherwise, residents tend to withdraw emotionally from the program, feeling the residence isn't a home but an institution.

5. If vocational services provided in the community ecosystem are of poor quality or in poor supply, the residence should not hesitate to secure its own vocational counseling staff to assist residents in developing work skills and formulating vocational plans, and to undertake assertive outreach into the community to develop employment sites, protected and competitive, including the model of supported employment as discussed in Chapter 3. In comprehensive rehabilitation programs, such as Knoedler's Program of Assertive Community Treatment (see Chapter 3), 50% of all professional and nonprofessional staff time is devoted to the development of work skills in the client group.*

6. A full aftercare program offers continued support, including respite beds and a source of social network to all alumni.

7. The community residence is an important component of the community support *team* (which replaces the single case manager), definitely during time of residence and when feasible for a period after discharge.

8. More collaborative research studies must be initiated by psychiatric hospitals and community residences to isolate as much as possible in this imperfect science those variables that are associated with effective care. Concurrently, more research is needed on the national level to focus on the etiologies and treatments of the major psychiatric illnesses.

9. The family can be the best support group for the psychiatrically disabled person if destructive patterns of dependency can be broken and if the son or daughter can reintegrate into the family so that members have different and more mature expectations of each other. When the family can provide a permanent home to the patient, the number of residential care facilities can be reduced. The community residence, as noted in Chapter 9, may function as the transitional facility which helps the resident grow and family

---

*Knoedler, W. (9/21/85) Speech delivered at the Third Annual Educational Conference of the Alliance for the Mentally Ill of New York State.

members adjust to the point where they can live together positively.

10. A strong organization such as the National Alliance for the Mentally Ill can advocate in the political arena for broader community attention, and funding for the unmet needs of the psychiatrically disabled. It can also provide information and support to consumers of mental health services and to their families.

Historically, community residences have reflected the unique needs of their communities and the personalities of their founding boards and directors. They have been small and individual, incorporating a variety of philosophies and operational techniques, attracting staff who are creative and untraditional and thus on the forefront of experiment and change. This flexibility and versatility have been crucial to the success of the community residence experience in reducing rates and lengths of rehospitalizations and in improving the quality of personal and community life for those who have come under their care.

Bibliography

Alpert, M., Blohm, T., Cotter, J., Grady, K., & Kresky, M. (1971). *A follow-up study of two psychiatric halfway houses in Washington, D. C.* Unpublished Masters Thesis, Catholic University of America.

American Psychiatric Association (1980). *Diagnostic and statistical manual of mental disorders (DSM-III) (3rd edition).* Washington, D.C.: American Psychiatric Association.

American Psychiatric Association (1987). *Diagnostic and statistical manual of mental disorders (DSM-III-R) (3rd edition, revised).* Washington, D. C.: American Psychiatric Association.

Anderson, C. M., Hogarty, G. E., & Reiss, D. J. (1980). Family treatment of adult schizophrenic patients: A psycho-educational approach. *Schizophrenia Bulletin, 6* (3), 490–505.

Anderson, C., & Stewart, S. (1983). *Mastering resistance: A practical guide to family therapy.* New York: Guilford Press.

Anthony, W. A. (1979). *The principles of psychiatric rehabilitation.* Baltimore: University Park Press.

Anthony, W. A., Cohen, M., & Cohen, B. F. (1983). Philosophy, treatment process, and principles of the psychiatric rehabilitation approach. *New Directions in Mental Health, 17,* 67–79.

Anthony, W. A., Cohen, M. R. & Farkas, M. (1982). A psychiatric rehabilitation treatment program: Can I recognize one if I see one? *Community Mental Health Journal, 18,* 83–95.

Anthony, W. A., & Margules, A. (1974). Toward improving the efficacy of psychiatric rehabilitation: A skills training approach. *Rehabilitation Psychology, 21,* 101–105.

Arieti, S. (1980). Psychotherapy of schizophrenia: New or revised procedures. *American Journal of Psychotherapy, XXXIV* (4), 464–476.

Atwood, N. (1985). Forgotten therapist? *Hospital & Community Psychiatry, 36* (4), 410.

Bakos, M., Bozic, R., Chapin, D., Gandrus, J., Kahn, S., Mateer, W., & Neuman,

S. (1979). Group homes: A study of community residential environments. Ohio Department of Mental Health and Mental Retardation.

Becker, E. (1973). *The denial of death*. New York: The Free Press.

Bellamy, G., O'Connor, G., & Karan, O. (Eds.) (1979). Vocational rehabilitation of severely handicapped persons. Baltimore: University Park Press.

Berman, N., & Hoppe, W. (1976). Halfway house residents: Where do they go? *Journal of Community Psychology, 4* (3), 259–260.

Bowden, C. L. (1985). Current treatment of depression. *Hospital & Community Psychiatry, 36* (11), 1192–1200.

Bowers, M. B. Jr. (1974). *Retreat from sanity: The structure of emerging psychosis.* New York: Human Sciences Press.

Brown, G. W., Birley, J. L. T., & Wing, J. K. (1972). Influence of family life on the course of schizophrenic disorders: A replication. *British Journal of Psychiatry, 121*, 241–258.

Budson, R. D. (1978). *The psychiatric halfway house: A handbook of theory and practice*. Pittsburgh: University of Pittsburgh Press.

Budson, R. D. (1979). Consultation to halfway houses. Mental health consultations in community settings. *New directions for mental health services, 3,* 41–57. San Francisco, Washington, London: Jossey-Bass.

Budson, R. D., Grob, M. C., & Singer, J. E. (1977). A follow-up study of Berkely House—A psychiatric halfway house. *International Journal of Social Psychiatry, 23* (3), 120–131.

Budson, R. D., & Jolley, R. E. (1978). A crucial factor in community program success: The extended psychosocial kinship system. *Schizophrenia Bulletin, 4* (4), 609–621.

Campbell, M. E. (1981). The three-quarterway house: A step beyond halfway house toward independent living. *Hospital & Community Psychiatry, 32* (7), 500–501.

Carling, P. J. (1978). Residential services in a psychosocial rehabilitation context: The Horizon House model. In J. Goldmeier, F. V. Mannino & M. F. Shore (Eds.), *New directions in mental health care: Cooperative apartments*. Adelphi, MD: Mental Health Study Center (DHEW Publication #ADM-78-685).

Carpenter, W. (1978). Residential placement for the chronic psychiatric patient: A review and evaluation of the literature. *Schizophrenia Bulletin, 4* (3), 384–397.

Christ, W., & Gitelson, A. (1983). *Diagnostic related groups—Threat or challenge to social work?* Unpublished manuscript. New York Hospital-Cornell Medical Center, Westchester Division.

Cohen, P. (1984). Community support system evaluation program for fiscal year 7/1/1983–6/30/1984. A report on studies of CSS programs and issues, *III*. New York State Psychiatric Institute.

Compton, B. R., & Galaway, B. (1976). *Social work processes* (Revised Edition). Homewood, IL: Dorsey Press.

Cotton, P. G., Drake, R. E., & Gates, C. (1985). Critical treatment issues in suicide among schizophrenics. *Hospital & Community Psychiatry, 36* (5), 534–536.

Coulton, J., Fitch, V., & Holland, T. P. (1985). A typology of social environments in community care homes. *Hospital & Community Psychiatry, 36* (4), 373–377.

Dellario, D. J. (1982). On the evaluation of community-based alternative living arrangements (ALAs) for the psychiatrically disabled. *Psychosocial Rehabilitation Journal, V* (1), 35–39.

Di Bella, G. A. W., Weitz, G. W., Poynter-Berg, D., & Yurmark, J. L. (1982). *Handbook of partial hospitalization*. New York: Brunner/Mazel.

Dixon V. Weinberger, 1974, 495 F 2nd 202.

Doane, J. A., Falloon, I. R. H., Goldstein, J. M., & Mintz, J. (1985). Parental affective style and the treatment of schizophrenia. *Archives of General Psychiatry, 42,* 34–42.

Easton, K. (May, 1978). Community residential programs for the mentally ill. *New York State Journal of Medicine,* 920–922.

Fairweather, G. W., Sanders, D. H., & Maynard, J. (1969). *Community life for the mentally ill: An alternative to institutional care.* Chicago: Aldine.

Fontana, A. F., Lewis, E., Klein, E. B., & Levine, L. (1968). Presentation of self in mental illness: Predicting course of illness and mental functioning. *Journal of Consulting and Clinical Psychology, 32* (2), 110–119.

Fountain House. (1974). *Progress report for 1974.* (Pamphlet.) New York: Fountain House.

Frances, A., Clarkin, J., & Perry, S. (1984). *Differential therapeutics in psychiatry: The art & science of treatment selection.* New York: Brunner/Mazel.

Futura House. (1985). Halfway House Pamphlet, White Plains, New York.

General Accounting Office (GAO). (1977). *Returning the mentally disabled to the community: Government needs to do more.* Washington, D. C.: Comptroller General of the United States.

Germain, C. B. (June, 1973). An ecological perspective in casework practice. *Social Casework, 54,* 323–330.

Germain, C. B. (1984). *Social work practice in health care: An ecological view.* New York: Free Press.

Gitterman, A. (1983). Uses of resistance: A transactional view. *Social Work, 28,* 127–131.

Gitterman, A., & Germain, C. B. (1976). Social work practice: A life model. *Social Service Review,* The University of Chicago, *50,* 601–610.

Glasscote, R., Cumming, E., Rutman, S., Sussex, J., & Glassman, S. (1971). *Rehabilitating the mentally ill in the community.* Washington, D. C.: The Joint Information Service of the American Psychiatric Association and the National Association for Mental Health.

Glasscote, R., Gudeman, J., & Elpers, R. (1971). *Halfway houses for the mentally ill.* Washington, D. C.: The Joint Information Service of the American Psychiatric Association and the National Association for Mental Health.

Goldstein, J. M., Cohen, P., Lewis, S., & Struening, E. (1984). Treatment environments: Effects of specific and non-specific ingredients on perceptions of outcome. A report on studies of CSS programs and issues by the Community Support Systems Evaluation Program of New York State Psychiatric Institute, for fiscal year July 1, 1983–June 30, 1984. *III,* 1–23.

Goldstein, J. M., & Phil, M. (1984). Conceptual issues in the definition of course of schizophrenia. A report on studies of CSS programs and issues by the Community Support Systems Evaluation Program of New York State Psychiatric Institute for the fiscal year July 1, 1983–June 30, 1984. *III,* CSS 1–23.

Golomb, A. L. (1984). The psychodynamics of anorexia nervosa and bulimia. Unpublished doctoral dissertation, Michigan State University.

Gomez, E. A. (1978). Small supportive treatment units and the problem of recidivism in indigent chronic schizophrenic patients. *Psychiatric Quarterly, 50* (3), 211–217.

Goodwin, F. (1984). Recent research in manic depression and schizophrenia. *The Newsletter of the Alliance for the Mentally Ill of New York State, 5* (12), 6.

Group for the Advancement of Psychiatry (1986). *A family affair: Helping families cope with mental illness—A guide for the professions* (Report #119). New York: Brunner/Mazel.

Gruenberg, E. (1982). Social breakdown in young adults: Keeping crises from becoming chronic. In B. Pepper & H. Ryglewicz (Eds.), *The young adult chronic patient, 14*, 43–50. San Francisco: Jossey-Bass.

Guide for board organization in social agencies. (1975). Child Welfare League of America, Inc. (revised edition). New York.

The Gutman House report. (1962–1965). Portland: Mental Health Association of Oregon.

Haier, R. J. (1980). The diagnosis of schizophrenia: A review of recent developments. *Special Report: Schizophrenia 1980* (pp. 2–13). Rockville, MD: National Institute of Mental Health.

Halmi, K. A. (1984). Anorexia nervosa. In M. Green & R. Haggerty (Eds.), *Ambulatory pediatrics, III* (pp. 267–273). New York: W. B. Saunders.

Harding, C. (1984). Hope, rational optimism, and empowerment. University of Vermont. (Unpublished monograph.)

Hendin, H. (1986). Suicide: A review of new directions in research. *Hospital & Community Psychiatry, 37* (2), 148–154.

Hierholzer, R. W., & Liberman, R. P. (1986). Successful living: A social skills and problem-solving group for the chronic mentally ill. *Hospital & Community Psychiatry, 37* (9), 913–918.

Holman, T., & Shore, M. F. (1978). Halfway house and family involvement as related to community adjustment for ex-residents of a psychiatric halfway house. *Journal of Community Psychology, 6* (2), 123–129.

Holzman, P. S., Shenton, M. E., & Solovay, M. R. (1986). Quality of thought disorder in differential diagnosis. *Schizophrenia Bulletin, 12* (3), 360–371.

Hospitals (1984). Management rounds, patient care services, *58* (15), 52.

Howe, C. (1984). Breakthrough-NIMH test may detect depression. *The Newsletter of the National Alliance for the Mentally Ill, 5* (5), 3.

Hull, J. T., & Thompson, J. C. (1981). Factors which contributed to normalization in residential facilities for the mentally ill. *Community Mental Health Journal, 17* (2), 107–113.

Joint Commission on Mental Illness and Health. (1961). *Action for mental health.* New York: Basic Books.

Jones, M. (1953). *Therapeutic community.* New York: Basic Books.

Knoedler, W. H. (1979). How the training in Community Living Program helps patients work. *New Directions for Mental Health Services, 2*, 57–66.

Kruzich, J., & Kruzich, S. (1985). Milieu factors influencing patients' integration into community residential facilities. *Hospital & Community Psychiatry, 36* (4), 378–382.

Lamb, H. R. (1976). Assessment of various residential programs for the mentally ill and disabled, presentation of a viewpoint. In *Community living arrangements for the mentally ill* (pp. 19–23). Rockville, MD: National Institute of Mental Health.

Lamb, H. R., & Goertzel, V. (June, 1977). The long-term patient in the era of community treatment. *Archives of General Psychiatry, 34*, 679–682.

Landy, D., & Greenblatt, M. (1965). *Halfway house: A socio-cultural and clinical study of Rutland Corner House, a transitional aftercare residence for female psychiatric patients.* Washington, D.C.: U.S. Government Printing Office, Department of Health, Education & Welfare, Vocational Rehabilitation Administration.

Lanin-Kettering, L., & Harrow, M. (1985). The thought behind the words: A view of schizophrenic speech and thinking disorders. *Schizophrenia Bulletin, 11* (1), 1–7.

Leighton, A. H. (1982). A recurrent millennium: The cure and prevention of mental illness. *Canada's Mental Health, 30* (2), 2–5.

Liberman, R. P. (1982). Assessment of social skills. *Schizophrenia Bulletin, 8* (1), 62–83.

Liberman, R. P., Massel, H. K., Mosk, M. D., & Wong, S. E. (1985). Social skills training for chronic mental patients. *Hospital & Community Psychiatry, 36* (4), 396–403.

Lieberman, C. (1979). Schizoaffective illness defies the dichotomy . . . And keeps DSM-III pondering. *Schizophrenia Bulletin, 5* (3), 430–440.

Lipton, F., Sabatini, A., & Katz, S. (1983). Down and out in the city: The homeless mentally ill. *Hospital & Community Psychiatry, 34* (9), 817–821.

London, D. B., & Docherty, J. P. (1979). How to manage the stages of psychiatric illness. *Behavioral Medicine, 6,* 29–37.

Lynch, V. J., Budson, R. D., & Jolley, R. E. (1977). Meeting the needs of former residents of a halfway house. *Hospital & Community Psychiatry, 28,* 585.

Lyons, R. (1984). How release of mental patients began. *The New York Times,* October 30, p. C4.

Mackinnon, R., & Michels, R. (1971). *Psychiatric interview in clinical practice.* Philadelphia: W. B. Saunders.

Matorin, S., & De Chillo, W. (December, 1984). Psychopharmacology: Guidelines for social workers. *Social Casework,* 579–589.

McCoy, K. (1985). Help on the way for homeless, but some say it's not enough. White Plains, New York: Gannett Westchester Newspaper, March 20, p. A1.

McCreath, J. (1984). The new generation of chronic psychiatric patients. *Social Work, 29* (5), 436–441.

Meissner, W. W. (1981). The schizophrenic and the paranoid process. *Schizophrenia Bulletin, 7* (4), 611–631.

Miles, C. P. (1983). Thoughts on "Expressed Emotion" and other research. *The Newsletter of the National Alliance for the Mentally Ill, 4* (5), 1–6.

Minkoff, K., Bergman, E., Beck, A. T., et al. (1973). Hopelessness, depression, and attempted suicide. *American Journal of Psychiatry, 130,* 455–459.

Minkoff, K., & Stern, R. (1985). Paradoxes faced by residents being trained in psychosocial treatment of people with chronic schizophrenia. *Hospital & Community Psychiatry, 36* (8), 859–864.

Mosher, L. R., & Keith, S. J. (1980). Psychosocial treatment: Individual, group, family, and community support approaches. *Schizophrenia 1980* (pp. 127–158). Rockville, MD: National Institute of Mental Health.

Neffinger, G. G., & Schiff, J. W. (1982). Treatment by objectives: A partial hospital treatment program. In B. Pepper & H. Ryglewicz (Eds.), The young adult chronic patient, *New Directions for Mental Health Services* (14) (pp. 77–83). San Francisco, Washington, London: Jossey-Bass.

Nelson, B. (1983). Nation's psychiatrists give high priority to the homeless. *New York Times,* May 10, pp. C1–C2.

Nielson, G. (1983). *Borderline and acting-out adolescents: A developmental approach.* New York: Human Sciences Press.

Ornstein, P. (1979). Remarks on the central position of empathy in psychoanalysis. *Bulletin of the Association of Psychoanalytic Medicines, 18,* 95–108.

Pepper, B. (1984). The young adult chronic patient and the high-EE/low-EE climate. In B. Pepper and H. Ryglewicz (Eds.), *Tie Lines, I,* 4.

Pepper, B. (1985). Where (and how) should young adult chronic patients live? The concept of a residential spectrum. *Tie Lines, II* (2), 1–8.

Pepper, B., & Ryglewicz, H. (Eds.) (1982). The young adult chronic patient. *New Directions for Mental Health Services, 14,* San Francisco, Washington, London: Jossey-Bass.

Pepper, B., & Ryglewicz, H. (1984a). Who is the young chronic patient? *Tie Lines, I,* 7.

Pepper, B., & Ryglewicz, H. (1984b). Families and clinicians of young adult chronic patients: How can we bridge the gap? *Tie Lines, I,* 1–3 & 6–7.

Pepper, B., & Ryglewicz, H. (1985a). The developmental residence: A "missing link" for young adult chronic patients. *Tie Lines, II* (3), 1–3.

Pepper, B., & Ryglewicz, H. (1985b). Guidelines for treating the young adult chronic patient. *Tie Lines, II,* (4) 1–5.

Peters, T. J., & Waterman, R. H., Jr. (1982). *In search of excellence: Lessons from America's best-run companies.* New York: Harper & Row.

Peterson, K. (December, 1979). Assessment in the life model: A historical perspective. *Social Casework,* 586–596.

Pierce, N. (1985). Why can't every American city do this much? White Plains, New York: Gannett Westchester Newspapers, November 25, p. A12.

Poque-Geile, M. F., & Harrow, M. (1985). Negative symptoms in schizophrenia: Their longitudinal course and prognostic importance. *Schizophrenia Bulletin, 11* (3), 427–439.

Procci, W. R. (1976). Schizo-affective psychosis: Fact or fiction? *Archives of General Psychiatry, 33,* 1167–1178.

Rabkin, R. (1977). *Strategic psychotherapy: Brief and symptomatic treatment.* New York: Basic Books.

Raush, H. L., with Raush, C. L. (1968). *The halfway house movement: A search for sanity.* New York: Appleton-Century-Crofts.

Rehabilitation Research and Training Center at Virginia Commonwealth University and the Specialized Training Program at the University of Oregon. (1985). *Perspectives on Supported Employment* (Special issue), *2* (2), 1–8.

Revell, W., Wehman, P., & Arnold, S. (October–December, 1984). Supported work model of competitive employment for persons with mental retardation: Implications for rehabilitative services. *Journal of Rehabilitation,* 33–38.

Roose, S. P., Glassman, A. H., Walsh, B. T., et al. (1983). Depression, delusions, and suicide. *American Journal of Psychiatry, 140,* 1159–1162.

Rose, G. (1984). In pursuit of slow time: A psychoanalytic approach to contemporary music. *Psychoanalytic Study of Society, 10,* 353–365.

Rothwell, M., & Doniger, J. (1966). *The psychiatric halfway house.* Springfield, IL: Charles C Thomas.

Ryglewicz, H. (1982). Working with the family of the psychiatrically disabled young adult. In B. Pepper & H. Ryglewicz (Eds.), The young adult chronic patient. *New Directions for Mental Health Services,* 14 (pp. 91–99). San Francisco, Washington, London: Jossey-Bass.

Sass, L. (1982). The borderline personality. *New York Times Sunday Magazine,* August 22, pp. 12–15, 66–67.

Scheflen, A. E. (1981). *Levels of schizophrenia.* New York: Brunner/Mazel.

Shulman, L. (1979). *The skills of helping individuals and groups.* Itasca, IL: F. E. Peacock.

Sivadon, P. D. (1957). Techniques of socio-therapy. *Psychiatry, 20,* 205–210.

Smith, M. B., & Hobbs, N. (1966). The community and the community mental health center. *American Psychologist, 21,* 499–509.

Solomon, R., & Solomon, L. L. (1982). *Residential home management: A manual for managers of community-living facilities.* New York: Human Sciences Press.

Stein, L., & Test, M. (1976). Training in community living—one year evaluation. *American Journal of Psychiatry, 133,* 917.

Stone, M. H. (1985). Analytically oriented psychotherapy in schizotypal and borderline patients: At the border of treatability. *Yale Journal of Biology & Medicine, 58,* 275–288.

Strauss, A. (1975). *Chronic illness and the quality of life.* St. Louis, MO: C. V. Mosby.

Summers, F., & Hersh, S. (1983). Psychiatric chronicity and diagnosis. *Schizophrenia Bulletin, 9* (1), 122–133.

Talbott, J. (1981). The chronic mentally ill. In S. Arieti & H. Brodie (Eds.), *American handbook of psychiatry* (2nd Edition) (pp. 369–387). New York: Basic Books.

Test, M. A., & Stein, L. I. (1977). Special living arrangements: A model for decision-making. *Hospital & Community Psychiatry, 28* (4), 608–610.

Tolman, R., & Rose, S. D. (1985). Coping with stress: A multimodal approach. *Social Work, 30* (2), 151–157.

Tomlinson, P. B., & Cumming, J. (1976). Coast Foundation apartment project. *Canada's Mental Health, 24* (1), 23–28.

Torrey, E. F. (1983). *Surviving schizophrenia: A family manual.* New York: Harper & Row.

Trop, J. L. (1984). Self psychology and the psychotherapy of psychotic patients: A case study. *Clinical Social Work Journal, 12* (4), 292–302.

Unger, K. V., & Anthony, W. A. *A university based treatment setting for young adult chronic patients.* (Unpublished monograph.)

Vaughn, C., & Leff, J. (1976). The influence of family and social factors on the course of psychiatric illness: A comparison of schizophrenic and depressed neurotic patients. *British Journal of Psychiatry, 129,* 125–137.

Velleman, R. (1984). The engagement of new residents: A missing dimension in the evaluation of halfway houses for problem drinkers. *Journal of Studies on Alcohol, 45* (3), 251–258.

Vermont Longitudinal Study of Chronic Schizophrenics (December, 1984). Principal investigator: Courtenay Harding, Vermont State Hospital, as reported in *The Newsletter of the Alliance for the Mentally Ill of New York State, 5,* 5.

Walsh, T. (1983). This month in OMH research. New treatment of bulimia. *This Month in Mental Health.* NY State Office of Mental Health, *5* (10), 2.

Ward, M. J. (1946). *Snake pit.* New York: Random House.

Wehman, P. (1981). *Competitive employment: New horizons for severely disabled individuals.* Baltimore: Paul Brooker.

Weinstein, A. S., & Cohen, M. (1984). Young chronic patients and changes in state hospital population. *Hospital & Community Psychiatry, 35* (6), 595–600.

Wheelis, A. (May, 1969). How people change. *Commentary,* 56–66.

Wilder, J. F., Kessel, M., & Caulfield, S. C. (1968). Follow-up of a "high expectations" halfway house. *American Journal of Psychiatry, 124* (8), 1085–1091.

Wilner, M. (1985). The young adult chronic patient in the day hospital. *Proceedings of the Annual Conference of Partial Hospitalization* (pp. 251–255). Boston: American Association for Partial Hospitalization.

Winston, A., Pinsker, H., & McCullough, L. (1986). A review of supportive psychotherapy. *Hospital & Community Psychiatry, 37* (11), 1105–1114.

Wintersteen, R. T. (1986). Rehabilitating the chronically mentally ill: Social work's claim to leadership. *Social Work, 31* (5), 332–337.

Wyatt, R. J. (1985). Q. & A. *The Newsletter of the National Alliance for The Mentally Ill, 6* (2), 11.

Zanditon, M., & Hellman, S. (1981). The complicated business of setting up residential alternatives. *Hospital & Community Psychiatry, 32* (5), 335–339.

Zelman, W. N. (1977). Liability for social agency boards. *Social Work, 22* (4), 270–283.

Name Index

Alpert, M., 193
Anderson, C. M., 107–109
Anthony, W. A., 45, 83, 130, 135
Arieti, S., 70
Arnold, S., 51
Atwood, N., 115

Bakos, M., 60
Beck, A. T., 150
Bellamy, G., 51
Bergman, E., 150
Berman, N., 193
Birley, J. L. T., 52
Blohm, T., 193
Bowden, C. L., 26
Bozic, R., 60
Brown, G. W., 52
Budson, R. D., 35, 36, 39, 40, 121, 193,
    195, 198, 209, 214

Campbell, M. E., 173
Carling, P. J., 171, 172, 216
Carpenter, W., 81
Chapin, D., 60
Christ, W., 10
Clarkin J., 14, 15
Cohen, B. F., 45, 130, 135
Cohen, M., 32, 130, 135
Cohen, P., 102, 104
Compton, B. R., 115
Cotter, J., 193

Cotton, P. G., 149
Coulton, J., 36
Cumming, E., 8, 209
Cumming, J., 173

DeChillo, W., 154
Di Bella, G. A. W., 104
Doane, J. A., 23
Docherty, J., 33, 34, 78
Doniger, J., 35
Drake, R. E., 149

Easton, K., 225
Elpers, R., 7, 35, 122

Fairweather, G. W., 37, 136
Falloon, I. R. H., 23
Farkas, M., 45
Fitch, V., 36
Frances, A., 14, 15

Galaway, B., 115
Gates, C., 149
Gandrus, J., 60
Germain, C. B., 36, 42
Gitelson, A., 10
Gitterman, A., 36, 42, 200
Glasscote, R., 7, 8, 35, 122, 209
Glassman, A. H., 150
Glassman, S., 8, 209
Goertzel, V., 9

Goldstein, J. M., 23, 104
Gomez, E. A., 173
Grady, K., 193
Greenblatt, M., 35, 193
Grob, M. C., 193
Gruenberg, E., 32
Gudeman, J., 7, 35, 122

Halmi, K. A., 30
Harding, C., 23
Harrow, M., 18
Hellman, S., 172
Hersh, S., 16
Hierholzer, R. W., 110
Hogarty, G. E., 107–109
Holland, T. P., 36
Holman, T., 193
Holzman, P. S., 24
Hoppe, W., 193
Hull, J. T., 65

Jolley, R. E., 193, 195
Jones, M., 5, 6

Kahn, S., 60
Karan, O., 51
Katz, S., 7, 9
Kinigstein, L., 158
Knoedler, W., 45, 50, 51, 228
Kresky, M., 193
Kruzich, J., 39, 46
Kruzich, S., 39, 46

Lamb, H. R., 9, 173
Landy, D., 35, 193
Lanin-Kettering, L., 18
Leff, J., 52
Leighton, A. H., 58, 225
Lewis, S., 104
Liberman, R. P., 110
Lipton, F., 7, 9
Lynch, V. J., 193
Lyons, R., 6

Margules, A., 83
Mateer, W., 60
Matorin, S., 154
Maynard, J., 37, 136
McCoy, K., 226
McCreath, J., 9, 32
Miles, C. P., 19
Minkoff, K., 150, 201, 217
Mintz, J., 23

Neffinger, G. G., 103, 104
Nelson, B., 9
Neuman, S., 60

O'Connor, G., 51
Ornstein, P., 200

Pepper, B., 31, 48, 52, 90, 172, 227
Perry, S., 14, 15
Peters, T. J., 197, 198, 199, 200
Peterson, K., 42, 43, 44
Phil, M., 104
Pierce, N., 226
Pynter-Berg, D., 104

Raush, C. L., 6, 8, 36, 38, 40, 42, 64,
   198, 218
Raush, H. L., 6, 8, 36, 38, 40, 42, 64,
   198, 218
Reiss, D. J., 107–109
Revell, W., 51
Roose, S. P., 150
Rose, G., 60
Rose, S. D., 206
Rothwell, M., 35
Rutman, S., 8, 209
Ryglewicz, H., 31, 90, 227

Sabatini, A., 7, 9
Sanders, D. H., 37, 136
Sass, L., 28
Scheflen, A. E., 70
Schiff, J. W., 103, 104
Shenton, M. E., 24
Shore, M. F., 193
Shulman, L., 202
Singer, J. E., 193
Sivadon, P. D., 76
Solomon, L. L., 208
Solomon, R., 208
Solovay, M. R., 24
Stein, L. I., 171
Stern, R., 201, 217
Strauss, A., 17
Struening, E., 104
Summers, F., 16
Sussex, J., 8, 209

Talbott, J., 9, 47
Test, M. A., 171
Thompson, J. C., 65
Tolman, R., 206
Tomlinson, P. B., 173

Torrey, E. F., 48
Trop, J. L., 200

Unger, K. V., 83

Vaughn, C., 52
Velleman, R., 208

Walsh, B. T., 150
Walsh, T., 29
Ward, M. J., 13
Waterman, R. H., Jr., 197, 198, 199, 200

Wehman, P., 51
Weinstein, A. S., 32
Weitz, G. W., 104
Wheelis, A., 53
Wilner, M., 103
Wing, J. K., 52
Wintersteen, B. T., 17

Yurmark, J. L., 104

Zanditon, M., 172
Zelman, W. N., 219

Subject Index

Acute Stabilization component, 103
Aftercare, 190–196
Alcoholics, 8
Alcoholics Anonymous (AA), 31
American Psychiatric Association (APA), U.S. Joint Information Service of, 8
Anorexia nervosa. *See* Eating disorders.

Belmont Hospital, 5
Berkely House, 35
Bipolar illness, as manic-depressive, 26, 27
Board of directors. *See* Halfway house.
Borderline personality disorder:
  characteristics of, 27, 28
  and halfway houses, 29
Boston State Hospital, 23
Boston University's Center for Rehabilitation Research and Training in Mental Health, 45
Bulimia nervosa. *See* Eating disorders.

Community Mental Health Act, 7
  and aftercare, 6
Community Support System (CSS), 192, 194, 195
Conard House, 7
Confrontation, 128–130

Depression:
  characteristics of, 25
  drug treatment of, 26
  and halfway houses, 26
Diagnostic and Statistical Manual (DSM-III-R), 23
  and anorexia nervosa, 29
  and borderline personality disorder, 27
  and depression, 25
  and schizophrenia, 23, 24
  and symptoms of paranoid schizophrenia, 21
Diagnostic Related Group (DRG), 10, 11
Discharge:
  destination:
    community, 165
    family, 165, 166
    supportive apartment, 164, 165
  final evaluation, 160–164
  steps toward, 166, 167
  transition, 168–170
Division of Vocational Rehabilitation, 51
Dixon v. Weinberger, 6
Drug abusers. *See* Substance abuse.

Eating disorders:
  anorexia nervosa, 29, 113, 157, 158

bulimia nervosa, 29, 30, 157, 158
Electroconvulsive therapy (ECT), 26

Fairweather Lodge, 37
Fountain House, 136

Gheel community, 7
Gould Farm, 7
Group for the Advancement of
   Psychiatry (GAP), 50
Guide for Board Organization in
   Social Agencies, 218–220
Gutman House, 35–37

Halfway house:
  authority issues, 156, 157
  board of directors, 218–222
  bonding, 76–81
  community meeting, 94, 95
  daily maintenance and rules, 62–65
  decompensation, 118, 119
  description of, 55–61
  ecosystem, 44, 45, 87–92, 117, 118,
    156
    day hospitals, 101–110
    family, 88–90
  evaluations, 95–100
  expressed emotion, 52
  historical review, 35–38
  life model, 42–44
  medications, 153–155
  milieu interventions, 38–42
  motivation, 52–55
  periods of crisis, 147–153
    suicide, 149–153
  physical setup of, 61, 62
  rehabilitation, 45–47, 109, 110
    coordination efforts, 113–118
    model, 130–134
    vocational planning, 134–139
  socialization, 84–87
  staff meeting, 146
  structure, 81–84
    chores, 82–84
  treatment guidelines, 47–52
  use of staff meeting for adjustment,
    91, 92
  violent patient, 92–94
Homeless:
  demographics, 8, 9
Horizon House, 172

Hospitals:
  acute care, 10
  day, 101
    and psychoeducation, 107–
      110
    and vocational planning, 110
  length of stay, 9
  psychiatric, 13–15

Institute for Living, 37
Intake, 66–75
  application questionnaire, 67–69
  initial interviews, 69–75
  family interview, 74
Intensive Day treatment, 103
Iowa 500 study, 23

Joint Commission on Mental Health
  and Illness, 6

Lithium, 27

Manic-depressive, 27
Medicaid, 9
Medicare, 9–11
Medications, 153–155
Mental illness:
  stages of, 33, 34
    equilibrium, 33
    overextension, 33
    psychotic state, 33
    restricted consciousness, 33
Mentally retarded, 8
Monoamine oxidase inhibitors
  (MAOIs), 26, 154

National Institute of Mental Health
  (NIMH), 8
New York State Homeless Housing
  Assistance Program, 226
New York State Office of Mental
  Health, 7, 8, 29, 219
Not-for-Profit Corporation Law, 219

Peer Review Organization (PRO), 10,
  11
Program of Assertive Community
  Treatment (PACT), 45, 51, 228
Psychiatric Rehabilitation Approach at
  Boston University, 110
Public Law 113, 5

Rehabilitation Research and Training Center at Virginia Commonwealth University, 51
Resident Congregate Care for Adults (RCCA), 172, 224
Rutland Corner House, 7, 35

Schizophrenia:
acute:
in hospitals, 16, 17
other characteristics of, 20–22
chronic:
symptoms, 18–20
course of, 22, 23
diagnosis of, 15, 24
and drugs, 18, 47
and expressed emotion, 23, 52
schizoaffective disorder, 24
Separation and individuation, 123–128
love relationships, 126–128
Specialized Training Program, University of Oregon, 51
Spring Lake Ranch, 7
Staff, 197–217
administrative support staff, 201
consulting psychiatrist, 215, 216
counselors, 206–215
volunteers, 215
director, 198–201
social work staff, 201–206
Substance abuse, 8, 31
treatment of, 50
Suicide, 149–153
Supplementary Security Income (SSI), 225

Supportive apartments, 164, 165, 171–189
adjusting to move into, 175–178
levels of supportive living, 173–175
movement toward discharge, 187–189
skills of supportive living, 178–187

Therapists, 109–120
attitude toward halfway houses, 110–112
and decompensation, 118, 119
Tricyclics, as antidepressants, 26

United States Department of Health and Human Services, 10
United States Department of Housing and Urban Development,
and Section 8 funds, 226
and technical information, 172
Utilization Review Board, 103

Vermont State Hospital Longitudinal Study of Chronic Mental Patients, 23, 48, 49, 193
Vocational planning, 134–139

Westchester County Social Services Department, 226
Westhab, 226
Woodley House, 7, 35

Young adult chronic, 31–33